Cold War on Ice

ALSO OF INTEREST
AND FROM MCFARLAND

*World Series '48: The Cleveland Indians
and Boston Braves in Six Games*
(John G. Robertson *and* Carl T. Madden 2023)

*The Bruins in 25 Games: Boston's Most
Unforgettable Wins and Heartbreaking Losses*
(John G. Robertson and Carl T. Madden 2023)

*The Mustache Gang Battles the Big Red Machine: The 1972
World Series* (John G. Robertson and Carl T. Madden 2022)

*Hockey's Wildest Season: The Changing
of the Guard in the NHL, 1969–1970* (John G. Robertson 2021)

*Amazin' Upset: The Mets, the Orioles and the 1969
World Series* (John G. Robertson and Carl T. Madden 2021)

*When the Heavyweight Title Mattered: Five Championship Fights
That Captivated the World, 1910–1971* (John G. Robertson 2019)

*Too Many Men on the Ice: The 1978–1979 Boston Bruins
and the Most Famous Penalty in Hockey History* (John G. Robertson 2018)

*The Games That Changed Baseball: Milestones in Major League
History* (John G. Robertson and Andy Saunders 2016)

*The Babe Chases 60: That Fabulous 1927 Season, Home Run by
Home Run* (John G. Robertson 2014; paperback 1999)

*Baseball's Greatest Controversies: Rhubarbs, Hoaxes,
Blown Calls, Ruthian Myths, Managers' Miscues
and Front-Office Flops* (John G. Robertson 2014; paperback 1995)

A's Bad as It Gets: Connie Mack's Pathetic Athletics of 1916
(John G. Robertson and Andy Saunders 2014)

Cold War on Ice

*The NHL versus the Soviet Union
in Hockey's Super Series '76*

John G. Robertson
and Carl T. Madden

McFarland & Company, Inc., Publishers
Jefferson, North Carolina

ISBN (print) 978-1-4766-9387-3
ISBN (ebook) 978-1-4766-5130-9

LIBRARY OF CONGRESS AND BRITISH LIBRARY
CATALOGUING DATA ARE AVAILABLE

Library of Congress Control Number 2023043744

© 2023 John G. Robertson and Carl T. Madden. All rights reserved

No part of this book may be reproduced or transmitted in any form or by any means, electronic or mechanical, including photocopying or recording, or by any information storage and retrieval system, without permission in writing from the publisher.

Front cover: Valeri Kharlamov (17) of CSKA during a Super Series game against the New York Rangers on December 28, 1975, at Madison Square Garden (Jo Ann Kalish/Hockey Hall of Fame)

Printed in the United States of America

*McFarland & Company, Inc., Publishers
Box 611, Jefferson, North Carolina 28640
www.mcfarlandpub.com*

To the great Soviet/Russian and North American hockey players of the past for giving all of us who enjoy the game such fond memories; the ones of the present for their continued excellence in the sport; and the ones yet to come who will have to carry the weight of such traditions and distinctions in the future.

Acknowledgments

The authors would like to gratefully acknowledge the following people and institutions for their help with this book:

- The staff of the public library systems of both Cambridge and Kitchener, Ontario, for their assistance in acquiring research materials, some of them quite obscure;
- The staff of the Dana Porter Arts Library at the University of Waterloo for their very helpful assistance in accessing their large collection of newspaper archives on microfilm;
- The diligent staff at the Toronto Public Library who helped with our acquisition of images from its *Toronto Star* collection of photographs;
- Dave Wilson for providing us with his copy of Harry Sinden's hard-to-find 1972 book about the famous Canada–Soviet Series played just a few months earlier.

Table of Contents

Acknowledgments — vi
Introduction — 1
Terms and Spellings — 6

1. The IIHF Years, Part One: Canada Seems Invincible — 7
2. The IIHF Years, Part Two: The Soviet Superpower — 16
3. The Awakening: The 1972 Summit Series — 33
4. The Often-Forgotten 1974 Summit Series — 56
5. The Making of Super Series '76 — 75
6. Soviet Lineups — 82
7. Game #1: Central Red Army vs. New York Rangers — 83
8. Game #2: Soviet Wings vs. Pittsburgh Penguins — 97
9. Game #3: Central Red Army vs. Montréal Canadiens — 108
10. Game #4: Soviet Wings vs. Buffalo Sabres — 126
11. Game #5: Soviet Wings vs. Chicago Black Hawks — 138
12. Game #6: Central Red Army vs. Boston Bruins — 147
13. Game #7: Soviet Wings vs. New York Islanders — 161
14. Game #8: Central Red Army vs. Philadelphia Flyers — 167
15. Aftermath 1976 to 1991: What It All Meant — 190

Chapter Notes — 201
Bibliography — 213
Index — 215

Introduction

It was the novelty of Super Series '76 that made it so compelling to hockey fans. For the first time in the sport's history, eight different National Hockey League teams would each play a single, mid-season game on home ice against one of two touring clubs from the Soviet Union. The contests were spread over two weeks during the holiday season in 1975–76 for maximum exposure. It was more than hockey on display, of course. Though unspoken, it was quite blatantly Cold War politics contested on a sheet of ice with the two opposing sides both seemingly at their best for the first time ever.

Seeing communist bloc athletes competing in person in Canada and the United States was a true rarity as 1976 approached. *Sports Illustrated* noted that the seven games played in the United States all had something akin to a sideshow aspect about them: *Step right up, ladies and gentlemen, boys and girls! For the measly price of a single hockey ticket, take a gander at some real live Russians!* The visiting players were foreigners. They were an exotic commodity … and they were the big, bad commies who had to be vanquished at all costs. If the Cold War could be contested indirectly in a revolution in Angola, as it was in late 1975, it could also be contested directly in North America with hockey sticks as the weapons of choice and hockey rinks as the battlegrounds.

The winter of 1975–76 was also a time of uncertainty and strangeness in both Canada and the United States. A growing separatism movement was engulfing Quebec, causing concerns about what Canada might look like in the near future. A country that had once been a showcase for how two different cultures and languages could co-exist superbly was now having to deal with disenchantment and strong regional sentiments. No matter how many times the top song of 1975, "Love Will Keep Us Together," was played on the radio, there was an ongoing fear that Canada was on the verge of falling apart along linguistic lines. Montréal was about to be put on the world stage as the host the 1976 Summer Olympics. The city's mayor, Jean Drapeau, dismissed all cynics who said the Games would create an enormous financial shortfall. Scoffing at such a possibility, Drapeau famously declared an Olympics could no more have a deficit than a man could have a baby. (He would be proven terribly wrong—and political cartoonists would have a field day drawing Drapeau in advanced stages of pregnancy.) Be that as it may, Canadians could overwhelmingly agree that hockey was a fine pastime and that those born and bred in the Great White North were the best in the world at playing it, all things considered.

In the United States, inflation, fuel shortages and urban decay were now parts of everyday life. Social breakdown manifested in rising crime statistics. People's disenchantment with the status quo could be seen in Hollywood's foremost antiheroes: Charles Bronson and Clint Eastwood. They seemed to operate on the premise that a satisfying end always justified the violent means. (Even the seashore becoming a dangerous place as *Jaws* was easily the highest-grossing film of 1975.) The White House was occupied by Gerald Ford, a man who was neither elected vice-president nor president. Nevertheless, fate had elevated him to be the leader of the Free World. The Vietnam War had ended in April with U.S. troops long gone from the scene, but the fall of Saigon still stung. It had been a thoroughly polarizing episode in American history. (At least Americans could still laugh at their political and social issues in 1975–76 as *All in the Family* remained the number-one TV program in the country.) A decline in prestige was now afflicting the country. In a year where both pet rocks and Pop Rocks were introduced, anything, including beating the Soviet Union in hockey at the club level, took on increasing importance for a nation searching for positives anywhere they might be found.

The Soviet Union of the mid-1970s largely remained a closed and secretive polity. Leonid Brezhnev was still the first secretary of the Communist Party and Alexei Kosygin still served as the USSR's prime minister. Both men had held those roles since 1964. Some strides toward détente had been made, however. In exchange for receiving most-favored-nation trading status with the United States in 1974, the Soviet Union liberalized its emigration policy. (It was not loosened enough, however, to please a portion of America's population: Picketers from the Jewish Defense League targeted three of the Super Series '76 contests to vent their displeasure. They dangerously disrupted two of those games.) Always looking to gain an edge on their ideological foes, the Soviet Union narrowly beat the French and English in the field of supersonic flight. They got their version of the Concorde, the Tuploev Tu-144, airborne in late December 1975, a month ahead of their aeronautic rivals. (Its flights carried cargo and mail only, however.) The Soviet Union remained a power in international sports on the "amateur" level. Of course, life as an amateur athlete in a communist country was completely different to being one in the western world. Some journalists began using terms such as "masked professionals" to describe the sports figures who resided behind the Iron Curtain.

Many Americans would learn first-hand from Super Series '76 that the Soviet Union produced superb hockey players. Canadian hockey fans were understandably a bit more cosmopolitan about the situation than their brethren down south. They fully knew what "Russian hockey" was all about, having recently endured the ground-breaking and emotionally stirring Canada–Soviet series, a thoroughly compelling sports event in September 1972 when the NHL's best players confronted the perennial IIHF world champions. (This was later followed in 1974 when the floundering World Hockey Association's stars did exactly the same thing with a lesser team that achieved a completely different result.) Older hockey enthusiasts had suffered through two decades of Canadian amateur teams at international events steadily becoming less and less likely to defeat the team with the letters CCCP on the front of their jerseys. The Soviets may have been robotic and lacked individual charisma, but any Canadian who cared at all about the sport realized these players with all the vees in their names and ragtag equipment were indisputably very fine hockey players. Fittingly, the best game of the eight Super Series clashes took place at the lone Canadian stop on the tour, the venerable Montréal Forum, on December 31, when Central Red Army faced the leading team in the NHL in 1975–76, the Montréal Canadiens. It may have been the single greatest hockey game ever played. The other seven contests were largely eye-openers for the more provincial American hockey fans residing in Pittsburgh, Chicago, Long Island, New York City, Buffalo, Boston, and Philadelphia.

"It was Us against Them," noted Rod Smith of the Sports Network in Canada on January 11, 2016. It was the fortieth anniversary of the Red Army facing the Philadelphia Flyers and Smith was trying to explain to viewers—many who were born well after the collapse of communism in eastern Europe—the importance of those eight international games in the grand scheme of North American hockey.

The same capitalism-meets-communism scenario was played out at seven other NHL arenas from December 28, 1975, to January 10, 1976. Only in Pittsburgh did the game not immediately sell out based on passions fueled by patriotic fervor—at least as much as can be generated by cheering on the local NHL team that was, in each case, overwhelmingly comprised of Canadians. Temporary alliances were formed. Never before or since have NHL fans openly rooted for teams that were normally their archrivals. It was all in the unifying spirit of standing strong against geopolitical enemies wearing Soviet hockey jerseys.

Introduction

Prior to the first game of the 1972 Canada–USSR Series, two Soviet coaches (Arkadi Cherneshev, left, and Boris Kulagin) lift the Stanley Cup during a visit to the Hockey Hall of Fame in Toronto. The very thought was frightening to many Canadian hockey fans (Toronto Star Photograph Archive, Courtesy of Toronto Public Library).

This book will, of course, take the reader through all eight hockey games that comprised what was called Super Series '76, but it will also include the origins of this unique sporting rivalry that dates back seven decades to the mid–1950s. That was when the Soviet Union emerged, literally out of nowhere, to take up ice hockey as a way of showcasing the superiority of their ideology. The fact that they achieved so much so fast frankly scared the bejeezus out of North American hockey followers. Repeated Soviet hockey successes inflicted huge amounts of angst and self-doubt on Canadians especially. It was entirely understandable. Since much of Canada's identity rode on being known as the country that produced the best hockey players in the world, any threat to that situation was perceived as nothing short of a national emergency.

Introduction 5

In 1994, Dick Irvin of *Hockey Night in Canada* discussed the Red Army–Montréal game played 19 years earlier. He noted, "It was an exhibition game—but it really wasn't. The tension in the Forum that night was unbelievable."[1] Indeed, nothing was at stake—and yet, at the same time, everything was at stake.

Terms and Spellings

During the Cold War era, the terms "Russia" and "Soviet Union" were frequently used as synonyms in North America—especially by sports writers. They were not the same thing either geographically or politically, but seldom was the difference pointed out. The quotes in this book often use the terms "Russia" and "Russian." In almost every instance, it should have been "Soviet Union" or "Soviet" instead.

The 1954 Allan Cup champions were officially called the Penticton V's, but the team's nickname was often written as Vees or Vs in newspaper accounts to the point where the names were interchangeable. We opted for the spelling with the vowels. It simply looks better. (Penticton's present junior hockey team calls itself the Vees.)

Although the Chicago franchise entered the National Hockey League in 1926 as the "Blackhawks" (one word) it was routinely written as "Black Hawks" (two words) for more than six decades. In keeping with the practice of sportswriters during the 1975–76 hockey season, the authors have opted to follow the common (albeit inaccurate) two-word spelling of the Chicago NHL team's nickname at the time.

The language of the Soviet Union was Russian. Russian uses the Cyrillic alphabet, also known as the Slavonic script. It has more characters than the English language in order to accommodate the different sounds common in Slavic speech. Thus, people's names were and are often translated to the closest-sounding English equivalent. Not surprisingly, there is/was a great variation of English-language spellings of these names: Alexandrov/Alexsandrov; Tretiak/Tretjak/Tretyak; Shluktov/Zhluktov; Anatoli/Anatoly; Dombrowski/Dombrowsky/Dombrovsky; and others. We have strived to use the most frequently written version of each Soviet individual's name. Sometimes it is only our best guess which one that is.

1

The IIHF Years, Part One

Canada Seems Invincible

Hockey, at least the version played on ice that we recognize today, was invented in Canada in the last third of the 19th century. Cities such as Victoria, Montréal and Halifax have all claimed to have been the birthplaces of the winter sport most associated with Canada, but the nationality of the game has never been seriously disputed by historians. Some folks say the love of the game is ingrained within the DNA of the population, kiddingly asserting that many Canadians can skate before they can walk and that they are often given a hockey stick before their first diaper change. Common signs displayed at international hockey games state, "Canada is hockey. Hockey is Canada" and "All ice is home ice for Canada."

The International Ice Hockey Federation (IIHF) was formed in France in 1908. For many years, it was primarily a European affair with Canada and the United States showing little interest in the IIHF or its tournaments. The first true world championship event, as recognized by the IIHF, was the 1920 Olympic tournament in Belgium. (As there were no Winter Olympics yet, the hockey event was held in April, four months ahead of the rest of the Olympic Games.) An amateur team, of course, represented Canada. It was comprised of just eight players of Scandinavian origin from a single city: the Winnipeg Falcons. They were no slouches, though. The Falcons had recently won the Allan Cup to claim the Canadian amateur hockey championship. In Belgium, the results put up by Canada's reps were very telling, to put it mildly. "The world suddenly realized hockey was not what they had thought it was," noted Brian Johannesson, the team's historian. His father, Konnie, played defense for the 1920 gold medalists. "The Canadians came along," Johannesson says, "and they steamrolled everyone."[1]

The Falcons cruised through the seven-team Olympic event, outscoring their opposition 29–1 in three games played on consecutive days. In accordance with IIHF rules, those games were divided into two 30-minute halves. Canada's first game was a 15–0 whitewash over Czechoslovakia.

Winnipeg Falcons: 1920 Olympic hockey champions.

"The Canadians at no time exerted themselves,"[2] reported William A. Hewitt of the *Toronto Star*. The 45-year-old Hewitt had been appointed as the Falcons' team chaperone, manager, and correspondent by the Canadian Olympic Association. He would hold the same duties for the next two Canadian Olympic hockey teams. Hewitt's son (Foster) and grandson (Bill) would both become nationally famous in Canada as hockey broadcasters.

In those three games, future NHL player Frank Fredrickson scored 12 of Canada's goals (with seven of them coming in the final); Haldor (Slim) Halderson was not far behind his teammate with nine scores. Only the Americans, who lost to Canada by just a 2–0 score, put up much of a contest against the Winnipeg lads. Sweden was soundly thrashed, 12–1, in the gold-medal game. (It was widely reported that the lone Swedish tally, scored by Elnar Svensson, was an act of mercy by the compassionate Canadians who allowed the Swedes to avert the embarrassment of being both routed and shut out. Goaltender Wally Byron conveniently fell down at an appropriate time, leaving a gaping net as an easy target for Svensson. The Swedes reputedly thanked the Canadians for graciously allowing them to score. "There was a lot of sportsmanship involved,"[3] Byron happily recalled.) The talent gap between North American and European hockey was obviously an enormous one as Canada won every Olympic hockey gold medal but one from 1920 through 1952. (Great Britain won top honors in 1936 at Garmisch-Partenkirchen, Germany, with a lineup replete with expatriate Canadians. The ex–Canadians beat the present Canadians 1–0 in the preliminary round. The unforgiving nature of the Olympic tournament's format made it difficult for the Canadians to recover from that tough loss—and they did not.)

It took decades for European hockey to approach its counterpart in North America. Whenever they chose to do so, Canadian teams, often with fewer credentials than the 1920 Winnipeg Falcons, utterly dominated world amateur hockey through the early 1950s. Typically, the Canadian Amateur Hockey Association (CAHA) would send local teams—such as the Port Arthur Bearcats, the Edmonton Mercurys or the Sudbury Wolves—to carry the nation's flag and honor at the IIHF world amateur championship tournament. They were hardly national selections of the best available hockey talent, but in most cases that was enough to win the IIHF tournament quite handily. Often the lopsided scores and the Canadians' love of physical play irked the European hosts, but Canada's games were always well attended. (At the opening game of the 1949 tourney in Stockholm, Canada thrashed Denmark by the remarkable score of 47–0, showing no mercy whatsoever to the badly outclassed Danes.) With few exceptions, only their absence from the tournament kept Canada from routinely winning the IIHF's laurels.

Such was the case in 1953 when the CAHA balked at sending a team to the tournament in Zurich, Switzerland. Canada, represented by the Edmonton Mercurys, had won the Olympic and IIHF world championship in Oslo in 1952, but the CAHA chose not to send a team to defend their title the following year. Its president, the headstrong W.B. George, explained why Canada had opted to pass on the event: "Every year we spend $10,000 to send a Canadian hockey team to Europe to play 40 exhibition games," he noted. "All these games are played to packed houses that only enrich European hockey coffers. In return we are subjected to constant, unnecessary abuse over our Canadian style of play."[4]

Also absent from Zurich and Basel were the Americans, and the Soviet Union. The latter were scheduled to make their IIHF debut but their introduction to international hockey was delayed. The Soviets did, however, send a team of observers to the small, four-team tourney. It is believed injuries to their key players—especially Vsevolod Bobrov—was the major reason for no Soviet participation at the 1953 event. (Bobrov was an earlier version of Bo Jackson, a distinguished, multi-talented, three-sport star, who exceled for the Soviet Union on the world stage in bandy, hockey, and soccer. Bobrov led the Soviet soccer team in scoring at the 1952 Olympic tournament in Helsinki, notching five goals in the USSR's three games.) Sweden won the 1953 IIHF tournament—one that certainly lacked star quality. It was scarcely mentioned in the Canadian media.

It seems odd today, but for nearly the first three decades of the Soviet Union's existence, the communist regime snubbed sports entirely. Deriding them as bourgeois activities, the Union of Soviet Socialist Republics preferred to showcase steel mills, hydro-electric dams, and other construction projects as their propaganda statements to the non-communist outside world. Athletes running races, throwing javelins, chasing balls, and shooting pucks did not fit the desired ideals of the new socialist state. By the late 1940s, however, attitudes behind the Iron Curtain began to change about such things. As the newest postwar world superpower, perhaps Soviet athletes excelling in elite international sports could be used to enlighten the world to embrace communist superiority. None would be considered professional; all of them would officially be "state-sponsored amateurs" of the Soviet Union, thus eligible to participate in the Olympics and other major events that, at the time, were often tightly restricted to non-professional athletes.

Before 1946, Russians/Soviets knew virtually nothing about ice hockey. Bandy, a close relative, had been widely played as far back as the tsarist regime. Contested on ice with players on skates brandishing field hockey sticks who attempted to direct a ball into soccer nets, bandy was the most popular winter sport in the country. However, ice hockey was steadily gaining in international popularity thanks to the quadrennial Olympic tournament. Accordingly, Soviet sports officials handed a bureaucrat named Sergey Savin a surprising mission. His task was to study this unknown game of ice hockey to determine if it had any potential in the Soviet Union. Savin traveled to Latvia. There he obtained Canadian-made ice skates, a stick, a puck, and a set of hockey rules. It was a very modest beginning, but Soviet hockey had its roots.

The first Soviet ice hockey championship game was played in 1946 on a chilly outdoor rink in Moscow. It was contested by bandy players. An official Soviet newsreel of the game can be seen on YouTube. To modern eyes, it is somewhat comical in nature. Thus, it is hard to believe that within two years the Soviets had quietly formed a national team at least as good as any found in Europe. The key was preparation and an ambitious program designed by an introverted hockey genius named Anatoli Tarasov. Aptly nicknamed "The Father of Soviet Hockey," Tarasov loved the Canadian version of the game and followed it as closely as he could from his home behind the Iron Curtain. Tarasov was greatly influenced by *The Hockey Handbook*.

An original copy of Lloyd Percival's *The Hockey Handbook* from 1951. Percival's ideas on fitness and training were often dismissed as quackery in North America, but they were fully embraced in the USSR.

Published in 1951, *The Hockey Handbook* is a 320-page tome about the sport's fundamentals. The book was written by a maverick 38-year-old Canadian coach named Lloyd Percival. A man of wide sporting interests, Percival was once a nationally ranked amateur boxer whose only loss was at the 1928 Canadian Olympic trials as a 15-year-old bantamweight. He had also competed in the Canadian Open junior tennis championships as a 16-year-old in 1929. Percival lost in the final to an American, Frankie Parker, who would rise to become the best male player in the world. The defeat puzzled the young Canadian because he believed himself the better athlete. Curious, Percival asked Parker's renowned coach, Mercer Beasley, why he had lost. Beasley bluntly told Percival his technique was bad, but it could be corrected with proper coaching. Percival took the advice to heart and began a passionate study of the scientific, physical and mental aspects of not only tennis but hockey and other sports. It was an obsession that would dominate his life.

Percival was decades ahead of his time. In the 1940s, as the autocratic coach at the North Toronto Track Club, Percival had his young athletes stretching, doing breathing exercises, and applying ice to their injuries—all novelties. Percival also had them eating an exotic food called yogurt. (It had to be ordered from a Quebec monastery. At the time, yogurt was not sold anywhere in Toronto.) His pupils began to dominate track meets. Percival's impressive record should have gotten him named as Canada's track and field coach for both the 1952 Summer Olympics in Helsinki and the 1954 British Empire Games in Vancouver, but he was snubbed each time by the selection committee because of his unconventional ideas that rankled the Canadian Olympic Association. One longtime associate humorously declared that Percival found himself involved in some sort of controversy as regularly as most people got out of bed.

Lloyd Percival was decades ahead of his time regarding athletes' training, diets, and mental preparation. Despite achieving great success, Percival often clashed with Canada's sporting bodies because of his maverick ways (Toronto Star Photograph Archive, Courtesy of Toronto Public Library).

Percival was also a true eccentric. Once he ran continuously until he dropped from exhaustion just to experience what it felt like. Although he strongly disapproved of the habit in all his pronouncements about healthy living, Percival himself was a lifelong smoker who quit and restarted puffing several times. (In fact, at age 50 he chain-smoked menthol cigarettes in a bizarre experiment to prove that a smoker who exercised regularly was in better physical shape than a non-smoker who did not!) Percival seemed to understand the important mental aspect of competition far better than anyone else of his era. Thus, he was probably Canada's first sports psychologist. Bill Gairdner, a hurdler and decathlete who trained under Percival for the 1964 Tokyo Olympics, spoke highly of him nearly 60 years later. Gairdner said, "He'd make you feel like you could fly, and you'd ask him where the window was so you could try it."[5]

Percival would later devise a workout regimen for Canadian heavyweight champion George Chuvalo. As a late substitute for Ernie Terrell, Chuvalo had only 17 days to prepare himself to fight Muhammad Ali in 1966 for the world title when the latter was at his absolute peak. The boxing establishment thought Percival's methods were downright crazy—a common theme in the coach's life—but they did wonders for the huge underdog, increasing both Chuvalo's punching power and stamina. Although he lost by decision, Chuvalo lasted the full 15 rounds and was punishing Ali by the end of the bout. The indefatigable Canadian, beaten but not disgraced, wholly credited Percival for his surprisingly competitive performance against the formidable world heavyweight champion.

The Hockey Handbook included radical ideas about the importance of physical fitness and proper diets—concepts that were barely considered in North American sports at the time. Both Percival and Tarasov believed that anger and hatred had no part in the game, each thinking that such emotions would inevitably detract from a player's skills on the ice. At home, Percival was regarded as something akin to an annoying quack among sports executives. His ideas were largely ignored in Canada, but Tarasov embraced them. Furthermore, Tarasov was convinced he could improve on Percival's views with distinctly Soviet innovations. Fortunately for Tarasov, the Soviet government now considered international sports to be a valuable propaganda tool. Accordingly, Tarasov was given a free hand to experiment with the USSR's national team's preparations and training in any way he desired. Tarasov thus became akin to an absolute autocrat in Soviet hockey. It was a role he zealously embraced.

Tarasov thoroughly controlled the lives of the young men who played under him. He was the sole arbiter as to whether or not a player could own a car or live outside the team's secluded training facility located about 12½ miles from Moscow. (The players' living quarters were adequate but not luxurious. They lived two men to a room. They had no private telephones. They ate their meals together in a common dining room. Contact with the outside world was restricted.) According to goaltender Vladislav Tretiak, Tarasov twice denied him a day off to get married, so twice his wedding had to be postponed. Yet the rustic, lonely setting consistently produced winning hockey teams. Tarasov seemed inspired by the site's isolation from the rest of the world—and he thrived on it. Tretiak later said of his coach in his autobiography, "I can honestly say there wasn't one practice to which Tarasov came without new ideas. He amazed all of us every day. One day he had a new exercise, the next an innovative idea, and the next a stunning combination to remove the effectiveness of our opponents."[6] Curiously, there was no ice surface at the facility where the Soviet players spent most of their lives; they had to be bused back and forth to a rink in Moscow from their twice-daily practices.

Even as late as the 1980s, the Soviet Union only had about a dozen indoor ice surfaces in their entire, huge country. This forced their national hockey program to significantly focus on off-ice training. It was a blessing in disguise. Under Tarasov's guidance, they did it far better than anyone else. The emphasis on overall fitness was certainly superior to anything happening in North America. Proper diet, weight training, flexibility exercises, and drills to build and enhance stamina were part of the normal Soviet training regimen. Most of these concepts were utterly foreign to Canadian hockey. Tarasov was also a huge believer in teamwork rather than individual creativity. As a strident communist, Tarasov firmly believed in the principle that the collective was more important than the individual—and he zealously applied that theory to building championship Soviet hockey teams. This he did with great success. According to Tarasov's 1995 obituary in the *New York Times*, during one faceoff drill he roughly slashed and speared his players so they could get used to what Canadian opponents might do to them when they finally met.

The Soviets' intention was to enter their hockey team in the 1952 Winter Olympic tournament in Oslo, Norway, but they were not quite ready yet. Their sudden, unexpected withdrawal from the world championships

Soviet goaltender Vladislav Tretiak.

in Switzerland in 1953 postponed matters for another year. However, the Soviets were ready for the 1954 IIHF tournament in Stockholm, Sweden where they would encounter a team from Canada for the first time.

With their grievances over traveling to Europe apparently settled, the CAHA sent the East York Lyndhursts, a Senior B hockey club of some repute. They were augmented with four other players to represent Canada in Stockholm. (The team's nickname came from its primary sponsor, Lyndhurst Motors, a Toronto automobile dealership owned by a passionate hockey enthusiast named Harry Crowder.) They were not exactly the CAHA's first choice. The problem was that no Senior A amateur team in Canada cared enough to go to Europe even if it was for the IIHF world championship. The Lyndies—as the press liked to call them—got the nod from the CAHA because they were the only capable team that seemed interested in traveling overseas to represent their country in 1954. For the most part, the Lyndhursts saw the chance to play for Canada as a free trip to Europe. Half a century later, player Earl Clements said the team was comprised of a bunch of young men from East Toronto simply trying to find their way in life. So, off the hopeful Lyndies went to Sweden to meet their collective fate, whatever it might be. Their journey began on January 22. The team sailed across the Atlantic Ocean from New York City on the British liner *RMS Queen Mary*, docking in France. They had no idea that they would become quite infamous in Canada for losing one very important hockey game.

2

The IIHF Years, Part Two
The Soviet Superpower

As was typical of previous IIHF tourneys, each of the eight competing nations in 1954 in Stockholm would play the other seven in a simple round-robin format to be contested over 10 days. The venues were outdoor rinks with natural ice. Whichever team finished atop the standings would be declared the IIHF's world amateur champions. There were no playoff rounds; they were not needed. Since it was a non–Olympic year, interest in Canada about the world championship event was minimal. Only one Canadian journalist, a writer employed by the Canadian Press, went to Stockholm to cover the tournament.

Alarm bells sounded when the Lyndhursts lost badly, 11-2, to a team of Canadian-born all-stars from the professional British Ice Hockey League in a special exhibition game played in Paris. (Years later the Lyndies recalled the Parisians as being marvelous hosts, even going as far as providing beer to players who were serving time in the penalty box!) Some reinforcements were sent overseas by the CAHA to strengthen the team. More were to come when two Lyndies were injured in subsequent exhibition games versus European clubs as the team made its way toward Stockholm. Still most Canadians figured the IIHF title was in the bag. As long as a halfway decent team showed up representing Canada, it automatically became the tournament favorite. That was the way it had always been. The inclusion of a team from the Soviet Union into the mix was thought to be a quaint novelty rather than a threat. Why should 1954 be any different?

According to some bookies, Czechoslovakia was the team to beat in Stockholm. However, Jaroslav Drobny, arguably the best Czech player at the time, had recently fled the communist country and was now residing in Egypt. (Drobny was an excellent tennis player, too. He would win the men's singles title at Wimbledon a few months later!) With Drobny unavailable to help the Czech hockey team in Stockholm, the Lyndies seemed poised to be the team to beat, despite their questionable pedigree and the doubts of some skeptical Canadians.

As in previous years at IIHF events, Canada rolled over its early opponents with little trouble. The scores of their first six games were 8–1, 8–0, 8–0, 8–1, 20–1, and 5–2, giving them a perfect record of six wins in six games with 57 goals scored and just five conceded. Their easy 20–1 rout of Finland on March 4—in which 23-year-old Moe Galand scored seven goals for the victors—may have lulled the Canadians into believing they could not be beaten. Czechoslovakia did put a scare into Canada in the sixth round of games, trailing only by a goal after 40 minutes and firing more rubber at goaltender Don Lockhart than he had seen at any time during the tourney. (Lockhart, age 23, was one of the players specially added to the Lyndhurst's roster by the CAHA.) Canada got two third-period insurance goals, however, to defeat the Czechs 5–2 and remain unbeaten and atop the standings.

Despite their excellence, the Lyndies, according to news reports coming from Stockholm, were not especially popular or well received by their European rivals or that continent's hockey establishment. Tommy Shields of the *Ottawa Citizen* wrote after the Lyndies' victory over Czechoslovakia in their penultimate game, "From all outward appearances, no royal welcome is extended to a Canadian team at the world tournament as it is now constituted. This attitude may be prompted by a feeling of resentment, an inferiority complex, if you care to put it that way. Canada is standing alone at this tournament for all things that are not European. Credit for their six straight victories has only been accorded grudgingly."[1]

Dramatically, the final game of the tournament pitted the heavily favored Canadians against the underdog Moscow Dynamo club of the Soviet Union.

The Soviets had already made a spectacular IIHF debut. Clad in bicycle helmets that looked similar to the headgear of the era that boxers wore in training, they wielded homemade sticks and were outfitted in second-hand, battered skates. The Canadian Press declared, "The Russian team made its bow in international competition, outclassing Finland"[2] by a decisive 7–1 score on February 26, in the second game of the first day of the Stockholm tournament. The conditions were less than ideal. The historic first match for Soviet hockey was played at an outdoor venue during a heavy blizzard. The accumulating snow gave the Soviets more trouble than their Finnish opponents for the first 20 minutes. When the weather improved, the Soviets certainly seemed right at home at the IIHF championship event, winning five games and tying one in their first six outings, although they had not looked especially daunting in their 1–1 deadlock with host Sweden nor in a listless 4–2 victory against winless Switzerland.

Those results left the Soviets with 11 points in the standings to Canada's 12. This meant the Soviets had to beat the Canadians in the tournament's climactic game to win the IIHF world championship. A tie would be sufficient for Canada to secure first place. Still, it was considered highly improbable that the newcomers to international hockey could beat or tie the Lyndhursts on Sunday, March 7. Tournament organizers were extremely doubtful such a scenario would occur. The event also doubled as the European championship event. Whichever European team finished highest in the overall tournament standings would be deemed the hockey champions of that continent. Assuming that Canada would summarily take care of the upstart Soviets, IIHF and Swedish hockey officials had already begun selling tickets for a Sweden–Soviet Union tiebreaking rematch to be held on March 8 to decide the championship of Europe.

They had to issue refunds. The result on March 7 was an absolute shocker: Soviet Union 7, Canada 2. The Lyndies had been totally outclassed and thoroughly humbled by the Soviet newcomers. "Their slowest skater was faster than our fastest skater,"[3] recalled Canadian forward Eric Unger in an interview 55 years later. (A 17½-minute, Soviet-made highlight film of the game exists on YouTube. It appears to back up Unger's assertion.) "The jubilant Russians were hugged and kissed by team officials at the end of the game while the disconsolate East Yorkers trooped back to their dressing room,"[4] declared the *Montréal Gazette*. The Soviets jumped out to a huge 4–0 first-period lead and never looked back. Incredibly, in less than a decade, the Soviet Union had gone from knowing absolutely nothing about ice hockey to being the IIHF world amateur champions. By any standard, the rapid rise of Soviet hockey has to be considered one of the most remarkable success stories in any sport at any time.

CAHA president W.B. George was among the stunned crowd of 16,725 spectators at the outdoor rink in Stockholm to see the heretofore unthinkable. He promptly criticized the Lyndhursts for their timidity, believing they were afraid of being penalized for aggressive play. (Over the course of the game, the Canadians were whistled for six penalties compared to just two for the Soviets.) The defeat was only the fourth a Canadian team had ever suffered in the 20 IIHF events they had entered. "What are they going to say in Canada?"[5] worried Lyndhursts coach Greg Currie sheepishly asked a reporter. He probably already had a fair idea.

They said plenty, of course. Most of it was harsh. The front page of the March 8 *Toronto Star* featured this blistering commentary by Robert Nielsen:

> There are at least 50 better hockey teams in Canada than the Toronto Lyndhursts, who were trounced 7–2 by Russia in the world championship match yesterday. On that the embarrassed brass and brains of Canadian hockey

2. The IIHF Years, Part Two

agreed today. So why was this country represented by its 51st (or worse) team? [It] was certainly Canada's most humiliating defeat ever in sport....

Other hockey writers too dumped on the vanquished Lyndies and the CAHA with equal vigor. Jack Howlett of the *St. John's Daily News* stated, "Canada thought she had the title in the bag before sailing [for Europe]. This might wake her up for another year."[6]

Harry Eisen of the *London Free Press* commented, "No one but the CAHA can be held responsible for Canada's defeat. The East York Lyndhursts were not strong enough to uphold Canada's prestige as a leading hockey nation. Unless Canada can send its best team to these so-called world hockey tournaments, the wisest course would be to pass them up."[7] That was a sentiment shared by many Canadian hockey fans—and would be for decades to come.

In a small southeastern Ontario city, 21-year-old Harry Sinden and his teammates on the Senior A Whitby Dunlops were riled up over the Soviets winning the world amateur hockey championship by knocking off a mere Senior B outfit. Four years later the Dunlops would try to do what the overmatched Lyndies could not do—defeat the Soviet Union at the IIHF tourney. Eighteen years later, Sinden would coach the most formidable group of players Canada had ever assembled on one team to that point in its hockey history.

Bill Westwick of the *Ottawa Journal* was especially critical of Canadian hockey leadership. He wrote, "The CAHA can take a bow today for a masterpiece of stubbornness and blundering that netted them exactly what they deserved. Canadian expatriates had given warnings that 'a Class B club would never do.' Once in Europe, the CAHA backtracked, admitting it had not made a good choice. It rushed over four more players, including a goalie [to strengthen the team]. It makes you wonder what the Russians would have done to the original Canadian team."[8]

Elmer Ferguson, a 69-year-old hockey writer who had been covering the sport even before the formation of the NHL in 1917, categorized the Lyndies' loss in his *Montréal Herald* column as "a national calamity, a national humiliation, and a mortifying experience."[9] Such comments were the norm and they were plentiful. At a fiftieth anniversary get-together in 2004, one East York player, Reg Spragge, recalled, "You would have thought we'd lost World War Three, not a hockey game."[10]

The Lyndhursts' defeat was even discussed in Canada's House of Commons by the notable Liberal member of parliament from the western Toronto riding of Trinity. He was Lionel Conacher, an esteemed figure in Canadian sports history. On the ice, on the baseball diamond, and on the football field, Conacher was so outstanding and versatile that he was named Canada's athlete of the first half century. He was also a proud Canadian. Conacher angrily called the upset defeat in Stockholm "a catastrophe for Canadian hockey." He said, "Canadian youngsters are brought up to believe that we have the best hockey players in the world. Now they only know that the Russians beat us."[11] (Conacher, 54, would be dead just two and a half months later, succumbing to a heart attack after legging out a triple in the annual government softball game played on Parliament Hill in Ottawa.)

Conn Smythe, who owned the NHL's Toronto Maple Leafs, was also vexed by Canada's runner-up status in Stockholm. He quickly volunteered to take his team to the Soviet Union (once the NHL season concluded) to restore Canada to the top spot in the world hockey pecking order. It never happened, but considering the Maple Leafs were merely a third-place club in the six-team NHL that was beaten rather soundly in the first round of the 1954 Stanley Cup playoffs by the Detroit Red Wings, perhaps it was fortunate they did not venture overseas to face the ascending Soviets. Be that as it may, Smythe's passion showed that seemingly overnight the average Canadian suddenly did indeed care very much about his country's performance in international hockey.

The *Montréal Gazette* said that the East York defense left goalie Don Lockhart to fend for himself on numerous occasions. Despite the seven goals he allowed in the finale, Lockhart was nevertheless named the tournament's best goaltender. He was given a crystal vase as a memento. (Lockhart died young, at age 51, in 1982, never being comfortable with the fact that he was the goalie of the Canadian team that was thumped by the Soviets in Stockholm in 1954. He always believed the Lyndhursts would have beaten the Soviets easily had North American–style body contact been fully allowed under IIHF rules in 1954.) The *Gazette* scribe, who did not merit a byline, was forced to concede that the Soviets had played a virtually flawless game to earn their surprise win. Hockey games between Canada and the Soviet Union now became matters of national pride. Remarkably, though, Canada's federal government steadfastly refused to get involved in the business of amateur hockey—even at the international level—and would not until 1968. The CAHA was on its own in financing the teams they sent overseas. Nevertheless, the seeds of an unexpected hockey rivalry had been planted.

Of course, the Soviet victory became a communist propaganda tool in Eastern Europe. The Soviet press made the most of their national hockey team's victory, claiming they had throttled a group of Canadian superstar players—calling them Team Canada—and not just a coterie of part-timers from a Toronto suburb who all worked real jobs and basically played the sport as a hobby.

The end result of the national hand-wringing and finger-pointing in Canada was a sensible CAHA decision to only send Senior A teams to future IIHF world tournaments. Furthermore, the embarrassment of losing to the novice Soviets created a sense of national importance in how Canada's hockey teams fared on the international stage. It became akin to an obsession. Top amateur clubs that once had shown little interest in travelling overseas were now begging the CAHA to let them take a crack at the Soviets as an act of patriotism and a service to their country. That plan worked for a time.

The 1954 Allan Cup champions, the Penticton Vees of the Okanagan Senior Hockey League in British Columbia, were sent to the IIHF world tournament as Canada's entry in 1955. They were a skilled but rough-and-tumble outfit who liberally threw their weight around as part of their strategy. A few of their players were former pros who had been reinstated as amateurs, a common practice in those days. The Vees' tactics thoroughly intimidated the many Canadian teams they played. They downright terrified their European opponents. The club had only been founded in 1951 in a region that was more famous for producing peaches than championship hockey teams. Despite the Vees holding the Canadian national amateur championship of 1953–54, and being comfortably in first place of their league well into the 1954–55 season, some haughty Canadian journalists openly declared the unfashionable, burly Vees were unsuitable to represent Canada in international hockey. "It was not a popular choice by a lot of people, especially in eastern Canada," recalled Penticton goaltender Ivan McLelland in a 2015 interview with CBC News on the sixtieth anniversary of their remarkable triumph. "Everyone said we weren't good enough. They didn't feel we were an adequate team."[12]

Indeed. Among the naysayers was a writer from *Weekend Magazine*, a popular Canadian newspaper supplement. He angrily roared, "So we have placed the prestige of Canada's hockey in the hands of a group of unknowns from a small town no one has ever heard of. What on Earth is the CAHA thinking? Or are they thinking at all?"[13]

There were others who were more supportive, however. Dick Beddoes, then a sportswriter on the staff of the *Vancouver Sun*, went as far as nominating the Vees as Canada's "Team of the Year" for 1954. He had watched them defeat the favored Sudbury Wolves to win the Allan Cup in a thrilling comeback. "As a spectacle," Beddoes commented on his nomination form, "the Penticton Vees must be cradled with the finest figures in sport. Hackneyed words are appropriate ... terrific ... fantastic ... pulsating...."[14]

The CAHA was not exactly providing the means for the Vees to travel first-class to Europe. In fact, they did not provide much in the way of financial assistance at all: The Vees basically had to foot the enormous

$30,000 bill to pay their costs to travel to West Germany and cover all their sundry expenses for five weeks. Somehow enough money was raised. The journey was long and complicated, beginning from the small airstrip in Penticton where about 1,500 local well-wishers showed up to offer their support. It included a cross–Canada flight from Vancouver to Montréal (with plenty of stops along the way), another flight across the Atlantic to London, a trip by ocean liner to Germany, and then a final flight to Berlin.

Ivan McLelland hoped to earn a little extra money on the side thanks to the largesse of his employer back in Penticton. The man, a generous hockey fan, promised McLelland $100 for every shutout he recorded in Canada's eight tournament games. Furthermore, the bonus would be doubled to $200 plus an extra week of paid vacation if he shut out the Soviet Union. That was a potential bonanza for the diminutive netminder, considering that McLelland's monthly salary at his day job was $300.

Prior to the start of the IIHF tournament, the Vees arranged to play a couple of exhibition games in Prague to warm up for the big event. Their two opponents were basically the first-string national team of Czechoslovakia followed by the second-stringers. Before winning the second game handily, 6–0, the Vees were shocked to be held to a 3–3 tie in the opener by a very strong Czech team. A huge, enthusiastic crowd of about 19,000 fans attended the game.

The next day, McLelland had a pleasant chat with an English-speaking interpreter who had been assigned to accompany the Vees around the Czech capital city. When McLelland casually mentioned it would not surprise him if the Czechs finished ahead of the Soviets in the tournament, the interpreter blanched and bluntly told him the Czechs would not defeat the Soviets. When McLelland tried to say the Czechs were probably at least the Soviets' equals, the agitated man interrupted him. "We *cannot* beat the Russians," he insisted. "It is not wise."[15] It took a moment, but McLellan finally understood the dangerous implications of life behind the Iron Curtain in 1955. In his 2012 autobiography, McLelland wrote, "Today that would be ridiculous, but I have no doubt it was true."[16] During the IIHF tournament, the Soviets beat a listless Czech team, 4–0. Even a new American publication called *Sports Illustrated* strongly hinted that the Czechs deliberately did not try their best in that game. *SI* was not alone with their suspicions. A Canadian documentary about the Vees did not say so directly, but absolutely insinuated that the important USSR–Czech game was not exactly on the level.

The Vees did not travel to Europe just to be glorified tourists; they were all business about regaining the IIHF world title for Canada—as their opening game clearly indicated. Actually, their focus on hockey was on display in the moments leading up to the start of the team's first contest on

February 25. While the Canadians and Americans were on the ice, a tournament dignitary also entered the rink to make a speech. The Canadians simply ignored his presence while he spoke and continued with their pre-game warmups. It was a disrespectful action that stunned their German hosts who culturally put a great value on deferring to authority figures. Be that as it may, the Vees must have warmed up well. They annihilated an optimistic and supposedly strong American team, comprised of players chosen from many states, 12–1. Remarkably, the Vees mercilessly fired 96 shots at overwhelmed American goaltender Don Rigazio. A Canadian Press reporter opined that had it not been for the 20-year-old Rigazio's heroic play, the score would have looked like a basketball result—on one side of the ledger. (Although the Americans eventually finished in fourth place at the tourney with a 4–2–2 record, the harried Rigazio was unanimously selected as the event's best goalie.) After the rout, when the Vees were asked by a CAHA official if their roster needed further bolstering with other top Canadian amateurs, they politely declined the offer for additional players, saying that that their team already seemed well stocked. American coach Al Yourkewicz certainly would have agreed. He grumbled after the game, "We might as well have been playing the National Hockey League's all-stars."[17]

In the Vees' first seven games at the nine-team IIHF event held in various outdoor locales throughout West Germany, only the Czechs (who fell 5–3 after leading 2–1 and 3–2 in the third period) and the Swedes (who lost 3–0) gave the Canadians much of a challenge. Everything was going as planned. The Vees' biggest complaint seemed to be a dislike of German milk. When news of this dietary calamity became public via a newspaper story, a dairy patriotically rushed a fresh supply of Canadian milk across the Atlantic Ocean to the grateful team's hotel. That same inn had copious amounts of Canadian beer in storage for the Vees as well.

On Friday, March 4, in their penultimate game, the Vees walloped their West German hosts, 10–1. The Canadians were surprisingly put through a rigorous workout immediately afterward because player-coach Grant (Knobby) Warwick thought the Vees had looked unacceptably sloppy even though they had handily beaten the Germans by nine goals.

To that point in the tournament, the Canadians had outscored their seven opponents by an impressive ratio of 61:6. Only the Soviet Union remained to be vanquished in the Vees' final game. Both teams had perfect 7–0 records. Canada had a far better goal differential than the Soviets, however, so a tie would be sufficient for the championship—but the Vees were not gunning for a deadlock. They wanted an outright victory. Grant Warwick firmly assured the hockey fans who were following the event from every corner in Canada that the IIHF world championship would surely be won by his club on Sunday, March 6. Bookmakers listed the Vees as 3:2 betting favorites. American coach Al Yourkewicz, whose team had fared much better against the Soviets (losing just 3–0) than versus the Canadians, figured the Vees would win by two goals but the contest would be a tough one for them.

Grant Warwick's boast was not a hollow one. The tournament concluded two days later. Among the overflow crowd of an estimated 12,000 hockey fans at the Krefeld Arena (located just outside of Dusseldorf) were about 1,500 prominent Canadian military personnel. They had been specially bused in from nearby army and air force bases to root the Vees on to victory. Armed with loud voices, and augmented by kazoos, trumpets, cow bells, drums and tin horns, they noisily supported the Canadians as they inflicted a decisive 5–0 shutout on the previously undefeated Soviets in the deciding game on March 6. Ivan McLelland, nearing his 24th birthday, recorded the shutout—a $200 feat for him—his fourth in eight games for the Vees. That whitewash gave him a minuscule goals-against average for the tournament of 0.75.

Before the puck was dropped, there was a nasty incident during the pregame skate. The Soviets thought nothing of extending their warmup laps through the Canadian zone. (This was not against IIHF rules at the time, but such a territorial transgression simply was not done in Canada.) One unnamed Vee put a stop to it by deliberately tripping an oblivious circling Soviet invader. The two Swiss referees threatened to eject any Canadian who did such a thing again—and none did—but the Vees got their message across.

Clad in predominantly white and blue uniforms (featuring a blue maple leaf!), the Vees began the game by complaining that the blades of the Soviets' homemade hockey sticks all exceeded the allowable IIHF length—which was patently obvious. (One can view them; the full game is available on YouTube.) When tournament officials basically refused to do anything about it, the Canadians simply dropped the issue and got on with the business of winning the world amateur hockey championship. However, the Soviets' sticks did provide comedic ammo for one vocal Canadian supporter. He got a big laugh from the crowd when he heckled a Soviet player, Alexander Uvarov, who, in the first period, broke two of his sticks in short order and twice had to get replacements. "Not sabotage!" yelled the wise guy. "Just inferior communist production!"[18]

One of the most memorable moments of the game was neither a goal nor a save. It was a classic, open-ice hip check delivered by Canada's sturdy, 210-pound defenseman, Hal Tarala. It spectacularly sent Soviet captain Vsevolod Bobrov airborne, separating the Soviet superstar from both his stick and his two gloves—all of which descended 20 feet from where he landed with a thud. Bobrov's teammates had to help him to the Soviet bench.

Since international hockey was now hugely important to Canadians, *Hockey Night in Canada*'s Foster Hewitt was hastily rushed across the Atlantic Ocean by CBC to do a live, national radio description of the climactic Canada–USSR game. (A small Penticton station sent its own play-by-play man there, too!) The opening faceoff was scheduled for 5 p.m. local time in Krefeld, 8 a.m. in Penticton, and 11 a.m. in Toronto and Montréal. Newspapers across Canada carried numerous stories about antsy people stampeding out of church services in order to hear every second of the broadcast, or of large percentages of typically dedicated congregations skipping worship altogether that Sunday morning. An estimated 1.5 million Canadian radios were tuned in to listen to Hewitt's description of the action. According to the British Columbia Sports Hall of Fame, the broadcast drew the greatest audience in Canadian radio history. Sixteen other countries were getting radio descriptions of the action, too. A CBC Television crew was present as well, with Steve Douglas at the microphone, to film the championship contest. Live TV coverage from Europe was not yet technically possible in 1955. The film was rushed across the Atlantic and swiftly processed and edited for broadcast in Canada the very next day.

Among those listening to Foster Hewitt with rapt attention were Formo and June Bregg. "I remember us sitting around the radio. Every time the Vees scored you could hear [cheering] all over the neighborhood," said Formo nearly 60 years later in a 2015 interview printed in the *Penticton Western News*. "Everybody was listening to that hockey game." June concurred. "You just glued yourself to the radio and listened and got excited,"[19] she said. June's father, Clem Bird, was the president of the Vees. Her husband, Merv, played on the team.

In that same 2015 interview, 84-year-old Ivan McLelland recalled that the Vees had endured a bit of a shaky start to the game, but survived it unscathed. The winning goaltender noted the match's frantic opening minutes. McLelland said, "Our defense gives up the puck in our zone, and Russia is handed two good scoring chances," he said. "Then, [after Canada took a 1–0 lead at 4:25 of the first period,] George McAvoy is given a penalty. The Russians try again, but [they got] no goal for their efforts."[20]

It seemed that Canada was destined to win the world title. Certainly, the key bounces of the game went the Canadians' way. The Vees' second goal was an absolute fluke. It was scored at 7:35 of the second period from *behind* the Soviet net. A blind pass from Bill Warwick struck a Soviet defenseman and ricocheted past startled goaltender Nikolai Puchkov. In another 2015 interview, 92-year-old Viktor Shuvalov, the lone surviving member of the 1955 Soviet national squad, said his team was "hopelessly unlucky" during the game. Shuvalov remembered the Soviets' top line of Yuri Krylov, Alexander Uvarov and Valentin Kuzin failed to convert on several good chances they had against McLelland.

Shuvalov said no one in the Soviet delegation knew anything about the Canadian team before the tournament began. He admitted that Canada had gathered a powerful team in West Germany for 1955 after their loss in Stockholm the previous year, and the game against them was a tough one. "I guess the [CAHA] understood that they couldn't beat us by hardly shedding any blood," he surmised, "so in Germany, Team Canada was much stronger than [it had been in 1954]."[21] He stated that the Warwick brothers were particularly impressive for the victors and played brilliantly throughout the championship game.

Soviet starting goaltender Nikolai Puchkov was pulled after the fifth Canadian goal was scored early in the third period. He was replaced by 32-year-old Grigory Mkrtychan. Actually, Puchkov pulled himself from the ice. Later, when the Vees were informed that the Soviets claimed Puchkov was allegedly "sick," Grant Warwick gleefully added, "...And for good reason!"[22] Mkrtychan managed to prevent any further Canadian scoring.

It was somewhat fitting that when the game ended, two Vees were sitting in the penalty box and the Soviets did not come close to scoring on McLelland. Over the course of the game, Canada accrued six minor penalties to the Soviets' one. The Vees scored a goal on their lone power-play opportunity.

Vees team president Clem Bird happily belittled the Soviets' efforts when asked to offer his views on the game. "I think those guys just quit cold. The Canadians tied them up and beat them at their own game."[23] American coach Al Yourkewicz readily concurred. "The Russians lost their spirit,"[24] he said.

CBC's Steve Douglas commented, "It was a good, rough, tough battle all the way. But the Canadian team very definitely showed its superiority. It was a well-deserved victory. I can promise you that Canada's players have got grins on their faces from ear to ear and back again," He continued, "All [of] Canada should be mighty proud of the Penticton Vees from British Columbia. It is, of course, tremendously sweet revenge for last year's 7–2 loss to the Russians."[25] In his summary, Douglas accidentally shortchanged goalie Ivan McLelland of a shutout, claiming he had three over the course of the tournament instead of four. Of course, much amusement derived from the fact that the Soviets had been shut out by a Canadian goaltender named Ivan.

There was one comical incident at the end of the game. Shortly after the final buzzer sounded, a very excited and very inebriated Canadian soldier vaulted over the boards, presumably to personally congratulate the

2. The IIHF Years, Part Two

victors. He lost his shaky footing after a few steps, however, and clumsily toppled backward onto the ice. A group of helpful Canadian military policemen got him to his feet and roughly hauled him away—presumably to sleep it off somewhere.

In some parts of West Germany, a public holiday was quickly declared for the following day to extend the celebrations of the glorious victory by the "Canadian heroes." A hockey result was *that* important to the locals. Whenever the despised Soviets suffered a setback in anything to a western ally, it was an appropriate occasion for smiles and cheering in Germany's democratic sectors. (Goaltender Ivan McLelland recalled when the Vees flew to Berlin three weeks earlier, the two-man German flight crew summoned him to the cockpit. They briefly lectured him on how important it was for Canada to defeat the hated Russians. Both men had aging parents living in East Germany whom they could no longer visit. It was the first true indication to the Penticton goalie of the large global impact that a single international hockey game could potentially have.)

Along with the general public, the Canadian media was thoroughly delighted by the result from Krefeld. The Toronto *Globe & Mail* crowed that the Penticton Vees "had erased a smudge on Canada's hockey reputation [from 1954]" and the victory "was a triumph for the way the game is played in Canada."[26] Arch MacKenzie of the Canadian Press wrote, "This time Canada sent a team worthy of the country which calls itself the home of hockey. The Vees fully avenged the setback from a year ago."[27]

Jack Stepler of Southam News Services joyfully reported on the Canadian hockey triumph in the German Federal Republic. His account of the game—which appeared on the front pages of numerous Canadian dailies on March 7, 1955—began with "What a championship! What a day! What a team!" Stepler glowingly continued,

> This crew of mechanics, café operators, and other small businessmen from British Columbia's fruitland broke the bubble of Russian hockey prestige with all the subtlety of a hydrogen bomb.
> What if their style of hockey does resemble a backyard shinny scuffle? It wins games and a world title.
> The outcome of the game was never in doubt after the Vees had scored the first of their five goals. It was just a question of how many [would be scored].[28]

Back in Penticton, nine times zones away, when news of their hockey team's tremendous victory was received on the morning of March 6, an impromptu parade of private automobiles, fire engines and police vehicles formed in the town of 10,000 residents. It stretched four cars wide and was 11 miles long. An official parade to welcome home the conquering heroes was held in Penticton ten days later.

Perhaps the most thoughtful comment on the game and its greater meaning came in an editorial published on March 8 in a British Columbia newspaper. It said,

> Everyone in Canada owes something to the Penticton Vees. The Vees brought back what rightly belongs to this land that gave birth to the thrilling sport on skates.
>
> Everyone thinks there was extra value in the victory in that the Canadians had to beat the Russians [for] the title. Even in sport, it seems, we have to live with the fact that Russia is a potential enemy. It's sad that this feeling has to pervade in athletics, but it's there.[29]

Canada's politicians gleefully jumped on the Vees' bandwagon, of course. From his residence in Ottawa, Governor-General Raymond Massey sent a cablegram to the team offering "his warmest congratulations." Prime Minister Louis St. Laurent sent a wire to coach Grant Warwick that said, "Your fellow Canadians are delighted with your splendid victory." Not to be outdone, George Drew, the leader of the opposition Progressive Conservative Party, forwarded his greetings as well. His message from across the Atlantic Ocean stated, "All Canadians are celebrating your great victory. You have brought credit to yourselves and to Canada."[30] All in all, it was quite a stunning contrast from the negativity and despair of the year before.

The Soviets, fully expecting to repeat as IIHF titlists, had arrived for the tournament in West Germany with a surfeit of confidence. The players cheerfully signed plenty of autographs for whomever asked for them, but they were otherwise kept on very short leashes. Among the Soviet delegation were no fewer than 17 "political officers" from the communist party whose job was to protect the USSR's hockey players from all anti-Soviet propaganda and offers to defect to the West. Two "special" soldiers were positioned near the team's bench to prevent anyone from harming the defending champions. Their returnees from 1954 were badly unprepared for how much better their Canadian opposition was in 1955 compared to the previous year in Stockholm. They were aghast that they had somehow lost for the first time in international play. One hyperpatriotic Soviet player, Yevgeny Babich, was so disconsolate over the defeat that he was heard muttering that he did not want to play hockey any more, after which he tossed his hockey equipment out the window of the Dusseldorf high-rise hotel where the Soviet team was staying.

To their dismay, the Vees later discovered the IIHF championship trophy had been smashed by the Soviets in a fit of anger. Canada's Grant Warwick—one of three brothers on the Vees—carefully collected the pieces, had the trophy repaired back home in British Columbia, and proudly displayed it for the rest of his life at the Penticton restaurant he owned. He sneakily sent an ersatz copy of it to the CAHA to be defended the following year. Nobody knew the difference ... until Warwick revealed the subterfuge in a 1983 interview.

However, the Soviets rebounded to win the IIHF world championship again in 1956. The Canadian team—the Kitchener-Waterloo Flying Dutchmen—surprisingly lost to both the Soviets (2–0) and to the Americans (4–1) at the Winter Olympic Games in Cortina d'Ampezzo, Italy to finish a disappointing third, despite Canada having three of the top four scorers in the tournament. Denis Brodeur—the father of NHL star goaltender Martin Brodeur—was Canada's first-string goalie at the 1956 tournament. The Flying Dutchmen never recovered from a bad goal that eluded Brodeur in their stunning loss to the underdog Americans.

The Americans and Canadians both boycotted the 1957 world tournament, held in Moscow, because of the Soviet Union's invasion of Hungary in 1956. Canada won the IIHF title in 1958, 1959 and 1961, but it was that country's last major hurrah on the world amateur hockey stage. The latter championship was won by the Trail Smoke Eaters, another British Columbia senior amateur outfit, who, for more than three decades, held the distinction of being the most recent Canadian team to win the IIHF world title. Many of the aging ex-players enjoyed their fame for the 33 years the drought lasted.

The 1962 IIHF world championship tournament was held in the United States for the first time in a non–Olympic year. The venue was mainly Colorado Springs, with Denver hosting some games too. However, the event was boycotted by both the Soviet Union and Czechoslovakia due to Cold War politics over the Berlin Wall and American policy on East German emigration. The Galt Terriers from southwestern Ontario were Canada's entry. The Terriers were the 1961 Allan Cup champions. The unforgiving nature of the round-robin format proved fatal for Canada that spring. They finished second because of a single 5–3 loss to Sweden on March 13 despite recording six rather lopsided wins in their other round-robin contests.

In the critical contest—each team's fourth of the tourney—the underdog Swedes jumped out to a daunting 4–0 lead with the first two Swedish goals coming 15 seconds apart in the final minute of the first period. Undisciplined penalties did not help the favorites. Nevertheless, the determined Terriers steadfastly whittled away at the large deficit. They rallied to get within a single goal with eight minutes to play, but with exactly 60 seconds left on the clock, the Swedes notched an empty-netter to seal the game—and Canada's fate. It was the first time the Swedes had ever bested a Canadian team at the IIHF event. The steady play of 22-year-old Swedish goaltender Lennart Haggroth was the difference: He made 35 saves, stopping several Canadian breakaways among them. Shortly after the final buzzer, Haggroth's joyful teammates tossed him into the air in celebration three times. "The better team did not win," moaned Canadian coach Lloyd Roubell afterward. "That goalie was their whole team."[31] By the time Canada defeated the United States, 6–1, in their final game on March 18, Sweden had already clinched the IIHF championship, compiling a perfect 7–0 tournament record, with an easy 4–0 shutout over West Germany the day before. Times were changing. Unlike in 1954, there was no subsequent national outrage in Canada and it was no longer front-page news in most dailies.

A year later, in 1963, the Trail Smoke Eaters were again Canada's reps, but they finished a horrendous *fourth* in the IIHF tourney in Stockholm with a mediocre 4–2–1 record in the eight-team round-robin, losing to both the Soviet Union (4–2) and host Sweden (4–1), and tying Czechoslovakia (4–4). Canada's defeats at the world championship event were no longer shocking. The only significant comment the Canadian Press made about the Canada–USSR game, the tournament finale, was that the Smoke Eaters were in the unusual position of having 16,000 Swedish fans raucously cheer for them, as a Canadian win over the Soviets would have given the host country the championship. The *Globe & Mail* frankly noted, "The Russians outclassed the Canadians by skating better and passing more accurately. Their precision teamwork contrasted with the Canadian attacks that appeared disorganized."[32] The Canada–USSR game was a seminal event for Soviet hockey as it was the first IIHF tournament game ever televised nationally in the Soviet Union. It is credited with creating a surge of interest in hockey, especially among youths. It was the first of nine consecutive world titles for the Soviet Union—hockey's version of the Big Red Machine.

Bobby Kromm, who coached the 1963 Canadian team, complained loudly to the media that the CAHA had not reinforced the Smoke Eaters with any other players. While that was true, it may not have made any difference. European hockey had advanced to the point where the presence of a Canadian Senior A team could no longer guarantee a world championship—or medals of any color—for the birthplace of hockey. The head of the CAHA, Art Porter, recognized this fact. He said, "It was obvious that the Russians were much fitter, in better condition than our boys. They had better bench power and they were skating better and shooting better."[33] "An editorial in the *Ottawa Citizen* pessimistically stated that Canada never again would win the IIHF world title unless it sends the pick of its players and gives them plenty of time to work as a team before the championship."[34] A new strategy was desperately needed.

By the time the 1964 Winter Olympics took place in Innsbruck, Austria, the CAHA was trying something completely different: the establishment of a full-time national amateur team. "The Nats," as the press like to call them, were to be comprised largely of college boys with a few exceptions. The National Team would be headquartered in Winnipeg and be under the control of Father David Bauer, a onetime junior star who gave up a career in professional hockey for the priesthood. Over the remaining years of the 1960s, the scheme did not bear much fruit. Canada's youthful amateur teams were now hard pressed to beat even the Czechs and the Swedes. Bronze medals were being brought home regularly by the team wearing the Canadian maple leaf on their jerseys, not gold ones.

After the 1968 Winter Olympics in Grenoble, in which Canada's national team finished third, 55-year-old Lloyd Percival appeared on the CBC television program *The Day It Is* in which he outlined his biggest ongoing frustration with the decline of Canadian hockey on the international scene. A vexed Percival vented,

> Why aren't we learning? Why aren't we doing the things that should be done and can be done to get back on equal terms with the Russians? I am so sick of hearing Canadian athletes, Canadian hockey players, Canadian coaches, Canadian observers saying year after year that the Russians were in magnificent condition. It's too bad we weren't. They beat us through conditioning. There is nothing stopping us from getting into condition. The Russians don't hold any premium on conditioning.[35]

A week after Percival died on July 23, 1974 at age 61, journalist Douglas Fisher called him "one of the half-dozen great Canadians of the past 30 years." Fisher ruefully wrote in the *Ottawa Citizen*,

The Canadian National Team (referred to as the Nats by the media), a full-time amateur team, was a six-year experiment that proved to be an insufficient answer to the domination of international hockey by the Soviet Union. The priest in the front row is Father David Bauer, the man who ran Canada's national team during the 1960s.

The prophet was unrecognized in his own country because his ideas were too radical and comprehensive. The art of managing and coaching in NHL circles is still primitive when contrasted with the empirical thoroughness of *The Hockey Handbook*. He was a challenging man. Lloyd was too experimental and eclectic on the scientific aspects of sport for the men in the physical education facilities in Canada. He frightened the senior administrators of government with the sweep of his plans.[36]

Bruce Kidd, another elite Canadian athlete who knew Percival well, concurred. "Those who loved Lloyd, loved him; those who hated him, hated him,"[37] Kidd said. Percival would have agreed. "People either swear by me or swear *at* me,"[38] he once said.

By the end of the 1960s, the Soviet players were now regarded as amateur hockey's unbeatable supermen—a title once automatically given to average Canadian hockey players by awestruck Europeans. The year-round training of the Soviets was too much of an obstacle to overcome for Canada's true amateurs who often held jobs or were full-time students. To level the competition, the CAHA asked that ex-professional players be allowed to be reinstated as amateurs with greater leeway. The IIHF granted this exception for a while—until the International Olympic Committee threatened to discontinue its quadrennial hockey tournament if the IIHF did not revert to rules requiring pure amateurism. (This rule would have disqualified a large percentage of the Penticton Vees, for example, had it been in vogue in 1955.) The IIHF caved—and, in protest, the CAHA angrily withdrew Canada from international hockey. The 1970 IIHF world championship tournament that was supposed to be held in Canada for the first time (in both Winnipeg and Montréal) was quickly shifted to Sweden. With their sole purpose for existing now gone, the Canadian Nationals disbanded shortly thereafter.

Few Canadians really cared. The days when the exploits of the Penticton Vees, the Whitby Dunlops and the Trail Smoke Eaters captured national attention were long gone. (The Nats truly never garnered more than occasional, peripheral interest.) For most of Canada's hockey followers, their prime passion was narrowly but firmly focused on the goings-on in the National Hockey League. Two years later, however, something even more dramatic caused Canadians to refocus their attention on the international aspect of hockey. Its impact would have profound ramifications on the sport that are still felt many decades later.

3

The Awakening
The 1972 Summit Series

By the early 1970s, with Canada in a state of self-imposed exile from international hockey, the luster of the IIHF world championship was lessened severely. Canada's absence certainly left a noticeable gap at the tournament. The endless string of Soviet titles grew monotonous and tiresome, even among their own sports officials. Domination of the amateur hockey world had been achieved spectacularly but it was somewhat hollow. Something drastic and innovative needed to be done to restore enthusiasm in Soviet hockey and inject life into the international game. The Soviets themselves came up with a novel idea.

One day in 1971 in the pages of *Izvestia*, an official Soviet publication, a sports journalist named Boris Fedosov wrote that the all-powerful Soviet Union national hockey team had grown tired of thumping all comers at the IIHF world tournament, at the annual *Izvestia* tournament in the USSR, and at the quadrennial Olympic Games. Accordingly, the Soviets needed a greater challenge to sustain their interest in international hockey. It was not specifically stated, but that could only mean one thing: competition against North America's professional players and teams. In Moscow, a Canadian embassy worker named Gary Smith—no relation to the well-travelled NHL goalie with the same name—read the article with surprise. Knowing full well that no Soviet journalist's words ever made it into print without severe government scrutiny and official approval, Smith assumed the article was designed to start a discussion about a Canada–USSR clash sometime in the near future. He promptly telephoned Fedosov, who happened to be a friend of his, to find out if this was truly a serious challenge. It was. Within a short time, negotiations were underway for a friendly series between the Soviet national team and a team of NHL all-stars sometime in 1972 as "a celebration of hockey." The details were finalized during the 1972 IIHF tournament in Prague that April: An eight-game event in September with the first four games contested in four different major Canadian cities followed by the final four games all being played in Moscow.

[Authors' note: The above is one version of the creation story of the 1972 Summit Series. In a 2022 interview, 89-year-old Alan Eagleson, who was the head of the NHL Players' Association and a director of Hockey Canada in 1972, maintained he had spoken to IIHF president Bunny Ahearne at its 1972 world hockey championship event in Prague, and it was his (Eagleson's) enthusiasm and connections that truly got the project off the ground. Eagleson said he was inspired by the exciting 1966 FIFA World Cup soccer tournament to bring the passion of international sports back to Canada.]

Upon hearing about this unique event, most NHL stars were eager to participate for Canada and generally expressed a high level of optimism. Tim Burke of the *Montréal Gazette* interviewed a handful of them who were still competing in the 1972 Stanley Cup playoffs when news of the upcoming series came from Prague. Dennis Hull of the Chicago Black Hawks was especially keen to be involved. "I'll go anytime, anywhere to play [the Soviets]. I'll go as a sub; I'll go as anything. I hope that the guys making up the team remember to include me. We've been hearing for a long time how good the Russians are. This is the ideal occasion to show them who's best."[1]

In contrast, his more famous older brother and teammate, Bobby, was originally opposed to participating. "I'll never go—especially at that time of year. The hockey season is too long as it is. We'd have to start practicing in early summer. If they're going to have a series like that, it should either be in mid-winter or at the end of the [Stanley Cup] playoffs."[2]

Bobby Orr, the NHL's biggest superstar in 1972, was very excited by the idea of a Canada–Soviet series. He said he would love to be on the roster "as long as the team has had an opportunity to play together [in advance]."[3] Brad Park of the New York Rangers said he too would be eager to play, but he expressed practical concerns about insurance and what might happen if he suffered an injury in the series. "A lot of things need to be ironed out," he insisted. "Don't forget we're pros."[4]

Vic Hadfield, also of the Rangers, said, "I'll go—as long as the best guys go. I don't want to get involved in any half-assed operation.... I guess if it comes down to national pride you have to go."[5] His Ranger teammate, Jim Neilson, disagreed with the patriotism angle. Neilson expressed caution because of the September dates. "I don't think it has anything to do with national pride," he insisted. "We're not going to be in condition at that time of year. Unless we practice all summer, there's a real chance we could get beaten. I don't intend to practice hockey all summer, no matter what the cause is."[6]

3. The Awakening

Red Berenson of the Detroit Red Wings, the president of the NHL Players' Association, figured most of the league's stars would be "honored" to go, but their motivation would be broader than merely playing for Canada. "We represent the best hockey in the world," Berenson noted, "but it's spread out now between Canada and the United States. It will be the NHL versus international hockey."[7]

In Canada the series was promoted as a "celebration of hockey." Part of its profits would go toward the NHL players' pension fund. Some NHLers were initially less than enthusiastic about sacrificing part of their precious summer vacations for extra hockey, but most of the 40 invitees came to training camp without too much grumbling. Paul Henderson was not sure he wanted to play, but he had his mind changed at a sports banquet when Canadian Olympic trap shooter Susan Nattrass chided him for not being enthusiastic about representing his country and sport on an international stage.

By the summer of 1972, all the pieces for the eight-game series had been put into place. Canada's head coach would be former Boston bench boss Harry Sinden, who led his club to the 1970 Stanley Cup and then abruptly resigned his position with the Bruins over a relatively small salary dispute. (He was now employed by a modular housing company based in Rochester, New York.) Sinden was still a young man; his fortieth birthday would occur during the series. He and other Canadian hockey executives journeyed to Moscow in July to hammer out the final details with the Soviets. Sinden was amused when the first question posed to him by a Soviet sports journalist was why Dave Keon of the Toronto Maple Leafs had not been selected for Team Canada! (Sinden later joked in his book about the series that the water-cooler-type query sounded like it could easily have come from the lips of a gas-station attendant in Oshawa.) He also realized the question about the popular Leaf veteran was unintentionally very telling: Despite their alleged aversion to professional sports, the Soviets followed the NHL extremely closely. They knew the league's notable players and what their individual strengths were.

At the meeting, Canada agreed to play by IIHF rules and have that organization's amateur officials work the games with its outdated two-man system in which both officials could call penalties, icings, offsides and other rules violations. No one thought that would be a problem—yet. Although helmets were mandatory under IIHF rules in 1972, the Canadians were granted exemptions for this one special occasion. Hardly anyone on Team Canada wore protective headgear in the NHL. Paul Henderson, Bill Goldsworthy and Red Berenson were prominent exceptions.

By 1972 there were about three million people playing organized hockey in the Soviet Union, approximately twelve times the number of registered Canadian players. It was the most popular sport in the USSR by far. Still, very few hockey fans or media personnel in Canada believed the eight-game series would be even slightly competitive. The Soviets were quite content to have their hosts for the opening four games think that way.

"We have come here to learn." That was the official, modest statement from Soviet hockey officials and players when their national hockey team landed in Montréal in late August 1972. It was a polite and thoroughly magnificent con job. The supposedly naïve, awestruck, and overmatched Soviet "amateurs" had been well prepared for this epic eight-game marathon encounter with the famous and glamorous Canadian professional hockey stars from the NHL. They had even gone as far as living on Eastern Standard Time in Moscow a month before the first game was played. "They [the Soviets] trained together 50 weeks per year. They were more professional than we were,"[8] Canada's Phil Esposito said in retrospect decades later. Uncharacteristically, the Soviets were not the reigning IIHF world champions. They had finished second to the Czechs in Prague in April (although they had won the Olympic tournament in Sapporo, Japan in February in what was coach Anatoli Tarasov's swansong).

In 1972, few Canadians knew much about Soviet hockey although the USSR had thoroughly dominated the Olympics and the world amateur tournaments for more than a decade. Canadians rationalized that the hockey teams their country had once sent to thump European competition but could no longer do so had been mere Senior A amateur clubs or overmatched college boys—not the vaunted and adored NHL pro stars who were more than household names. How could the Soviet amateurs possibly compete against Canada's highly skilled professionals? Canadians, by and large, refused to take the Soviet invaders seriously as September approached.

This Canadian ignorance of their opponents played right into the hands of the Soviets. In *The Red Machine*, Lawrence Martin's book on Soviet hockey, the author declared, "The march of the Red Machine to the 1972 series took place behind closed doors. All Westerners saw of the Russians was their infrequent foreign ice appearances, and that was not enough."[9] Hockey writer Todd Denault further commented, "In a time before satellites and the Internet, and at the height of the Cold War, the Soviet Union truly was a closed society, shielded from all external influences, and a mystery to those in the outside world, including Canada."[10]

When Team Canada's lineup was announced, it only reaffirmed most people's confidence. Canada had assembled the greatest hockey team ever: Yvan Cournoyer, Brad Park, Jean Ratelle, Stan Mikita, Bobby Clarke, Ron Ellis, Phil and Tony Esposito, Frank and Peter Mahovlich, and a dozen other

3. The Awakening

high-profile players! Sure, a petty dispute with the nascent World Hockey Association (WHA) had disqualified a handful of potential Team Canada players—most prominently the popular Bobby Hull—but who cared? And did it really matter that Bobby Orr—unquestionably the best player in the NHL—was unfit to play, recuperating from yet another knee surgery? The series was going to be a complete rout! At least that was what Canadians were led to believe by almost everyone in the national sports media.

Dissenters were largely dismissed as alarmists or pinkoes and their voices of caution were quickly silenced. Coach Harry Sinden had represented Canada as a member of the winning Whitby Dunlops at the 1958 World Championship in Oslo. He knew the Soviets were talented. However, when Sinden tried to show old game films from that IIHF tournament to his 1972 Team Canada players, they simply laughed at the black-and-white images they saw on the screen. Their sentiment was unanimous: If the Whitby Dunlops could beat the dastardly Russians, why should we worry?

Illusions of invincibility were fostered. A soon-to-be infamous report on the Soviets—based solely on two intra-squad games—was filed by two Toronto Maple Leaf scouts: Johnny McLellan and Bob Davidson. It declared the Soviets would present absolutely no threat to the vaunted Canadian professionals. Their top goaltender, 20-year-old Vadislav Tretiak, was thought to be especially vulnerable. Furthermore, the Soviets did not look especially good in their practices when Canadian journalists were watching closely. A cakewalk was surely in the making.

Jacques Plante, one of the greatest goalies in NHL history, reputedly pitied Tretiak.

A few days before the 1972 Canada–Soviet Series, Canadian coaches John Ferguson (left) and Harry Sinden display their Stanley Cup rings. Past NHL championships meant little when the Soviets proved their mettle (Toronto Star Photograph Archive, Courtesy of Toronto Public Library).

Plante visited Tretiak in the Soviet dressing room before the first game to give him some helpful pointers on how to deal with the avalanche of shots he was certain to face form the talented array of the NHL's top stars. Years later Tretiak would comment in his autobiography, "I am still puzzled by what motivated him to do that. He probably felt sorry for me, the little guy, in whom Phil Esposito was going to shoot holes. I will always be grateful to Jacques Plante whose suggestions helped me so much."[11]

Most everyone was conned. Francis Rosa, the longtime and distinguished hockey writer from the *Boston Globe*, was just one of several veteran hockey followers who was completely fooled too. He predicted an easy eight-game sweep for the Canadians—and a corresponding 8–0 victory in Game One to get the rout underway. Jerry Eskenazi of the *New York Times* agreed, predicting the NHLers would "slaughter" the Soviets in all eight games. Some generous sports writers, including Mark Mulvoy of *Sports Illustrated*, thought the Soviets possibly might win a game in Moscow if they got a few breaks. Jim Coleman cautiously suggested that the Soviets might earn a tie in one of their home games. Foster Hewitt and Red Storey both confidently predicted Canadian sweeps, with the latter predicting the first game would be the toughest. Goaltender Ken Dryden was conned in a roundabout way. He initially suspected the Soviets were deliberately looking bad in their practices to give Team Canada a false sense of security—but then he dismissed the notion from his mind.

Colorful sports journalist Dick Beddoes loudly scoffed at the idea of the Russians playing the NHL's best and succeeding, calling them "a Russian team in decay."[12] A chagrined Beddoes admitted shortly before his death in 1991, "I had been at the '72 Winter Olympics in Sapporo. Canada had boycotted the hockey tournament. I saw the Soviets play, but I wasn't able to transpose what I saw there to the NHL."[13] In one pre-series article, Beddoes arrogantly forecasted an easy eight-game Canadian sweep. Furthermore, he vowed to publicly eat his column with a bowl of borscht if the Soviets so much as won a single game. (To his credit, Beddoes later kept his promise, scarfing down a shredded version of what he had penned, in front of the amused staff at the Soviet embassy in Ottawa! Photos of Beddoes' conspicuous act of contrition were circulated widely in the USSR.)

To hockey writers who attended the visitors' practices on Canadian ice, the comrades seemed to be a thoroughly odd bunch. The Soviets appeared to be from another planet. Every player wore a helmet (a recent IIHF requirement, but still a rarity in North American hockey). The goaltenders donned odd cage-style masks. Their skates were battered antiques; some of them had repaired blades crudely soldered into place. Surely these fellows named Evgeny, Alexander, Boris and Yuri would be cannon fodder for the famous and fearsome Canadian stars from the glamorous NHL.

3. The Awakening

Eager to witness the anticipated rout, 12 million Canadians (out of a population of 21 million) tuned in on the warm Saturday evening of the Labor Day weekend to watch a rare September hockey game from the Montréal Forum. Prime Minister Pierre Trudeau—hardly a fanatical sports fan—performed the ceremonial faceoff. (Phil Esposito made sure he won it.) At 8:29 p.m. the puck was dropped for real. Hockey was never the same again. Ray MacSkimming, in his excellent 1996 book, *Cold War*, declared, "In one evening, a large piece of the cherished bedrock of Canadians' understanding of ourselves exploded. A more influential hockey game has never been played."[14]

Just thirty seconds into Game One, 30-year-old Phil Esposito, the perennial NHL scoring champion from the Boston Bruins, batted home an airborne rebound during a goalmouth scramble to give Canada a fast 1–0 lead. Six minutes later, Toronto's Paul Henderson made the score 2–0. All was well; Canadians from coast to coast were smiling with confidence. Within moments, though, everything changed. Peter Mahovlich remembered, "When we got up by a couple of goals, we were all saying, 'Here we go.' Then, all of a sudden, it was, 'There *they* go.'"[15]

The Soviets, who had geared their hockey program toward this golden opportunity, were initially nervous and intimidated by their surroundings and the enormous crowd at the Montréal Forum, but halfway through the opening period, their jitters subsided. They began to skate, pass, and stickhandle superbly. Their outstanding physical conditioning was clearly evident. Evgeny Zimin narrowed the gap to 2–1 at 11:40. Before the period ended, Vladimir Petrov scored a shorthanded goal to even the score. "At that point," Paul Henderson recalled, "there was a sickening feeling."[16] Ken Dryden now had reasons to worry. He was having flashbacks to when he faced the Soviet national team in Vancouver on December 20, 1969, as a collegiate athlete. That day the Soviets severely outclassed his Canadian Nationals (in one of that team's final games) in every department, comfortably winning an exhibition game, 9–3. Dryden was in goal for all nine Soviet scores.

The Soviet style of play was confusing to the Canadians. They rarely went offside. They seldom committed icing infractions. Once they possessed the puck, they did not give it away cheaply. One trademark Soviet maneuver really startled the fans and Canadian players alike. In a typical North American hockey game, if an attacking team approached the opposing team's blue line and could not find an opportunity to gain the zone, the man with the puck would invariably take a long, hopeless shot on goal or simply dump it into a corner and he and his teammates would chase it from there. The Soviets did neither. Instead, they calmly retreated with the puck, reorganized their offense, and renewed their attack afresh.

Phil Esposito (#7) opens the scoring in Game One after just 30 seconds and is embraced by Yvan Cournoyer. The Soviets fell behind 2-0 before steamrolling Team Canada 7-3—a shocking defeat for the vaunted NHL stars. The player wearing #4 for the Soviet Union is Viktor Kuzkin (Toronto Star Photograph Archive, Courtesy of Toronto Public Library).

It was a common tactic in soccer. To North American hockey observers, however, it was a revolutionary idea.

Other oddities had Canadian fans bewildered. Whenever the vaunted New York Rangers' line of Rod Gilbert, Jean Ratelle and Vic Hadfield were on the ice, they were uncharacteristically impotent. Practically invisible, they seldom touched the puck, much less had scoring chances. Canada's best threesome was a pleasant surprise: Bobby Clarke, Ron Ellis, and Paul Henderson. They were supposed to be Team Canada's checking line. In the broadcast booth, analyst Brian Conacher opined, somewhat hopefully, that Team Canada needed to get Bobby Orr into the series to control the tempo of the game because they could not compete with the Soviets' fast pace otherwise.

The Canadians were badly outclassed over the last two periods, although the Soviets held a mere one-goal lead with six and a half minutes to play. Team Canada began to press for the tying goal. Yvan Cournoyer's

3. The Awakening 41

low shot from close in went past Tretiak and nicked the right goalpost. However, on the subsequent counterattack, Boris Mikhailov scored a fifth goal for the Soviet Union on a backhand from the slot that went between Ken Dryden's legs. Brian Conacher somehow concluded that Dryden had no chance on the routine shot. Foster Hewitt remained silent on the topic. Typical of the times, Hewitt opted not to contradict his broadcast partner's observations.

The Soviets now held a 5–3 advantage and proceeded to score two more late goals (by Evgeny Zimin and Alexander Yakushev) to add to the NHLers' Game One humiliation. Dryden—who played for the hometown Montréal Canadiens—looked shaky on both of them and was lustily jeered by the Forum crowd. The final score was Soviet Union 7, Canada 3. The shots on goal were 32–30 in favor of the visitors. The supposedly weak Soviet netminder, youthful Vladislav Tretiak, had played very well. "We were stunned—absolutely stunned," a rueful Sinden conceded to the swarming Canadian media, a group that was as equally bewildered by the game's outcome and was grasping for an explanation. "We lost to a very fine hockey team tonight."[17] In recapping the series for a book published late in 1972, Sinden wrote that Team Canada became completely "unglued" when confronted by the Soviets' foreign style of hockey. He had wrongly anticipated the reverse—that the Soviets would unravel upon facing NHL players for the first time.

There was the other side of the coin, of course. "Our players found out after ten minutes that the Canadians were just human beings,"[18] said a delighted Vsevolod Bobrov, the former outstanding player who was now the head coach of the Soviet national team. Indeed, one of the most lasting impressions of Game One was Soviet superstar forward Valeri Kharlamov blowing past three big-name NHL defensemen, Rod Seiling, Don Awrey and Brad Park, on three separate occasions "with amazing facility,"[19] noted Ted Blackman of the *Montréal Gazette*. (Seiling and Awrey were both left off Team Canada's roster for Game Two.) Toronto Maple Leafs owner, Harold Ballard, a feisty sexagenarian, and a vocal anti-communist, was duly impressed by that special Soviet player. He surprised hockey scribes by announcing he would gladly pay $1 million for the rights to sign Kharlamov to an NHL contract with Toronto. That was an astronomical sum in 1972.

When apprised of the final score from the Montréal Forum at his home in Great Britain, John (Bunny) Ahearne, the Irish-born, 74-year-old president of the IIHF whom Canadian hockey fans loved to hate, was reputedly delighted by the surprising result.

At the end of the game, an oversight in protocol embarrassed everyone connected with Team Canada. As was (and is) customary in international hockey, the Soviets lined up for a traditional postgame handshake. Meanwhile, the majority of the Canadians hustled off the ice to their dressing room, utterly oblivious to the ceremonial nicety they were supposed to observe. Ken Dryden, who had experienced some international hockey with the Canadian Nats, stuck around for the handshakes. He was joined by a few dawdling teammates. According to a book written by Harry Sinden, Alan Eagleson stormed frantically into Team Canada's dressing room to try to get the players back onto the Forum ice to save face—bit it was too late. When the Canadians returned, the Soviets had already left.

"I'll take the blame," conceded Sinden when apprised of the blatant faux pas. "I've played in international games. I was the first man in the dressing room, but I was never told about the ceremony [applying to this series]. It was an honest oversight. I hope the Russians understand."[20] To the rest of the world, it appeared the Canadians were sore losers. Several Team Canada players did not improve matters by telling reporters they thought the postgame handshake ritual was an insincere and pointless gesture. Perhaps it is worth noting—according to at least one source— that Soviet coach Vsevolod Bobrov, as team captain in 1955, did not stick around to shake the hands of the victorious Penticton Vees in Krefeld, West Germany 17½ years earlier.

The humbling defeat played very hard on the psyche of Canadian hockey fans. "The public was totally devastated," remembered CTV's Johnny Esaw in an interview years later. "[The Canadian] people were in a state of shock. Deep down inside they were scared to death—and so was I."[21]

Esaw was not exaggerating. To some people the defeat went beyond Canada just being on the wrong end of a hockey score. It was absolutely cataclysmic. The headline on Ted Blackman's brutally frank sports column in the September 4 *Montréal Gazette* read, "A dark day: Sept. 2, 1972; when pride turned to trauma." Blackman pessimistically told his readers, "When our national institution crumbles with one Bolshevik bodycheck, what can preserve the adjacent out-buildings of our culture? Nothing. Our national inferiority complex, defended only by our hockey, may now become terminal neurosis. We'll never be the same again."[22]

Blackman focused on a few seconds of play in the second period as an example of how the mighty had fallen and the hockey world had been turned upside down in one shocking night:

> It was 3–2 [for] Russia. None of us was convinced that Team NHL wouldn't soon bring down its wrath on the impudent invaders. Then it happened: Alexander Yakushev ... jolted Ron Ellis with a classic check. Seconds later, Valeri Kharlamov sent Guy Lapointe to the ice with a thump. And then Gary Bergman ... iced the puck.

3. The Awakening

Whatever Team Canada had presumed about the Russians, their notions had altered with the manifest admission: Ice the puck, brother. These cats have got us on the run.[23]

Everyone involved in Canadian hockey had some sort of explanation, flimsy or otherwise, for the debacle of Game One. Another journalist, Douglas Fisher of the Toronto *Globe & Mail*, blamed the Canadian defeat on arrogance and conceit. Coach Sinden was more pragmatic. He believed the superior conditioning of the Soviet players was largely responsible for the game's remarkable outcome. It was the old refrain that Lloyd Percival had preached about for decades. Sinden optimistically figured his squad's fitness would improve as the series progressed.

American reporters in traditional hockey hotbeds were equally shocked by the Soviet win in the series opener. "Count me among those who thought Harry Sinden and his men would be needing bigger hats on Sunday instead of alibis," wrote Harold Kaese of the *Boston Globe*. "The 7–3 defeat for the Canadians in the opening game ... was about as much as could be borne by anyone who thinks a National Hockey League player [is] a combination of Hercules, Lochinvar, Thor and John Wayne."[24]

After the game, the Soviets themselves could scarcely believe the 7–3 score. The word "fairytale" was uttered several times by the players and coaching staff inside the visitors' dressing room. The dominant result surprised even the top Soviet government officials back in Moscow. Originally cautious about their team's chances versus Canada's top professionals, they now saw the series as a huge propaganda opportunity that was well within their grasp. Word filtered from the Kremlin to Bobrov's men in Canada: The national hockey team of the Soviet Union was now ordered to win the series for the glory of their country and worldwide communism.

At least one business had a sense of humor about Team Canada's staggering loss in Montréal. On September 2, in a special series preview insert in the *Toronto Sun*, a Canadian distillery ran an ad that proclaimed, "If they can play hockey, we can make vodka." The next time the ad ran, the word "if" was prominently crossed out.

The Canadians proved to be a resilient bunch, however. Two nights later they won crucial Game Two at Maple Leaf Gardens in Toronto by a solid 4–1 score. Wayne Cashman of the Boston Bruins, known for being an edgy player, roughed up the Soviets thoroughly. Cashman's physicality, and a steady dose of persistent forechecking by the Canadians, disrupted the Soviets' passing that had been so efficient and dominant in Montréal. In the key moment of the game, Peter Mahovlich, while playing shorthanded, scored the prettiest goal of the entire series. On an individual rush, he stickhandled around Soviet defenseman Evgeny Paladiev and goaltender Vladislav Tretiak and tucked the puck into the net to give the Canadians an important insurance goal. Unlike Ken Dryden in Game One, Tony Esposito was excellent in net for Team Canada in Game Two.

Francis Rosa of the *Boston Globe* reported the huge sense of relief that spread among the worried fans in Toronto's famous arena as the final seconds of Game Two evaporated from the clock. He wrote that most of the 16,485 ticketholders were "hugging their neighbors and waving the Canadian flag at the end of the game. Canada's hockey prestige was restored—at least for a couple of days."[25] Indeed, in the space of 48 hours the advertised "exhibition series" with the Soviet National Team had morphed from a sporting curiosity into a deadly serious, we-must-win proposition for anyone in Canada who cared about hockey. That was just about everyone.

The famous Canadian vodka ad that ran before and during the 1972 Summit Series. This is the version that appeared in newspapers prior to the eye-opening first game.

Game Three was played at the Winnipeg Arena. Manitoba's capital city did not have an NHL team in 1972, but it had been the home base for the Canadian Nats for its brief, unsuccessful existence in the 1960s. Bobby Hull, now of the new Winnipeg Jets of the WHA—and barred from playing in the series because of it—was among the sellout crowd with his wife (Joanne) and his new boss, Jets owner Ben Hatskin, which had to be a little bit on the awkward side for the NHL brass. The 33-year-old Hull intended it to be that way (according to his 2023 obituary in the *Toronto Star*). He deliberately wanted to be a conspicuous presence in the building that evening. Journalist Dick Beddoes wrote years later, quite accurately, that "Hull had been ostracized by a spiteful NHL establishment."[26]

Harry Sinden put Tony Esposito back in net for Team Canada for Game Three. Few fans today recall much about it, but it may have been the most entertaining contest of the entire eight-game series. It ended in a 4–4 tie, a fair result for both teams. (Nobody in 1972 dreamed of playing overtime or having a godawful shootout to settle matters.) Neither team could muster a tie-breaking goal in the final 20 minutes of play. Despite the expected success eluding Team Canada, Sinden retained his sense of humor. He amusingly commented afterward, "Someone once said a tie is as exciting as kissing your sister. Well, for the last ten minutes tonight, that game looked like Raquel Welch to me."[27] Prior to the game, Paul Henderson witnessed something in a hallway near the visitors' dressing room that he had never seen before: Soviet goaltender Vladislav Tretiak repeatedly bouncing tennis balls off a wall with both hands and catching them. It was a simple yet terrific exercise to improve netminders' hand-eye coordination created by … Lloyd Percival. Soviet goalies had been using this basic drill, invented by a Canadian coach, for two decades. Henderson promptly summoned Team Canada's three goaltenders—Dryden, Esposito, and Ed Johnston—to watch it. None of them had ever seen it before.

Despite the series clearly not being the romp that the Canadians had figured on, the team still went ahead with their original plan to showcase youthful players in Game Four in Vancouver. It proved costly as the Soviets won, 5–3. That score actually was flattering to the Canadians as the Soviets dominated the action from the opening faceoff. Coach Harry Sinden wholly admitted Team Canada was never in the contest. Bill Goldsworthy of the Minnesota North Stars took two silly, obvious penalties early on which the Soviets promptly converted into a pair of power-play goals, both netted by Valeri Kharlamov. Goldsworthy, despite getting two assists in Game Four, had his ice time reduced thereafter. Sinden could not trust him to keep a level head.

As the clock wound down, loud boos descended on Team Canada from all corners of the Pacific Coliseum. Vancouver was something of a leftist haven, even in 1972, and a handful of pro-communist spectators began taunting the Canadians. "Admit communism is superior to capitalism!"[28] one repeatedly yelled. An angry and sweat-soaked Phil Esposito was being interviewed on the ice immediately after the game by CTV's Johnny Esaw. In the most famous rant in Canadian television history, Esposito passionately slammed his countrymen who were criticizing Team Canada. He assured the nation that every player was giving total commitment, therefore he thought the booing they were receiving was unfair. Espo told the country to "face facts"[29] that the Russians were good but the series was not over. He was right. The Series was not over—only the Canadian-based portion had been completed. The two teams headed to the Soviet Union with the "Russian amateurs" surprisingly ahead 2-1-1 after four games. What the Canadian contingent could expect in Moscow was anyone's guess.

Not long afterward, Esposito told Milt Dunnell of the *Toronto Star*, "Hell, half the press said we should win [all] eight games. Most of our guys never had seen the Russian team. Whoever scouted the Russians should get out of the scouting business. They said we should have no trouble. Is it our fault if they were wrong?"[30]

Dunnell described the negative feeling at the Pacific Coliseum throughout most of Game Four. He wrote,

> Many of the 18,000 partisans hooted the Good Guys, whom they had hoped to send on their way to Europe with a resounding victory over the comrades.
> Bill Goldsworthy, whose two penalties helped the Soviets practically sew up their 5-3 win before the first period was half gone, was a special target of fan abuse. Their displeasure spread to other members of the team. Ken Dryden, MVP of the [1971] Stanley Cup series, was jeered when he made routine saves.[31]

The next day's *Toronto Star* featured this front-page headline: "Canada loses its home series—amid a thunder of boos." It was a good time for Team Canada to quietly exit their hockey-mad country and its disappointed and disillusioned citizens.

Before landing in Moscow, Team Canada had an extended stopover in Stockholm to play two exhibition games versus the Swedish national squad. The Canadians were called gangsters and thugs by the Swedish newspaper for their rough style of play. Even Canada's ambassador in Stockholm made unkind remarks about them. Oddly, the team began to gel while away from the spotlight of Canadian media and passionate hockey fans. A handful of players who grumbled about inadequate ice time—most notably New York's Vic Hadfield—quit Team Canada and returned to North America where their club teams were now preparing for the upcoming 1972-73 NHL season. (Fans in Canadian buildings would routinely boo Hadfield thoroughly for the rest of his career for his decision.) However, the departure of the malcontents had the effect of further unifying those players who chose to stay and face whatever adversities—and there would be many—might come in the Soviet Union.

After a two-week hiatus, the remaining four games of the series would all be played in Moscow at the Luzhniki Ice Palace, one of the few indoor hockey arenas in the entire Soviet Union. The Canadians quickly discovered that everyday life there was far different than it was in Canada. Some of Team Canada's prized imported food—including steaks

3. The Awakening

and a large supply of beloved Canadian beer—mysteriously vanished in the labyrinth of Soviet customs. Hotel rooms were said to be bugged—and some certainly were. Jackhammers were going full tilt outside Moscow's Intourist Hotel in the wee hours of the morning, disrupting players' sleep. Some Canadian players received phantom phone calls in the middle of the night to further disrupt their rest. On one occasion, a scheduled Team Canada practice was delayed by a children's shinny game. The unsporting shenanigans had some effect on the visitors. One Canadian player, Frank Mahovlich, seemed to become paranoid. He was convinced that somewhere deep within the huge Soviet Union a team was secretly being specially trained to beat the Super Bowl–champion Dallas Cowboys in American football.

On the positive side, the Canadian contingent was heartened to receive hundreds of telegrams via their embassy from well-wishers back home. Some of them literally featured thousands of fans' names. The messages were taped to the walls of Team Canada's dressing room for inspiration. Years later, Brad Park would marvel at their length and the fact that they covered every possible inch of space. Apparently, Phil Esposito's fiery postgame rant in Vancouver had struck a chord with a great many Canadians.

Canada played very well in Game Five to begin with, having no trouble adjusting to the wider European ice surface. Toronto Maple Leaf owner Harold Ballard attributed their strong start to the players' wives having recently arrived in Moscow "with mattresses strapped to their backs."[32] However, Team Canada's hard-earned 3–0 lead evaporated in short order as the Soviets eventually rallied in the third period to win, 5–4. Nevertheless, the nearly 3,000 rowdy Canadian hockey fans who travelled to Moscow to witness the four games, sang a rousing version of "O Canada" at the end of the game to raise the players' spirits. In the Canadian dressing room, Phil Esposito calmly told his teammates they would not lose another game. They all nodded in agreement. Whether or not they all truly believed Espo will never be known for certain.

Esposito indeed proved to be a prophet. Horrendous officiating by the duo of West German Josef Kompalla and Czech Franz Baader—whom the Canadian players dubbed "Baader and Worse"—marred Game Six. (Canada was assessed 31 minutes in penalties to the Soviets' four. but Canada still won the game, 3–2, to stay alive in the series. Harry Sinden said it was the worst officiating he had ever seen at any level of hockey and publicly denounced the two officials as incompetent.) All the game's scoring occurred in the second period. Paul Henderson scored the winning goal for Canada. He would be heard from again. To the surprise of many observers, the Soviets did not pull Vladislav Tretiak for an extra attacker late in the game—even when Ron Ellis was serving a penalty. There was a reason for this: Pulling the goalie was perceived as an act of desperation in the USSR. Desperation was a dangerous emotion that ran contrary to the controlled play preached in Soviet hockey theory.

Game Six turned nasty on a couple of occasions. The apex was when Bobby Clake whacked Valeri Kharlamov across his ankle with what journalist Dick Beddoes described as a "wicked two-hander."[33] Clarke was assessed a major penalty for slashing, but Kharlamov was disabled for the rest of Game Six and all of Game Seven. When he returned for Game Eight he was ineffective. After the game, Clarke was unapologetic, saying he never would have gotten out of small-town Flin Flon, Manitoba if he had not learned how to deliver such a blow when the occasion called for it. In 1976 Clarke insisted, "It wasn't premeditated. [Kharlamov] had speared me. It wasn't a clean series from the start."[34]

Former NHL player Brian Conacher, who was doing color commentary beside Foster Hewitt for Canadian television, wrote in his 2007 book,

> [From] the broadcast booth I was shocked and disgusted when I saw Clarke viciously chop at Kharlamov's left ankle. Emotionally these games had clearly gone beyond sport for Team Canada. [It] had truly become unrestricted war on ice.[35]

Game Seven was another one-goal Canadian triumph. Late in the third period, Paul Henderson—who had earlier been helped off the ice after slamming headfirst into the boards—scored on a remarkable one-against-four attack on the Russian net. It was easily his best goal of the series. (Henderson, in the decades to come, would insist he never scored a better goal in his life.) It came with 2:06 left in the game. Again, the Soviets stubbornly refused to pull Tretiak for a sixth attacker. Henderson's goal gave Canada a spectacular 4–3 win to level the gripping series at 3–3–1 after seven matches. But it would soon be overshadowed.

More on-ice nastiness ensued a few minutes before Henderson's heroics when Boris Mikhailov repeatedly kicked Canada's Gary Bergman who was attempting to freeze the puck along the boards. Bergman, who played for the Detroit Red Wings, kicked (and punched) Mikhailov right back. Veteran hockey scribe Francis Rosa of the *Boston Globe* could scarcely believe the level of nasty play Soviets were getting away with. He penned, "The Soviet hockey team [is] under the cloak of immunity that international referees give to such things as kicking, spearing and interference...."[36]

In Canada, the public was thoroughly engrossed and emotionally invested in the titanic games being played in Moscow. With the time difference in that part of Europe, the contests were being aired live in the

3. The Awakening 49

early afternoon on the Eastern time zone and the late morning on the West coast, but Canadians were still tuning in by the millions. For Game Eight, played on a Thursday, the country effectively shut down as three-quarters of Canada's population of 21 million tuned into the CTV television broadcast to see how things would turn out. Today, virtually every living Canadian who was at least 10 years old at the time knows exactly where he or she was on September 28, 1972. One United Press report in the *Boston Globe* claimed, "Hardly ever was so much beer drunk or were so few people working ... from coast to coast in Canada. Millions kept their eyes glued to TV sets."[37]

Game Eight very nearly did not happen as Swedish referee Ove Dahlberg, scheduled to work the deciding game, was reported to be feeling ill. Dahlberg was one European official whom the Canadians liked and respected. (He was also a capable soccer referee who was held in high esteem throughout the continent.) The Soviets instead announced that the detested twosome of Baader and Kompalla would be back to work the climactic contest. The Canadian delegation angrily threatened a walkout over their appointments, but they eventually relented. Team Canada's assistant coach John Ferguson called the shenanigans a form of psychological warfare—which they certainly were. Later, Dahlberg was spotted as a spectator in the arena. He appeared to be the picture of health. (Apparently NHLPA boss Alan Eagleson, a Team Canada executive who would oddly become a peripheral figure during Game Eight, claimed that Dahlberg was told by the Soviets he had better call in sick or he would never officiate another hockey game. Taking the personal threat to his well-being very seriously, Dahlberg acquiesced.)

Another peripheral issue arose. The 2,700 noisy Canadian fans—whose antics and unwavering support of their team had become a factor in the three previous games in Moscow—learned there were suddenly no tickets for them to attend the deciding game—even though they had already paid for them well in advance. They instead were offered free passes to the ballet, a ridiculous compromise which would have been amusing had the increasingly volatile situation allowed for any levity. When the Canadian embassy in Moscow intervened, suddenly the Canadian fans rightfully got their tickets for Game Eight.

Team Canada's Gary Bergman boldly displayed confidence during the player introductions. The bald-headed defenseman brazenly flashed the "V for Victory" sign from the Second World War when his name was announced. The gesture merely added to the tension permeating the Luzhniki Ice Palace.

Within four minutes of the opening faceoff, all hell nearly broke loose. Canada's J.P. Parisé of the Minnesota North Stars was whistled for a debatable interference penalty. It was the third infraction called by Kompalla against Canada already. Parisé banged his stick on the ice to complain—and was given a 10-minute misconduct penalty too. The infuriated Parisé—who had never received a misconduct during his professional hockey career to that point—lost his composure entirely. He threatened to decapitate Kompalla with his stick, and promptly earned a game misconduct for his actions. Team Canada's American trainer, John (Frosty) Forristal of the Boston Bruins, angrily threw a stool at Kompalla to signify the Canadians were not going to tolerate what they perceived as horribly biased officiating. Harry Sinden began flinging furniture too. All the while, the enraged and vocal Canadian fans in the Luzhniki Ice Palace began chanting, "Let's go home!" Things eventually settled down, but the tension in the arena remained palpably thick.

In a gripping see-saw affair, the Soviets led 5–3 entering the third period. Phil Esposito scored early to narrow the Russian lead to a single goal, giving Canada a ray of hope. With seven and a half minutes to play, Yvan Cournoyer scored on a rising backhand from a goalmouth scramble in front of goaltender Vladislav Tretiak to tie the game—except the red goal light failed to come on. Team Canada official Alan Eagleson sensed, perhaps with good reason, that a dastardly plot was afoot. He leapt from his seat to do something about it. He tried to get the public-address announcer (a communist from Edmonton who had emigrated from Canada!) to confirm Cournoyer's game-tying goal. He did not get very far. Eagleson was quickly and roughly apprehended by several uniformed Russian soldiers and was being hustled off to God-knows-where. Peter Mahovlich promptly led the Canadians off the bench and across the ice to the area where Eagleson was being corralled and roughed up. The Soviets possessed machine guns, but the Canadians liberally whacked at and poked the gendarmes with their hockey sticks until Eagleson was set free. The Canadian players then escorted Eagleson across the ice to their bench to watch the final few minutes of play, but not before Eagleson made a threatening gesture to Leonid Brezhnev and other top Soviet government officials. Trainer Frosty Forristal was less subtle. He flipped Brezhnev and company the middle finger of both hands. The situation was becoming surreal. Later the goal judge, Victor Dombrowski, would state that the goal light had simply malfunctioned. To this day, few Canadians believe that explanation.

The omnipresent Phil Esposito assisted on the game-tying goal. Decades later, hockey blogger Maurice Tougas would marvel at the remarkable tenacity of the feisty Boston Bruin center, "Esposito was a force of nature. He exemplified why Canada won the series; we simply … wanted it more. We had to win it. Esposito simply would not allow Canada to lose the series, and for his efforts I am forever grateful."[38]

3. The Awakening 51

In the dying seconds of the third period, with the game and series looking to conclude in a tie, the omnipresent Paul Henderson took charge again. He picked up a loose, bouncing puck in the Soviet zone near the net, firing it once at Tretiak who made the initial stop with his pads. But Henderson got to the rebound first and slid it past the sprawling Soviet netminder. The time of the winning goal was 19:26. Henderson has always classified it as a "garbage goal" compared to the much prettier ones he had scored earlier in the series. Be that as it may, somehow Canada had won the game, 6–5, and the series 4–3–1. Again, Tretiak remained on the ice for the final 34 seconds without being pulled. Francis Rosa, one of the few American reporters who went to Moscow to cover the epic series, reported the celebrations in the stands among the visiting fans.

> [They] yelled themselves hoarse as they counted down the time, and the [Canadian] players on the ice turned into fans. They thrust their sticks in the air in a gesture of victory. The made the victory sign with their fingers. And they held up one finger [to indicate] who's number one in the world.
> And the Soviet players lined up on their blue line, waiting patiently for the celebration on the ice to end so they could shake hands with their conquerors.[39]

Toronto Star photographer Frank Lennon snapped the image of a joyful Henderson being embraced by Yvan Cournoyer—a French-Canadian hugging an English-Canadian. It became the most famous picture in Canadian history—and the most reproduced. Over the years, many people have argued that September 28, 1972, was the greatest day in the country's history. It is difficult to debate the point with a hockey fan. Canada went berserk with both joy and relief. Regional, cultural, and linguistic differences among Canadians ceased to exist on that special day. When the game was shown in its entirety again that night in prime time on CTV, 10 million people happily watched the replay and rejoiced a second time. Author Ray MacSkimming would comment years later, "The series did more for [Canadian] national unity than a dozen royal commissions and any number of constitutional conferences."[40]

Fifty years later, Vladislav Tretiak—who played every second of all eight games for the Soviets—bitterly recalled for a documentary about the 1972 Series, "We were leading 5–3 after two periods. Who beats us when we are leading by two goals going into the third period? Nobody. Never. Canada made magic."[41]

The result was, of course, front-page news across Canada. Even the *Boston Globe* gave it the same coverage. Veteran *Globe* sports scribe Francis Rosa happily gushed, "Wow! Was this a night in Moscow! Forget Bobby

Thomson's home run. Forget the Red Sox Impossible Dream [1967 American League pennant]. Remember instead Ken Dryden skating the length of the ice with 34 seconds left in the game to embrace Paul Henderson...."[42]

From his home in Moscow, the recently retired 53-year-old Anatoli Tarasov was impressed by the Canadians' display of grit and resilience against the Soviet team he had largely built, claiming the NHLers had played liked caged animals. The remark was meant as a compliment to the victors.

In some remote parts of the Soviet Union without television—and where dissemination of the truth was not a high priority—it was reported by the state media that Bobrov's team had won all eight games against the Canadian professionals! That was an outright lie, of course, but the Soviets claiming overall victory because they had outscored Canada, on aggregate, 32–31 was at least factually accurate.

Phil Esposito (left) and Paul Henderson, Canada's heroes from 1972, reunite in January 1985 (Toronto Star Photograph Archive, Courtesy of Toronto Public Library).

Canadian political pundits went as far to predict that Team Canada's victory was a positive sign for Prime Minister Pierre Trudeau and his ruling Liberal government. There was going to be a federal election in Canada on October 30. "It's not good to have discontented people,"[43] said one unnamed party strategist who said he feared the political ramifications of a hockey defeat at the hands of the Soviet Union.

Henderson was Canada's hero, but even the Soviet players knew that Phil Esposito was the outstanding player of the series and the heart and soul of the Canadian team. As a token of respect, they gave him a samovar—a decorative tea urn. Esposito had no idea what it was but he appreciated the gesture. Years later Esposito said bluntly, "The '72 series was not fun. It was a deadly serious business. It was the only time in my life I would have killed another human being to win—and that frightened me."⁴⁴

As the decades passed, Esposito became very friendly with many of those dastardly communist hockey players he had wanted to exterminate in 1972. He has also made many trips to post–Soviet Russia, in various capacities, where he was treated like royalty by the locals. "I've become close friends with [Alexander] Yakushev," Esposito confessed on the 40th anniversary of the Summit Series in 2012, even though a language barrier still exists between them. "Let me put it this way: He doesn't speak English very well; I don't speak Russian very well. It seems to me, the more we drank vodka, the more we understood each other. I don't know why that matters. That's the truth."⁴⁵

It had been a wild, tremendous, thrilling series, full of entertainment, incidents, and unbelievable twists and turns. Author Roy MacSkimming, in his book *Cold War*, accurately tabbed the eight games of the Summit Series "one of the great mythic dramas in the history of sport."⁴⁶ Joe Falls, a baseball writer from Detroit, generally cared little about hockey. But he came across the Canada–Soviet series by accident while channel surfing at his Michigan home—and was instantly hooked by the unfolding, thoroughly gripping drama. At a time when his hometown Detroit Tigers were involved in an exciting pennant race, Falls penned a column in *The Sporting News* in which he readily stated the hockey games he had witnessed on Canadian television were easily the most compelling sports event he had ever seen in his life.

In Toronto, shortly after Game Eight, the joyful switchboard operators at Maple Leaf Gardens immediately began including the phrase "the home of Paul Henderson" when answering phone calls. Plans for a public welcome-home reception in that city for Team Canada were switched from the famous Toronto arena to an enormous outdoor venue—Nathan Phillips Square—because organizers believed the 16,000-seat building could not accommodate the expected turnout. It proved to be a very good idea: On Sunday, October 1, more than 80,000 giddy people from all walks of life turned out in a driving rainstorm to greet their hockey heroes. They carried a wide array of homemade banners that ranged from the pithy ("Hurray!") to the comical ("Canada is Beaver Power!") to the mildly sacrilegious ("Jesus Saves but Esposito Knocks in Rebounds!"). One soaked attendee was an elderly local woman, Mabel Roadknight, whom the *Windsor Star* described as "silver-haired." She told a reporter, "I wouldn't have missed this for the world. I was all by myself when they won and I just ended up crying. I may [cry] again tonight."⁴⁷

The throng's loudest cheers were, predictably, reserved for Paul Henderson and Phil Esposito. In his brief speech to the crowd, Espo alluded

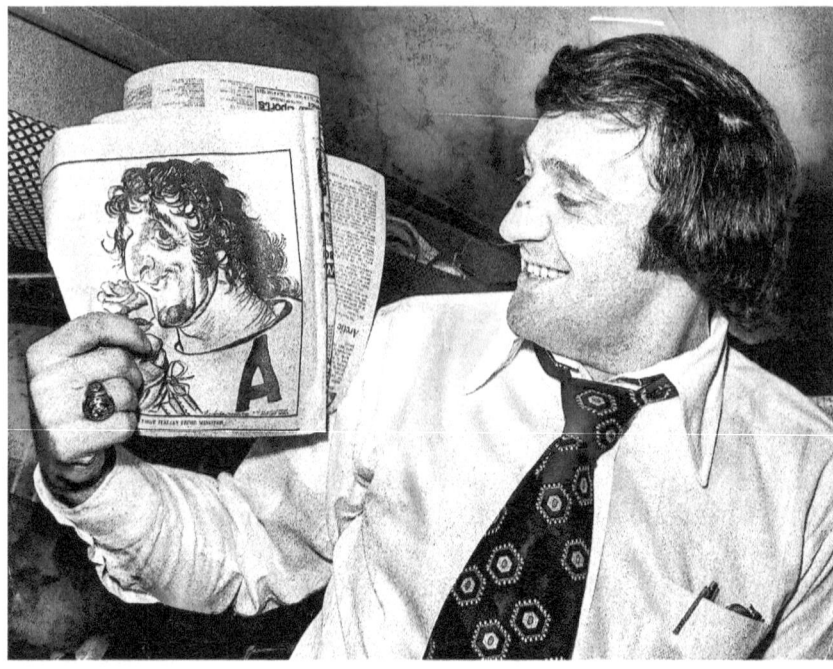

On the flight home from Moscow in 1972, Phil Esposito is amused by a newspaper caricature of himself (Toronto Star Photograph Archive, Courtesy of Toronto Public Library).

to his harsh remarks after Game Four in Vancouver three weeks earlier by saying, "You people have proved me wrong and proved the rest of us wrong. Thanks for all your support."[48]

The huge love-in on display in Toronto was actually the second stop of the day for Team Canada. Earlier, an equally large and boisterous crowd had greeted the entire team at Mirabelle Airport in Montréal. Among them was Canadian prime minister Pierre Trudeau. The players, coaches and staff were paraded through the streets of the city atop fire engines. Those players who lived in Quebec said their goodbyes to their short-term Team Canada teammates and stayed behind while the rest of the victorious group headed westward to Toronto for further celebrations. Regardless of which NHL clubs they were affiliated with for the remainder of their careers, there would always be a special kinship between the players who represented Canada in those trying days of September 1972.

The hard-fought triumph had been a national feel-good moment for all of Canada, but the eight-game series had clearly shown that Canada was not the lone hockey superpower on the planet—and never would be again. Quebec journalist Louis Arpin accurately wrote, "Hockey fans in

Canada had been lulled to sleep and led to believe, in a mythical way, that their idols were Greek gods. We now know that other countries have bred players who can rival anyone."[49] Most of them had CCCP on the fronts of their hockey jerseys.

More than three years later, during Super Series '76, Jack Dulmage of the *Windsor Star* declared,

> The 1972 series was tremendously emotional and nationalistic. It was Canada versus the Soviet Union at the highest possible level. It was played under amateur and diplomatic rules. The Canadian government virtually expropriated the NHL to form its side.
>
> It was an exhibition series won by the narrowest of margins by Canada. Yet, had the final game ended in a tie, the Russians were prepared to claim the championship of the world [based on aggregate] goals.
>
> It wasn't an exhibition series at all....[50]

Harry Sinden later wrote in his 1972 book, one of the first of numerous tomes that would be penned about the famous series by its Canadian participants, "How did we beat them? I don't have the answer." Despite his admitted uncertainty, Team Canada's head coach proffered this interesting theory anyway:

> Canadian pros are definitely more accustomed to playing in games with more at stake than the Russians [are]. Just look at the way we won the last three games—games we couldn't afford to lose. We won them all in the closing minutes. Our mental conditioning—the kind of toughness that comes only from playing for the Stanley Cup—is the thing that, in the end, proved to be the difference.[51]

Ken Dryden would thoughtfully note in his hockey journal, "I think we have all grown up these past six weeks [since training camp]. From the unswerving commitment to the belief that Canadians are unquestionably the best in the world and that our style is right because we invented the game and developed it, the feeling now seems to have changed to the awareness that the Russians now have something going, too. Both the Russians and the Canadians have an amazing amount to learn."[52]

Echoing Dryden's written comments, hockey historian Todd Denault wrote in 2010, "The reality is that in the course of one month the course of hockey had been forever changed."[53] Indeed, it unquestionably had.

4

The Often-Forgotten 1974 Summit Series

> "In 1972, it was bare bones, Cold War, Us versus Them hockey. In 1974, the series wasn't just seen as a fight over hockey supremacy. It was also about the messy political battle between the NHL and WHA."
> —Russell Field, University of Manitoba sports historian.[1]

Given the overall success and emotional roller coaster ride of the 1972 Canada–Soviet series, it was no surprise that shortly afterward there was talk of a follow-up meeting between the Canadian professionals and the defeated Soviet world amateur kingpins.

Negotiations began in April 1973. Lou Lefaive, the executive director of Sports Canada; and Gordon Juckes, a former president of the Canadian Amateur Hockey Association (CAHA), met with Andrey Starovoytov, the General Secretary of the Soviet Ice Hockey Federation. Discussions would intensify in January 1974 in Leningrad where the World Junior Ice Hockey Championship was being held. On the morning of April 26, 1974, both the Soviet Union and Canada would simultaneously announce the exciting rematch to their respective nations. There was one major difference this time, however: Unlike in 1972 when Bobby Hull, J.C. Tremblay, Gerry Cheevers, Derek Sanderson and other mavericks who jumped to the World Hockey Association (WHA) were disqualified from participating, in 1974 any NHL, WHA, or Canadian amateur player would be eligible for selection to represent Team Canada. The inclusivity was certainly a step forward.

However, just because Hockey Canada and the Canadian federal government were able to publicly make such a proclamation, it would still be up to the NHL to release their players for the 1974 series. Unfortunately for hockey fans, the NHL steadfastly refused to do so for legal reasons. At the time, hockey's premier professional league was engaged in a nasty dispute with the WHA over the enforceability of the reserve clause in the contracts of NHL players—a contentious issue already occupying the courts in the United States with baseball players seeking free agency. Absolutely the last thing the NHL wanted was to have the WHA viewed as an equal entity or something close to it. With or without the NHL's stars, the 1974 Canada–Soviet clash was initially planned to be a six-game affair, but it was later extended to eight games to mimic the successful format used two years prior. It would start about two weeks later than the Summit Series had in 1972—on Tuesday, September 17—at an arena somewhere in Canada. The games would conclude three weeks later in the Soviet Union on Sunday, October 6.

Also mimicking the 1972 confrontation, the 1974 Summit Series would feature four different Canadian sites playing host to the Soviets with each new game moving westward across the vast country. Those four WHA cities were Quebec City, Toronto, Winnipeg, and Vancouver. As was the case in 1972, the remaining four games of the series would all take place in Moscow at the Luzhniki Ice Palace. Team Canada would also add three exhibition games—one each in Helsinki, Gothenburg (Sweden), and Prague—as part of their European tour to prepare themselves for the larger European ice surface.

Team Canada's roster would be selected wholly from the WHA instead of the National Hockey League as the NHL had refused to release its players for the event. (There were no amateurs selected, of course.) This would provide an opportunity for such players as 35-year-old Bobby Hull (who was assigned to the team in 1972 but not allowed to play) and Gordie Howe (who had retired in 1972 at age 44) to finally test their mettle against the mighty Soviet Union players. This would also help give more clout and credibility to the financially struggling WHA. As a September 4, 1974, headline in the Toronto *Globe and Mail* succinctly and accurately put it, "Success against Russians would prove parity with NHL."[2]

Entering the 1974 series, the WHA had just completed its second season. Over its checkered history, the league largely consisted of players dredged from the minor leagues with a few NHL stars and aging veterans mixed in for good measure. The WHA was certainly a mobile outfit in the seven years it existed. It was the goal of the WHA to capitalize on North American markets left untapped by the NHL. Eventually 30 different teams were WHA members, some for comically short times. Two teams would change locations before the first season began, the Dayton Arrows became the Houston Aeros and the San Francisco Sharks would head north of the border and across the continent to become the Quebec Nordiques. Two other teams—the Miami Screaming Eagles and the Calgary Broncos—would fold outright before playing a single WHA game, being replaced by the Philadelphia Blazers and the Cleveland Crusaders respectively. With all the problems faced by the league, including only minimal TV coverage on both the local and national levels, it was a wonder how the circuit survived as long as it did. It came to no real surprise to anyone when the league finally folded in 1979, with four of its six remaining clubs merging with the NHL. But in the spring of 1974, the WHA was still very much an optimistic organization, perhaps in a Pollyannaish sort of way. The league's series versus the powerful Soviet National team would be its apex.

On July 31, 1974, William (Wild Bill) Hunter, the Saskatoon-born owner and sometimes coach of the Edmonton Oilers, hosted a press conference. It was to introduce the WHA's 1974 version of Team Canada: head coach Bill Harris and the 25 players he had chosen to combat the Soviet Red Army. The smaller roster size was a notable difference from the 35 who played in 1972 that negatively produced dissention and disappointment among the underused NHL stars. Harris had coached the 1973–74 Toronto Toros of the WHA to a 41–33–4 record. Team Canada II, as they had been dubbed by the Canadian media, would feature a mixture of rugged wisdom, dominant scoring finesse, and wily youth. John Gault wrote in a piece for the September 1, 1974, issue of *Maclean's*, a popular Canadian news magazine,

> Billy Harris is taking a team of Canadian professional hockey players into an eight-game series with the Soviet Union for reasons quite different from those that drive almost any other coach to take any other team into any other competition. His mission is nothing less than to restore ... an image for Canadian hockey teams abroad that runs contrary to one existing now: sort of street gangs on skates. "I'm looking for guys with class," Harris told me.

Assisting the 39-year-old Harris at the bench would be a pair of player-coaches in his age range: Bobby Hull of the Winnipeg Jets, who had just come off a fine season in which he netted 53 goals in 75 games; and defenseman Pat (Whitey) Stapleton of the Chicago Cougars. Stapleton was one of just three returning players for Canada following their 1972 triumphant series. Also returning were Paul Henderson and Frank Mahovlich. Conversely, the Soviets would have 17 returning players from 1972. Gerry Cheevers, a two-time Stanley Cup–winner with the Boston Bruins, would be called upon to play the bulk of the games in goal for the Canadians. Hull was featured on the cover of *Maclean's* wearing a stereotypical Russian fur hat while performing a squat dance on skates. Full marks go to the photographer for creativity.

There was a change atop of the USSR's national team: Boris Kulagin, a likable and quotable chap, would now be the man behind the Soviet bench.

4. The Often-Forgotten 1974 Summit Series

The 49-year-old Kulagin was certainly no stranger to Canada–Soviet hockey, having served as the Soviet Union's national team's assistant coach during the 1972 Summit Series.

At the start of the 1974 Canada–Soviet series, there were several storylines and key questions to be answered. Could the WHA players duplicate the success of the more celebrated 1972 NHL squad? How would Gordie Howe, an ageless wonder to be certain, fare at the ripe old age of 46 (an age well past what the Soviets believed any athlete was capable of playing competitive hockey)? Would Bobby Hull dazzle the fans as expected? Could Paul Henderson produce heroic magic once again? Would the Canadians receive fair and impartial officiating in Moscow? Perhaps most importantly, could the Canadian team be game-ready in time to face a formidable Soviet Union team that practiced together virtually year-round?

In 1974, North America's pro athletes often spent their off-seasons living the high life and shirking their fitness. Pro hockey players may have been the least diligent of all regarding their bodies. To combat the Soviets, who were always in shape and game-ready, on August 1, a special workout regimen was sent to each member of the Canadian squad. The program was apparently designed by Harris along with the team trainer, and the team doctor. It was expected that each player would arrive ready to play or they would be sent home. To their credit, many of the Canadian players had already been skating on their own and working out through their own routines which involved weightlifting and running.

Because of Bill Hunter's connections to the Western Hockey League (WHL) and proximity to their training camp in Edmonton, a few training games were set up against some junior teams from that circuit. Many of these young players had been playing together for some time. Accordingly, it was thought that facing their youth and speed would be a good warm-up for Team Canada for their upcoming games against the Soviet Union. Canada's WHA all-stars would also be subjected to something quite novel to hockey players: a NASA-designed 30-minute workout to improve speed and conditioning. It was also revealed that Canada's medical advisors had ordered 960 cans of the orange-flavored soda pop, C-Plus, to keep their players hydrated throughout their games. Years later, Mark Howe shared his thoughts. "I remember looking at the Russians drinking water on the bench thinking, 'Maybe they're ahead of us with that.'"[3] Each player was also given a new pair of skates to break in prior to their first game against the Soviets—which may not have been a great idea.

Game One was set for Tuesday night, September 17, at Le Colisée in Quebec City before an enthusiastic, sold-out crowd. It was the only venue that was different from the Canadian stops in 1972 when Game One in that series was held at the Montréal Forum. (Montréal never had a WHA team.)

Tickets for the opening game were so precious that two million hopeful fans purchased special lottery tickets that were sold at $2 apiece. From that enormous pool of applicants, the names of 15,000 lucky buyers were drawn at random. Only then were they permitted to purchase seats for the game. Full marks go to whomever came up with that lucrative idea, too.

As in 1972, Canadian prime minister Pierre Trudeau was on hand to drop the puck for the ceremonial pregame faceoff. The home team intended to counter the fitness of the Soviets with shorter shifts to keep their legs as fresh as possible. Canada opened the scoring at 12:13 of the first period. John McKenzie, formerly of the Boston Bruins now of the Vancouver Blazers, received a nifty pass in front of Soviet netminder Vladislav Tretiak and skillfully tucked the puck behind him. The Soviets countered with a strong second period, taking advantage of five Canadian penalties, outscoring the home team 3–1 to take a one goal lead into the third period. Undaunted, Canada scored in the final twenty minutes, dramatically tying the match with 5:42 remaining on the clock. They outshot the Soviet squad 34 to 28 in earning a 3–3 tie in a game they probably would have won if not for allowing two costly Soviet power play goals in the second period. Bobby Hull finished the game with a pair of goals and an assist. As was very familiar from 1972, Tretiak was superb. He made several game-saving stops in the final five minutes to keep the score level. Jim Coleman admiringly wrote, "[Tretiak] rises to extraordinary heights of goaltending perfection whenever he plays in international hockey matches against Canada. On his handling of Frank Mahovlich in the final minute alone, Tretiak should be rewarded with a 24-karat gold watch and, at least, a platinum-plated replica of the Order of Lenin."[4]

Francis Rosa, covering the series for the *Boston Globe*, praised what he had witnessed. He wrote, "Do you know what was up here [in Quebec City] last night? The hockey game? It was the ninth game of the '72 Canada–Russia series. And all those old men and so-called fringe players from the WHA, who have been put down so often by so many, played a great game of hockey against the Soviets."[5]

Indeed, to the surprise of many hockey pundits, it had been an excellently played opening game with an enthusiastic crowd that frequently sang songs to inspire their team as if it were a European soccer match. A headline in the next day's *Ottawa Citizen* suggested that if the high standard of play continued, the 1974 Series perhaps could surpass the landmark 1972 classic. It was a combination of both high praise—and high hopes.

In retrospect, the Soviets may have been lulled into underestimating the aging WHA stars prior to Game One. After the game, the visitors were quietly sitting in their dressing room. They had been amused by negative

4. The Often-Forgotten 1974 Summit Series   61

Canadian pre-series newspaper stories that predicted the Soviets would handle Team Canada 1974 easily. "What a game," Tretiak admitted. "And those [players] are called the old-timers! Are those considered weak Canadians? Seems to me it is going to be harder than it was two years ago."[6]

Bobby Hull, the best player on the ice who was not wearing goalie equipment, noted to reporters that although Team Canada had not achieved its optimum fitness level yet, the Soviets seemed to be taking shorter shifts than the Canadians by the end of the game. Francis Rosa concurred, noting, "The most surprising aspect of the game was that the Canadians actually outskated the Soviets in the third period. The Russians ... played the last two minutes as if they were protecting a one-goal lead. Who's in shape?"[7]

During the post-game interviews, Bobby Hull was asked about the NHL's decision to ban him from playing in the 1972 Canada–Soviet series. "It was childish to blackball me, but I don't hold much grudge," he opined with a wry smile. Then he added, "You have to forgive children."[8]

Two nights later, on Thursday, September 19, a crowd of 16,485 fans piled into Maple Leaf Gardens in Toronto for the second game of the series. Team Canada got off to a positive start by scoring a pair of goals in the opening frame. The first goal was courtesy of some pretty passing between the father and son duo of Gordie and Mark Howe. After the play, Gordie was injured with some bruised ribs. "He actually told me I did it to him," Mark Howe later confessed. "After the goal, I went and hugged him hard, and he had his arms up in the air."[9] The bizarre injury from a teammate's embrace would knock the senior Howe out of the rest of the game.

The two teams would exchange goals in the second period and head to the final frame with the host Canadians in the lead, 3–1. Roughly two minutes into the third period, the Soviets apparently had managed to put the puck behind Gerry Cheevers for a second goal. The red goal light game on and remained on for a solid 15 seconds before referee Tom Brown waved it off. J.C. Tremblay, the Montréal Canadiens' alum now playing with the Quebec Nordiques, added the only tally in the third period to preserve the victory much to the appreciation of the hometown crowd. The 4–1 triumph also precisely matched the score by which the desperate 1972 Canadian squad had won Game Two in Toronto.

Goaltender Gerry Cheevers, who had a superb night guarding the pipes, was named "Canadian Player of the Game" for stopping 29 of the 30 shots he faced. Cheevers was awarded a color television for his effort, but he was unable to celebrate. He learned shortly afterward that his father-in-law, John Sciamonte, had suffered a major heart attack while attending the game and had to be rushed via ambulance to a Toronto hospital. He passed away there. Meanwhile Vladislav Tretiak was so battered by the constant barrage of Canadian attacks he had faced, that he had collapsed, exhausted, on a bench in the Soviets' dressing room.

As in 1972, the Winnipeg Arena would play host to the third game in the series on Saturday, September 21. Canadian coach Billy Harris opted to make some notable changes in the lineup he put out that evening. Proving the adage that one should not fix things that are not broken, some of Harris' unnecessary tinkering proved very costly. Out of the net was Cheevers, who was attending to his father-in-law's funeral arrangements with his bereaved family. In his place would be backup goaltender Don McLeod. That change was unavoidable. Gordie Howe was also scratched to give his ailing ribs some additional recovery time. Frank Mahovlich, Réjean Houle, Brad Selwood and Rick Ley were also scratched. Those radical moves caused many of the senior players on the roster to lose a little trust and faith in the wisdom of their coach.

For the third straight game Canada would open the scoring in the first period but this time the visitors would level the score before the opening frame concluded. Mirroring the first game, the Soviets would outscore the host nation by a 3–1 margin in the second frame. The third period

Alexander Yakushev (#15) scores a goal in the 1974 clash against Canadian goaltender Don McLeod. Canada's #17 is Rick Smith and #19 is Paul Henderson (Toronto Star Photograph Archive, Courtesy of Toronto Public Library).

would see the talented visitors extend their lead to an insurmountable 7–2 score. Canada would make things interesting by earning three goals within a minute and a half to close within two including a pair from Paul Henderson but the home team's rally would be too little and too late as the Soviet Union would ultimately prevail with an 8–5 drubbing of the Canadians.

Lanky Alexander Yakushev led the way for the Soviets with a timely hattrick including the game-winning goal. With many of the veteran players for Canada sitting this game out, the visitors had no trouble controlling the play as the replacements had a difficult time contending with the Soviets' speed and skill. Despite that, the five goals scored by the Canadians would match their highest total of the eight-game series. With the loss, the 1974 version of team Canada sported the identical 1-1-1 record as their 1972 counterparts had after three home games had been contested.

Years later Paul Henderson did not hold back sharing his disgust with coach Harris' somewhat radical personnel moves for the Winnipeg game. "Changing the lineup was ridiculous," he said with bitterness in his voice. "After that, I pretty much treated it as a vacation, going to Russia. I didn't get a chance to look around in 1972 at museums or the sights, so when I went over with my wife in 1974, after Harris made the lineup change, and told us basically it was a joke, I guess I decided to play tourist."[10]

Game Four, the final game on Canadian ice, was held at Vancouver's Pacific Coliseum on Monday, September 23. Back in the lineup for Team Canada were the controversial scratches from Game Three. It did not take them long to make a huge impact on the game. Gerry Cheevers returned to the team to guard the Canadian goal. For the first time in the series, the visiting team opened the scoring but Canada tied the score less than a minute later on a goal by Gordie Howe. The Soviets found themselves up 2-1 less than six minutes into the game before the home team came alive by scoring four goals in a five-minute span including a hattrick by Bobby Hull and another goal by a Game Three scratch Frank Mahovlich. Alluding to the pedigree of the Canadian goal scorers, broadcaster Don Chevrier giddily declared it was "Hall of Fame night in Vancouver."[11] Despite a clearly shaky start by goaltender Gerry Cheevers, Canada rode a 5-2 lead into the second period. Few people sensed the turning point of the whole series was about to occur.

The second period featured the visitors scoring the only goal to narrow Canada's advantage to 5-3. (This was also the first period thus far in the series where Canada had failed to score a goal. That drought would be duplicated in the third period.) The Soviets narrowed the score to 5-4 with just under four minutes left in the game courtesy of a goal scored by Alexander Maltsev. Less than a minute later Alexander Gusev notched the

Canadian Paul Shmyr (#18) gives Alexander Yakushev a "face wash" during the 1974 Canada–Soviet Series. Rick Smith is #17 Paul Henderson is #19 (Toronto Star Photograph Archive, Courtesy of Toronto Public Library).

tying goal. Canada had a power play late in the game but was unable to score with the man advantage. After a flying start for the home team, the final score was a 5–5 draw, certainly a disappointment for Team Canada and their fans.

Immediately following the final buzzer, as the teams lined up to shake hands, Tretiak paused when he came to Hull to embrace the superstar who had beat him soundly in the first period with three shots from three different angles. It was a tremendous display of mutual respect from the two superstar players from the opposite ends of the hockey world.

Despite the letdown of Game Four and the disastrous result of Game Three, Team Canada Two was heading to Moscow with a slightly better

4. The Often-Forgotten 1974 Summit Series

record than that of the original Canadian Summit Series team of 1972 (1–1–2 as opposed to 1–2–1). The previous squad comprised of NHL players had managed just 14 goals in the four games on home ice; the WHA players had bettered that mark with 17. The Soviets had done no better this time around, but no worse, exactly matching their 1972 mark with 17 goals after four games were in the books. The series was level in every possible way.

The first of three exhibition games versus European teams, designed to familiarize the Canadians with the continent's wider IIHF ice surfaces, occurred on September 27 in Helsinki, the Finnish capital city, before approximately 7,000 curious fans who seldom got to see Canadian-style hockey up close. Team Canada rested goaltender Gerry Cheevers. Flaky Gilles Gratton, the team's third-string goalie, played the first half of the game; Don McLeod guarded the nets for the final 30 minutes. In contrast, Jorna Valtonen played the entire game in net for the home side who were taking the game very seriously. The clearly superior Canadian visitors exploded to a strong 3–0 lead by the conclusion of the first period. Gordie Howe took a mere three shifts, picking up a goal and an assist in the process, then took the rest of the game off. After the Canadians switched their goalies in the second period, the two teams traded goals and headed to the third with Canada seemingly well in control, 4–1. However, just a little more than four minutes into the third period, the home town fans were thrilled to see a pair of Finnish tallies that trimmed the deficit to a single goal. Canada rebounded and finished very strongly with four more goals—two came courtesy of Frank Mahovlich—to take the exhibition contest by an 8–3 score. It was a game in which Canada never had to give 100 percent effort. Whenever they needed a goal against the Finns, one was seemingly never too hard to find.

Two nights later, the traveling Canadians were back in action. It was in nearby Gothenburg before a fully packed arena (called the Scandinavium) of 12,273 Swedish fans. As was the case in Finland, the Canadian goaltending duties would again be shared. This time Gerry Cheevers worked the game's first half and Don McLeod the other. Leif Holmqvist suited up in goal for the home side. As in Helsinki, the visitors took an early 3–0 lead in the first period with "Iron Grandpa" Gordie Howe picking up one of Canada's goals. The Swedes tallied the only mark of the second frame to trail 3–1 heading into the third period. Once more, late action by the home crowd made things interesting. Sweden managed to tie the game with less than five minutes remaining. Frank Mahovlich was the hero, however, scoring the late game-winner as the Canadians eked out a tough 4–3 victory over Sweden in an entertaining contest.

After securing that pair of much-needed, morale-boosting wins in Finland and Sweden, the team was headed to Moscow to finish the second half of the eight-game series with the Soviets. As in 1972, the visiting squad would not have to wait long for the Cold War mind games and shenanigans to begin. Perhaps it would be more accurate to say that the mind games would begin with a long wait. An apparent three-hour delay at customs caused Team Canada to conveniently miss their appointed practice time at Moscow's Luzhniki Arena.

Ralph Backstrom, a 37-year-old member of Team Canada 1974, would reflect decades later about the notion that many of the Canadian players' hotel rooms were bugged, especially teammate Gordie Howe's room. "Whatever he said he wanted, it mysteriously was sent up to his room right after," Backstrom recalled. "Gordie had felt the room was bugged. A lot of funny things like that happened. The Russians knew exactly what they were doing (to rattle the Canadian players). But there was no use whining about it or using it as an excuse."[12]

The mood in Moscow was perceptibly different than it had been in 1972. The keen eye could notice splashes of color where there had just been cold, drab shades of grey the last time that the Canadian contingent was in town. However, for the many changes that could be seen, there was still a distinct harshness to the Soviet society. Mark Howe recalled, "I remember us all in a bus going from the rink in Moscow, and there are fans around outside and lots of police and Paul reaches out the window to hand a package of gum to a kid. All of a sudden, police grabbed the kid, bundled her into the back of a police van, and she was gone."[13]

Game Five, in Moscow, got off to a fine start for the home team. The Soviets took a 1–0 lead in the first period, holding Canada to just four shots on goal and keeping them off the scoreboard for the third consecutive period. Both teams exchanged tallies in the second and third frames but it was not the goals that were the story of this game. Polish referee Voitech Shchepek quickly earned the ire of the Canadians for a few questionable calls. Canada received seven minor penalties plus a back-breaking third period misconduct penalty to Ralph Backstrom. With all the time spent defending the Soviet power plays, it was difficult for the visitors to generate any sustained pressure against their highly skilled opponents. A missed call early in the third period that should have given Canada a slightly truncated power play went unseen by the Polish referee. Toward the end of the third period, several hits and potential penalties went uncalled for both sides which only added to the increasing tenseness between the two teams. Canada finished the game with just 16 shots on goal and yet the visitors only lost by a close 3–2 score. Incredibly, contrary to all pre-series predictions, the WHA players still maintained a slightly better record through five games against their Soviet adversaries compared to the vaunted NHL all-stars from two years prior: 1–2–2 as opposed to 1–3–1.

4. The Often-Forgotten 1974 Summit Series

After Game Five, Canadian coach Billy Harris mentioned to reporters that he did not he think Bobby Hull was playing at 100 percent health. Harris was uncertain if it was a nagging knee injury from training camp or perhaps something else that he declined to mention. Both Harris and Bill Hunter would take the high road, suggesting that their team was still adjusting to the larger IIHF-sized rinks and the time zone change as the reasons why their players had seemed off their game. Both expected better things from their WHA-filled roster in the next game.

However, dissention was beginning to take form in the Canadian squad. Prior to Game Six, Billy Harris blew up at his players during a practice, complaining about them staying out too late and partying way too much.

The sixth game of the 1974 Canada–Soviet Series followed a similar script to Game Five. The home team pressed hard from the outset, scoring a pair of quick goals. Canada bounced back and, by the midway point of the second period, trailed the Soviets only by a single goal, 3–2. That is when more poor IIHF officiating—and Canada's inability to rise above it—ultimately decided the outcome of the crucial match.

Soviet referee Victor Dombrowski sent Canadian Mark Howe off for cross-checking Boris Mikhailov at 12:22—an infraction that had happened several times earlier to players on both teams without it being whistled. Paul Henderson and Bruce MacGregor were sent out by Billy Harris as the forwards to kill the penalty. This is when things got confusing and controversial.

Just 22 seconds later, Valeri Vasiliev and MacGregor clashed on the side boards near the center red line. Dombrowski raised his hand, signaling a pending penalty to the Soviet defenseman who promptly dropped his gloves and began tossing punches at a very startled MacGregor. The veteran, 33-year-old Canadian recalled, "I saw him drop his gloves and I backed off. International rules say that the guy who throws the first punch gets a game misconduct and his team has to play short for ten minutes. There was no sense my getting into it at all. The referee was right there."[14]

When the two players separated, Dombrowski sent each man off for five minutes, perhaps conveniently forgetting all about the two-minute minor he had just called on Vasiliev less than a minute earlier! MacGregor, who had never even taken his gloves off, felt that this moment was the pivotal moment of the entire 1974 series. Had the proper penalties been assigned, Canada would have been poised to tie the game with the man advantage for nearly ten minutes, setting the stage for an exciting third period. Instead, the offsetting major penalties still left the Soviets a man up with Mark Howe already in the box. They would capitalize, scoring a power play goal to go up, 4–2.

Frustration was mounting on the Canadian bench. Team Canada had been assessed 33 minutes in penalties to only nine for the Soviets. When the final horn sounded, the score firmly favored the home team, 5–2. However, things were not yet over. Valeri Kharlamov, the star Soviet forward, skated near Rick Ley, a former member of the Toronto Maple Leafs, and allegedly said something rather unpleasant to him in English, rubbing in the home team's victory. An irate Ley responded by beating Kharlamov into a bloody mess, tackling him to the ice and continuing to lay on the punches. Kharlamov suffered a nasty cut near his eye.

There were calls to have Ley jailed for his assault on Valeri Kharlamov. Under the Soviet Union's criminal code, Ley could have been jailed for up to 15 days for his actions once the final buzzer had sounded but had there been time left on the clock, the on-ice arbiters would be the ones to have the final say. Ley did seek out Kharlamov the following day to apologize; the Soviet player accepted it. The Canadian squad was clearly growing increasingly frustrated over the unbalanced officiating. Years later, Gordie Howe would reflect on an intimate moment shared with one unnamed Soviet player who had sliced open the ear of his son, Mark Howe. "The next shift when we were out together, I said, 'Oh you want the puck? Well, here it is.' I threw it in the corner and when he went to get it, I broke his arm. After the game, he had to shake hands (with his opposite limb)."[15]

The 5–2 loss by a team incapable of outplaying the curious officiating gave the WHA version of Team Canada a disappointing record of 1–3–2 after six games. This meant they would need victories in each of the two remaining games in Moscow just to earn an overall split in the eight-game series. It also ensured, that despite playing some fairly competitive hockey for six games, the WHA contingent could not duplicate the NHL version of Team Canada's success from two years earlier. Controversy was far from finished with this series, however, as Game Seven soon revealed.

Game Seven was set for Saturday, October 5. Billy Harris benched 36-year-old Frank Mahovlich, who had played poorly thus far in the series, but it mattered not. Once more the Soviet Union got off to an impressively quick start, surging ahead 2–0 in the first period. Canada added one goal in response before the end of the frame. Seizing the momentum, the Canadians came roaring out of their dressing room for the second period. They scored a pair of early goals to suddenly take a 3–2 lead—their first on Soviet ice. Undaunted, the Soviets managed to beat Gerry Cheevers twice to take a 4–3 lead into the third period. As the teams took to the ice for the third period, Soviet defenseman Valeri Vasiliev did something curious: He was seen skating over to the timekeeper's bench and exchanging nods with him. Vasiliev then skated over to the Soviet bench to further exchange nods with his coach, Boris Kulagin. While it is entirely possible that nothing nefarious transpired between the Soviet defenseman and the timekeeper, the implications of the shared moment were soon felt by the edgy and suspicious visitors. Ralph Backstrom's goal tied Game Seven early in the third period and, for the next 15 minutes, the Canadian players were furiously searching for a much-needed go-ahead tally. There was a stoppage in play with 92 seconds left in the game. This was the moment when cynical observers first noticed something might be amiss with the game clock at the Luzhniki Ice Palace.

Television viewers in Canada suddenly saw something unexpected: an irate Gerry Cheevers skating swiftly and purposefully to the timekeeper's bench to accuse him of wrongdoing. He violently rapped his stick against the protective glass. On the alert for any sort of funny business, Cheevers had been closely watching the clock in preparation to come off the ice for an extra attacker. That was when he noticed that the clock had not stopped precisely on the referee's whistle as it should have. The Canadian goalie figured at least four full extra, precious seconds had been allowed to tick away. In the Luzhniki Arena press box, esteemed Canadian sports journalist Jim Coleman, his suspicions aroused, was scrutinizing the clock even more closely than Cheevers was. He figured there were several incidents of timekeeping shadiness over the third period that may have shaved as much as 15 seconds off the clock.

Canadian IIHF referee Tom Brown, who was already no stranger to controversy in the series, was able to restore just two seconds to the clock based on what he had seen. (He later claimed that no one had mentioned to him that the dispute was about more than two seconds.) Those two stolen seconds would prove to be very important and costly ones indeed.

With time winding down and Cheevers now at the Canadian bench in place of an extra attacker, Bobby Hull received a pass and rifled a shot past Tretiak for the apparent game winning goal. The red light came on, indicating a goal, the green light, indicating the end of the game had not yet come on. Brown, however, immediately waved the goal off claiming that it was scored after the game had been concluded.

The role of the goal judge is to indicate when a goal is scored regardless of whether or not the puck crosses the goal line after the game is over. He had seen a goal and signaled one. However, the system is set so that the goal light cannot come on if the green light is already on indicating the period is over. Brown posited that perhaps the lights and the timer in Luzhniki were not synchronized. The scoreboard was a sparkling new $250,000 piece of Finnish technology, built specifically to Soviet specifications and to Olympic standards. It included a timer that showed tenths of a second—a rarity in 1974. It is highly improbable that it did not have the lights synchronized as the official had suggested. However, the Soviets officially went on record the following day announcing that, indeed, the lights and the timer were somehow not synchronized properly.

After the game, Team Canada manager Bill Hunter demanded and received a meeting with the Soviet Ice Hockey Federation officials, incensed and resolute in the position that his Canadians had been cheated out of the game and should have been declared 5–4 winners. Hunter vowed that his players would not be taking the ice for Game Eight unless there was a formal hearing to investigate the shenanigans surrounding the clock, the timekeeper, and how they impacted the outcome of Game Seven. He did not get such a hearing. Hunter eventually calmed down and retreated from his position. Coach Billy Harris was immensely frustrated and near to tears as he pondered why suddenly the tenths-of-a-second timer was not showing those fractions of time as they had done so in each of the first two games in Moscow. He correctly noted that the only way the red goal light goes on when the game clock shows zero is if there are fractions of a second left in the period. If such was the case, as it certainly seemed to be, then the Soviets had clearly stolen not only the game but the series as well.

Alan Eagleson, the director of the NHL Players Association, who was present in Moscow to discuss future Canadian participation in IIHF events, said about Team Canada 1974, "I hope they learned the same lesson we learned in 1972. There's no point in coming over here trying to compete with these people on their terms. They'll do anything to screw you. Now maybe people will understand why I went nuts in 1972." Eagleson said that Canada should have quit the series after the Game Seven shenanigans and went home without playing Game Eight. "I wouldn't have put the team on the ice after they moved the clock. You can't handle these people with a lot of idle threats."[16]

Game Seven featured something that that the previous two games had not: The Soviets had been called for more penalties (two) than the Canadians (one). This was why, before the last contest, the visitors, who were already rankled after three hotly contested and controversial games in Moscow, were incensed even further upon receiving a message from the Soviets prior to Game Eight. It suggested that the Canadians would be wise to not retaliate on the ice with aggression or the Soviet players would refuse to take the ice! Whether this was an unnecessary step in the continuing mind games that the Soviets continued to play or it was a direct response to Bill Hunter threatening not to allow Team Canada to take the ice without getting his hearing will never truly be known.

Wild Bill Hunter went through the motion of having his Canadian players vote on whether they should take to the ice or not following the disastrous and contentious conclusion to Game Seven. The players were unanimous in their decision: For the sake of the 15,000 fans in Moscow who bought tickets, for their obligation to the World Hockey Association, and for the millions of hockey fans back home watching on television, they voted to play as scheduled.

Not quite knowing what to expect from the angry and volatile Canadians, the Soviets opted to rest many of their regulars and bring in their lesser-known players for Game Eight. Soviet Ice Hockey Federation chairman Andrey Starovoytov stirred the pot further by making an incendiary announcement prior to the game over the arena's public-address system. It declared that the Canadians had already violated the signed agreement adhering to IIHF rules with their dirty play and that Game Eight would be stopped at the first infringement of the above-mentioned agreement.

"Thus, the Canadians found themselves on the defensive again," wrote Wayne Overland of Southam New Service. "[It was] another psychological ploy by the Soviets who continually kept the visitors upset with poor accommodations, food and tickets, to say nothing about rigged officiating and timekeeping."[17] Jim Coleman agreed, penning, "In view of the fact that the Russians scarcely had been without sin in the previous seven shinny contests, Starovoytov's threat was an overt act of intimidation. It was the low point of the week in Moscow during which Team Canada had been subjected to considerable harassment...."[18]

An enraged Bill Hunter promptly responded to Starovoytov's fiery announcement by declaring his Canadians would leave the ice if the Soviets exhibited any unnecessary roughness. Later, Team Canada coach Billy Harris denied this was ever truly a serious consideration by his squad.

Game Eight was played the very next night after Game Seven—a Sunday—for the benefit of weekend television viewership. It was not without its own controversy as once again the score would take a back seat to questionable officiating. With the score tied 1-1 early in the third period, Vladimir Shadrin drew blood from the face of Canada's Pat Stapleton with his stick. Initially, it appeared that West German referee Josef Kompalla—the same official who was reviled by the Canadians in 1972—was going to let the infraction go without calling a penalty. Then Stapleton, a veteran of the 1972 Canadian team, did something quite remarkable and probably unprecedented: He briskly skated to the referee to inquire about the non-call—and wipe his dripping blood on Kompalla's cheek! Kompalla got the message. He sent Shadrin off for five minutes, but Stapleton was given a ten-minute misconduct for Canada for his highly creative method of making his point. It was the fourth Canadian misconduct penalty of the Series—against none for the Soviets. Jim Coleman sarcastically wrote in his Game Eight report, "Referee Josef Kompalla's officiating was up to his usual standards."[19]

Curiously, when the periods ended in Game Eight, there were no issues with the arena clock or its green or red lights. Apparently, the lights and timer were somehow perfectly synchronized again. The Soviets won the game by a slim 3–2 margin. The Canadians, for the most part, were just more than pleased to get back on the airplane and fly out of Moscow and the growing acrimony.

At the conclusion of the series, Jim Coleman criticized "the idiocy of Team Canada officials" in agreeing that the seventh and eighth games should be scheduled on consecutive nights which "undoubtedly took a heavy toll on the squad which was comprised chiefly of players in their mid-thirties."[20] Coleman did, however, single out three remarkable oldsters—Gordie Howe, Ralph Backstrom and Gerry Cheevers—as the top Canadian stalwarts who were never intimidated by the Russians at any point in the series.

When all the dust had settled, Team Canada Two had scored a total of 27 goals over the eight games, four shy of what their 1972 counterparts had accrued. Each of the two Canadian delegations surrendered the identical sum of 32 goals to the Soviets. For the most part, as it was two years prior, the games were generally competitive and really could have gone either way with a little bit of luck and, certainly, with more reliable standards of officiating.

There was one more game to be played before the WHA players could return home to Canada. As was the case in 1972, the final stop on Team Canada's European trek was Prague, Czechoslovakia for a single exhibition game versus the Czech national team. Don McLeod and Gilles Gratton would share duties in goal for the visitors while Jiri Holocek and Jiri Crha would do the same for the home team. Unlike the Soviet national team, the Czech squad was not a year-round collection of players. It had been brought together less than a week in advance in preparation for the exhibition match. Yet, the Czechs were still able to dominate the first half of the game against a Canadian team that was flat, stale, and understandably indifferent about playing the exhibition game as a meaningless coda to the eight games versus the Soviets. The Czechs cruised to a fairly easy and somewhat surprising 3–1 victory, much to the delight of the 14,000 cheering fans who did not know what to expect from the home team. Newspapers in Canada reported that the Canadian players were treated very hospitably by their hosts upon their arrival and throughout their entire brief stay. Copious amounts of high-quality Czech beer and stacks of tasty finger foods were presented to Team Canada. It was a kind gesture that pleased the tired visitors greatly and was fondly remembered by them years afterward.

Wild Bill Hunter had but a single regret on his decision making for the 1974 Canada–Soviet series. "This was a holiday series, not a hockey series. If there is a next time for the WHA, there won't be wives along."[21]

4. The Often-Forgotten 1974 Summit Series

Not every player and spouse felt the trip was akin to a vacation. Reports of loud arguments between Bobby Hull and his wife Joanne were commonplace. The combative couple would eventually split in 1977 and formally divorce in 1980.

Years, later Ralph Backstrom would reflect rather fondly about the 1974 series. "A few breaks and things could've been very different for us." He added. "But it was an honor to play in it. I was in about 1,300 games in my [professional hockey] career, but memories of that series are among the most vivid."[22]

Paul Henderson, Canada's hero from 1972, took a completely opposite stance. He felt that the 1974 series was a rather forgettable moment in Canadian hockey history, even for him as a participant. Decades later, when asked by the Sports Network (TSN) for an interview about the lesser-known WHA-Soviet tilt, Henderson was briefly stunned by the request. He began by saying, "My goodness, I honestly can't remember the last time anyone asked me about 1974. I just don't ever talk about it."[23]

That is generally the same view held by most Canadians who are old enough to remember the 1974 Series. It has largely been pushed out of their minds or it is barely recalled. The fact that the WHA players only won one of the eight games served to reinforce the general notion that Canada had sent a second-tier group of players to face the mighty Soviet national team—and the disappointing result was what NHL fans fully feared and expected. The well-publicized nonsense the Canadian players had to endure during the four games played in Moscow that October also makes it less than a fondly remembered experience.

In the Soviet Union, of course, the eight games of the 1974 Canada–Soviet series *are* fondly remembered by its citizenry because of the positive outcome. Seva Kukushin, who covered both the 1972 and 1974 series for the Tass (the Soviet Union's official news agency), stated in a 2014 interview with TSN,

> In 1972, we learned our hockey players were as good as those in Canada. In 1974, we learned our hockey players could beat [Canada's] best players. It wasn't celebrated with parades in the street, but it wouldn't have been like that in 1972 even if we had won. It just wasn't how our country acted at that time. Hockey was great, but it wasn't the only thing we had. We had [other] accomplishments, such as sending a man into space.[24]

Certainly, Kukushin's claim that Canada had its top players facing the Soviets in the autumn of 1974 would be quickly challenged by North American hockey historians today as laughable, politically motivated hyperbole. The absence of the NHL's star players is too blatant for anyone to overlook or dismiss.

Do you remember the 1974 Canada–Soviet series? If so, do you have fond memories of it? Should you? That is not for the authors of this book to decide. Nevertheless, despite the acrimony and bitterness that pervaded at the end of the 1974 series, the allure of international hockey's two distinct superpowers clashing was still an attractive and lucrative proposition. It would not be long before the Soviets would challenge North American talent once more—this time in a much different format.

5

The Making of Super Series '76

The seeds for Super Series '76 came during the 1975 IIHF world championship tournament in West Germany. It was still an amateur event—hopelessly outdated, completely devoid of drama, and having no appeal for even that year's host country. Of course, with Canada still boycotting the IIHF tournament, thoroughly miffed over the organization's continuing refusal to embrace professional players and former pros, the nation where hockey mattered the most was noticeably absent. No prominent sporting event on the planet needed a major overhaul more desperately than international hockey's annual showcase event.

The 1975 IIHF world championship tournament ran from April 3 to April 19 with Dusseldorf as its headquarters. The event's A Pool that would crown the overall winners was comprised of six teams: The Soviet Union, Czechoslovakia, Sweden, Finland, Poland, and the United States. Twelve other nations were there, too, but they were competing in the lesser B and C pools. Thus, the hosts, West Germany, who were in the B Pool, were thus ineligible to win the world title. It hardly made for must-see viewing amongst the locals. The six nations in Pool A played a double round-robin. After 10 games, whichever team was on top would be the world champions. The Soviet Union cruised to an embarrassingly easy championship, winning all 10 games they played, and outscoring their overmatched opponents 90–23. In their last game, they blasted the best Swedish amateurs 13–4—and the Swedes were the bronze medalists! In contrast, the American team—wholly comprised of eager but inexperienced college all-star players—finished at the bottom of the heap in Pool A. In basically a statistical reverse of what the Soviets did, the Americans lost all ten of their games, averaging just 2.2 goals per game while allowing 8.4. It was far from compelling entertainment. Public interest in the IIHF world championship tournament was at an all-time low, especially in North America. Even the victorious Soviets complained about it.

"We wish we could have more competition,"[1] griped Boris Kulagin, the head coach of the Soviet Union's superb national team. The Soviets' victory reinforced their utter domination of world "amateur" hockey. It marked their 12th IIHF title in the past 13 years. Winning was becoming too predictable and monotonous. The silver medalists from Czechoslovakia—who finished the event with an 8–2 record, with both losses coming at the hands of the Soviets—were equally bored with the tournament, the format, and the lack of drama attached to it. The IIHF vice president was a Czech, Miroslav Subrt. He also expressed desire for meaningful change in international hockey. On April 20, Subrt told a correspondent from the *Montréal Gazette*, "We want to play against the best in the world—and that includes Canadian pros. We are not afraid of anyone."[2]

Canada did send a delegation to the IIHF meetings in Dusseldorf—but it was not a hockey team. (The IIHF had generously offered Canada a spot in the tournament's A Pool, but it was politely declined.) The visitors who traveled to West Germany were representatives of the Canadian Amateur Hockey Association. The top CAHA man to make the trip was 60-year-old Gordon Juckes. He had been the organization's liaison for international hockey since 1960. Juckes was trying find some reasonable pathway to return Canada to international hockey for the first time since 1969, but it would not be under the present format. Canada was not going to give in to the IIHF dictates that continuously put their national teams at a disadvantage. The CAHA would not go along with the present system that forbade openly professional hockey players from competing but allowed for communist bloc, state-employed "pro amateurs" whose only true occupation was to play hockey. The 1975 IIHF tournament results made it patently obvious that legitimate amateurs, in the western sense of the word, could not fairly compete against opposition that was thoroughly professional in everything but name.

IIHF president Bunny Ahearne, a strict advocate of amateurism, naïvely thought that just a smidgen of minor tinkering with the format would restore the old luster to the IIHF event. He suggested expanding the A Pool to eight nations, as it once had been, and have those teams compete in a single, seven-game round-robin with a playoff round featuring the top four teams. Such a format might be more dramatic, but it did absolutely nothing to correct the problem that Canada and the United States could not send their best players to the IIHF tourney.

Juckes was hopeful that he could persuade the IIHF to allow pros to play and move its annual world championship tournament from April to December. The calendar change, he argued, could at least present the possibility of the NHL shutting down its season to send a squad similar to Team Canada 1972 to play for the IIHF title without any impact on the

Stanley Cup playoffs. Juckes fully knew in his heart that such a plan would probably be a tough sell to the NHL owners as any innovation that stopped their gate receipts during the season would be frowned upon. Nevertheless, he was still optimistic that the promise of big television revenues that could be shared would offset any financial losses of suspending play in the NHL around Christmastime.

Predictably, Juckes' plan did not fly with the NHL magnates, but such was the sentiment for change among IIHF members that major, significant overhauls were on the horizon. By the time the summer IIHF meetings had closed in 1975, the door at least was now open for professional hockey players to compete in IIHF events for the very first time in the organization's history. Canada agreed to send a team to the 1977 IIHF tournament in Vienna in exchange for hosting an open six-team international tourney in September 1976 (which would be called the Canada Cup) and having two Soviet clubs tour North America to take on the NHL's best teams just after Christmas 1975. Thus, Super Series '76 was given the green light by the IIHF.

On the evening of May 28, 1975, NHL president Clarence Campbell officially announced that two touring Soviet clubs would play eight different NHL clubs on their home ice between late December 1975 and the middle of January 1976. "This series fits into our schedule," Campbell declared, "and for the time being I believe it is the only way to develop the game of hockey."[3] When asked why the NHL did not form another version of Team Canada to play in all eight games versus the Soviets, Campbell replied, "It is simply too costly. We can't afford a national team the way the Russians do." What Campbell meant was it would be too costly for NHL owners to give up their usual gate receipts if league play had to be suspended for two or three weeks to accommodate such a series. He said, "The NHL, during the season, pays out $1 million a week in salaries. That's for players only."[4]

By the end of July, some of the details of the Soviets' tour were finalized and advertised to hockey fans throughout the world. (There was one potential hitch: The extra games needed to be okayed by the NHL Players' Association, which happened in October.) The NHL and the Soviets agreed that all eight games would feature a three-man on-ice officiating crew. This would be something new to the Soviet clubs who were used to the IIHF's two-man refereeing system. One of the three officials in each game would be from the USSR, who, like the Soviet hockey players, would be making the trip as a learning experience. In at least four of the games, the Soviet man would be the game's referee. In the other four contests he would serve a one of the two linesmen. NHL rules would be used to govern play—not the IIHF's. In Canada, CBC Television would be the host broadcaster, televising all four games involving the Central Red Army team and one game with the Wings of the Soviet—their encounter with the Buffalo Sabres.

How would the participating teams be selected? The Soviets agreed to send the two highest-finishing teams from their domestic league in 1974–75. One squad was HC CKSA Moscow—better known as the Central Red Army Hockey Club. It was the perennial champions of the Soviet Elite league because it featured a disproportionately huge percentage of players who also played internationally for the Soviet Union's national team. The second-place club was Sovetov Moscow, known in North America as the Wings of the Soviet (or Soviet Wings). Sometimes the North American media mischaracterized it as the USSR's Air Force team. That was not the case. The club was called the Wings because it was sponsored by the Soviet aircraft industry. Founded in 1947, the Wings' jersey featured the abbreviation "KC" on its front, undoubtedly confusing later generations of NHL fans. Many wrongly assume the players are the Kansas City Scouts when they see photos and clips of the Soviet Wings from Super Series '76.

The Soviets were also generously granted permission to augment the two touring clubs' lineups with players from the other teams in their domestic league. The Wings, for example, picked up five. As it turned out, it was roughly akin to the Montréal Canadiens being allowed to "borrow" the top stars of the Toronto Maple Leafs for a couple of weeks. Thus, it was not exactly a true test of Soviet clubs versus NHL clubs. The reverse did not happen. The NHL clubs were not permitted such a perquisite, of course. It was plainly impossible anyway because the NHL schedule would proceed as usual while Super Series '76 occurred in eight different one-night-stand venues. Any idea of NHL teams lending players to other clubs in the middle of the season was preposterous.

The exact schedule was not finalized until well into November. That gave the NHL time to analyze which of their teams ought to play which Soviet squad. Unfortunately, it may have affected television viewership in the United States. By the time it was settled when and where the games would be played, many American television stations at the local level had already locked in their programming schedules for late December 1975 and early January 1976.

The final schedule was announced on November 21 for now what was being called by the hockey media "Super Series '76"—a term Campbell personally disliked and seldom used. He preferred to perceive them as eight separate exhibition games rather than a cumulative endeavor. Whatever the case, this is what the dates would be along with the competing teams:

Sunday, December 28: Central Red Army vs. New York Rangers
Monday December 29: Soviet Wings vs. Pittsburgh Penguins
Wednesday, December 31: Central Red Army vs. Montréal Canadiens
Sunday, January 4: Soviet Wings vs. Buffalo Sabres
Wednesday, January 7: Soviet Wings vs. Chicago Black Hawks
Thursday, January 8: Central Red Army vs. Boston Bruins
Saturday, January 10: Soviet Wings vs. New York Islanders
Sunday, January 11: Central Red Army vs. Philadelphia Flyers

It was an event that hockey fans in Canada would certainly embrace despite 7/8 of the games being played south of the border. It was also an opportunity for the Soviets to finally compare themselves with the professionals of the National Hockey League when the latter were in mid-season form. Furthermore, it would provide the Soviets a timely warmup for the 1976 Winter Olympic Games in Innsbruck, Austria, which still featured an IIHF amateur-only hockey tournament. (It would be another 22 years before that competition was finally modernized enough to welcome the NHL's pro athletes, if they chose to participate.) The Soviet Ice Hockey Federation would be paid $25,000 per match for the eight-game tour. That was an enormous and thoroughly enticing sum of money in 1975. It was agreed that the NHL would also cover all the Soviets' sundry expenses while they were in North America. The remaining revenues would be split between the NHL and the NHL Players' Association.

"This series presents a new potential for hockey internationally," Clarence Campbell would decree prior to the opening game in New York City, where the host Rangers would face off against the Central Red Army club at Madison Square Garden on Sunday night, December 28, 1975. The optimistic Campbell continued, "We hope this new development is the forerunner to international competition on a continuing basis."[5]

The NHL wanted, of course, to showcase its best teams for the marquee event, but interest in some non-traditional American hockey markets was lacking. The league had to come up with eight host clubs that were both competitive and excited about the prospect of hosting one of the Soviet teams—and they had to confirm it well in advance so the game could be slotted into the already crowded 1975–76 NHL schedule within a tight 15-day window starting on December 28.

Some of those choices were obvious ones. The two-time defending Stanley Cup champion Philadelphia Flyers would host the final, climactic game on Sunday, January 11. The Buffalo Sabres, Cup finalists in 1975, were an ascending team with exciting, young, high-scoring stars. They fit the bill nicely. The always-competitive Montréal Canadiens' lineup had many players who were part of Team Canada 1972. Also, at the time the

Series was first planned, the Boston Bruins, perennial Cup contenders for the better part of a decade, had both Bobby Orr and Phil Esposito. (As it turned out, neither marquee player would be wearing a Bruins jersey when Boston played Central Red Army on January 8.) The Habs and Bruins would logically both be host clubs, too. The other four teams chosen were two Original Six clubs (Chicago and the New York Rangers), the rapidly improving New York Islanders, and the Pittsburgh Penguins. Only the latter club had trouble selling every possible ticket for its Super Series game.

Conspicuous by their absence were the Toronto Maple Leafs who probably could have sold out their 16,000-seat building a dozen times over. However, Toronto's confrontational owner, Harold Ballard, hated all things communist; he was not prepared to pay the Soviet Ice Hockey Federation a rusty nickel to play his club at Maple Leaf Gardens. (Thus, a day trip across the border to Buffalo became the best option for hockey fans in populous southern Ontario to see a Super Series game. Thousands of them did just that.) North American geography worked against the remaining Canadian team, Vancouver, from hosting one of the games. The Canucks were a middle-of-the pack team in 1975–76, as well, which did not boost their credentials. Chicago turned out to be the most westerly city on the Soviets' travel itinerary.

Despite the huge hockey rivalry between the two countries, the only Canadian stop on the Soviets' ballyhooed tour was in Montréal, perhaps the world's greatest hockey city. With the Canadiens beginning to dominate the NHL in the 1975–76 season, many people thought the marquee game of Super Series '76 would be the one slated for New Year's Eve 1975 at the stately Montréal Forum. Many people were correct.

It was unclear how much international politics would be a factor when the puck was dropped at each NHL arena. In the Cold War era it certainly would not be absent. The middle of the 1970s was supposedly a new era of détente between the world's two superpowers, but most everyone knew it would be difficult to separate sports from conflicting geopolitical ideologies once the teams took the ice for what would surely be eight spirited and intense hockey games. Decades later, Philadelphia hockey writer Brad Kurtzburg recalled the unique atmosphere around the series, especially in the City of Brotherly Love where the Soviet teams tour would come to its memorable conclusion against the NHL's reigning Stanley Cup champs on January 11 in a Sunday matinee. "The Cold War was still very hot in 1976," he accurately wrote. "It was [less than] one year after the fall of Saigon, and the idea of the world being divided between American and Soviet spheres of influence was still a reality to most observers."[6]

Montréal's Peter Mahovlich acknowledged that the NHL players would be in midseason form unlike the situation in September 1972, but

5. The Making of Super Series '76

he stressed that mental preparation for games against Soviet teams would be equally important, too, perhaps more so. "You can be physically prepared," Mahovlich acknowledged, "but that is not enough. Being mentally prepared is the key. When we played them the last time, we weren't mentally prepared." Mahovlich did support the idea of the NHL's individual teams playing Soviet clubs rather than forming another Canadian national team. He told the *Calgary Herald*, "Early in the winter when the Canadiens were on our winning streak, we felt we could have beaten anybody, even the Russians."[7]

Journalist Al Strachan of the *Montréal Gazette* got to the essence of Super Series '76 in a piece for his newspaper on November 11. It was a bit of a warning regarding what was really at stake when those eight games would be played. Strachan opined that the NHL would be embarking "on the most critical two-week period of its 50-year-history [*sic*]." He exposited,

> If they [the NHL teams] win, they will be saying to their detractors, "Look, you say that we don't play hockey the way we used to, but we just beat the much-heralded Russians. The NHL brand of hockey must therefore be a good-quality game." If, on the other hand, the NHL teams get thumped by the Russians' sound, programmed play, the NHL has no excuses. It is only sending its best teams against the Russians anyway. It is their best against our best.[8]

In truth, that was the basic appeal of Super Series '76: It was best versus best. It was also, on some level, perceived as a showdown between good and evil, the white hats versus the black hats, to be contested eight times on eight different sheets of NHL ice surfaces. It was Us against Them.

6

Soviet Lineups*

Central Red Army

1. Nikolai Adonin (goaltender)
2. Alexander Gusev
3. Vladimir Lutchenko
4. Viktor Kuzhkin
5. Valeri Vasiliev
6. Gennady Tsygankov
7. Boris Mikhailov (captain)
8. Alexander Maltsev
9. Alexander Volchkov
10. Viktor Kutyergin
11. Boris Alexandrov
13. Alexei Volchenkov
14. Vladimir Popov
15. Vyacheslav Solodukhin
16. Vladimir Petrov
17. Valeri Kharlamov
18. Vladimir Vikulov
20. Vladislav Tretiak (goaltender)
21. Sergei Glazov
22. Viktor Shluktov

Wings of the Soviet

3. Sergei Bobinov
4. Yuri Turin
5. Yuri Liapkin
6. Sergei Glukov
7. Vladimir Rasko
8. Sergei Kotov
9. Gennady Maslov
10. Alexander Yakushev
11. Vladimir Repniev
12. Viktor Kuznetsov
13. Vyacheslav Anisin
14. Sergei Kapustin
15. Alexander Budonov
16. Yuri Lebedev (captain)
17. Vladimir Shadrin
18. Yuri Tyerhin
19. Alexander Sidelnikov (goaltender)
20. Alexander Kulikov (goaltender)
21. Viktor Shalimov
22. Vladimir Krukinov

---

*Lineups are presented in numerical order. Wings of the Soviet did not have a player #1 or #2.

7

Game #1

*Central Red Army
vs. New York Rangers*

Sunday, December 28, 1975
Madison Square Garden

If one believed what the Soviet hockey officials were publicly saying upon their arrival in Montréal just before Christmas 1975, the eight games about to be played in Super Series '76 were merely friendly warm-up matches for them. Their real interest, they insisted, was preparing their top players for the all-important, upcoming hockey tournament in February at the 1976 Winter Olympics in Innsbruck, Austria. Nobody in North America who followed hockey closely took that statement seriously. The Olympic hockey tournament had lost much of its luster. Doing well against NHL opposition was of paramount importance to the two touring Soviet teams. Downplaying Super Series '76 was wholly disingenuous.

Those two Soviet clubs, Central Red Army and Wings of the Soviet, had arrived in North America well in advance to avail themselves of practice facilities in Montréal and to acclimate themselves to the narrower NHL-size rinks but much larger buildings. (Two men who would serve as on-ice officials for the eight Super Series games, Yuri Karandin and Victor Dombrowski, were on the flight too.) Both Soviet teams had bolstered their lineups with players from the capable Dynamo and Spartak clubs. Despite the official proclamations form both the Soviet and NHL organizers, this was no mere exhibition series—and everyone knew it. The esteemed visitors intended to win every game. As in 1972, it was all for the glory of the Soviet Union and the promotion of world communism as a superior system to western-style capitalism.

The *New York Times* described the two Soviet clubs' first public appearance in Montréal on December 24. That city would serve as both teams' headquarters. Robin Herman, a rare female scribe on the professional hockey beat in 1975, duly reported,

> The Soviet team members comported themselves in conservative fashion at first, acknowledging greetings ... with nods and firm handshakes, but nary a smile. They all requested Coca-Cola and then sat stoically at circular tables enduring the stares of their, hosts and the glare of television lights.
>
> [Initially], the hosts and guests were frustrated in their conversations. But [as soon as] interpreters went to work, the natural warmth of the Russians began to penetrate their solemn, state-imposed manner as the sun on a hazy spring day.[1]

In her article, Herman noted that the Soviet players and coaching staff were only allowed to answer questions that had been preapproved by their Ice Hockey Federation, which, of course, was strictly controlled by the government of the USSR. As Super Series '76 progressed, the two clubs' head coaches, Konstantin Loktev and Boris Kulagin, seemed more willing and often eager to answer off-the-cuff questions tossed their way by Canadian and American media. Their players, however, fearful of running afoul of Soviet protocols, stayed on script and generally were dull interview subjects. Their on-ice performances did their talking for them.

Two New York Rangers on their current 1975–76 squad had played on Team Canada 1972: Phil Esposito and Rod Gilbert. Both men told the press that they would not underestimate the Soviets this time around. They had learned the hard way not to do so back in September 1972. Esposito ruefully told Frank Brown of the Associated Press, "Before that [1972] series we had some scouts tell us that [Vladislav] Tretiak couldn't stop a puck—which was a lie; that the Russians couldn't shoot—which was another lie; and that the Russians couldn't skate—which was absolute nonsense. That series not only opened my eyes, it opened the eyes of a lot of people in the United States and Canada."[2]

"Esposito is aware that the Rangers are guinea pigs, so to speak, since they are playing the first game,"[3] noted Brown. Esposito accepted that reality with pragmatism. "If we lose it, it's not going to be the end of the world for me," he claimed. "We've got 45 to 50 regular-season games to go [sic] and a playoff spot to win. Unfortunately, we only have one chance against the Red Army and they have three chances [versus three other NHL teams]. It's an exhibition series that is darn good for hockey, but let's not get carried away."[4]

Esposito had injured his right ankle shortly after arriving on Broadway and it was not quite yet 100 percent. Stan Fischler wrote in *The Sporting News*, "[Esposito] is determined to play as much as possible, yet each time he skates, the ankle injury becomes aggravated."[5]

Frank Brown had been following the Soviets' preparations closely since their plane touched down in Montréal. They were intense workouts—and somewhat foreign to him. One particular drill impressed him. Each Soviet player took a turn standing on his own goal line. His task was to fire a hard, perfectly placed pass to another player positioned 60 feet away in the neutral zone. The player who made the pass then had to defend a two-on-one rush with the player who now had the puck, plus a teammate. The idea was to teach both offensive and defensive skills within the same drill. It was both simple and brilliant.

"This will be the first time a Soviet club has competed against a team from the National Hockey League—certainly an historic event...."[6] That is how the New York Rangers' public-address announcer, Carl Martin, began the evening's festivities ... after which each of the Soviet players and team officials was booed lustily by the 17,500 Ranger fans upon their being introduced. It was almost as if the Philadelphia Flyers or the Boston Bruins were the visitors at sold-out Madison Square Garden on that last Sunday night of 1975.

The New York Rangers were in a season-long funk entering the game, although they had won their last two NHL contests. The club sported a mediocre 15–17–4 record after 36 games and were sitting dead last in the four-team Patrick Division, six points out of a playoff spot. Perennial Cup challengers for the first half of the decade, the Rangers badly disappointed in the 1975 Stanley Cup playoffs in April, shockingly losing to the New York Islanders in a best-of-three opening-round series. When things began badly in 1975–76, the Rangers orchestrated a huge trade with the Boston Bruins in early November: the main component of the deal was that Phil Esposito and Carol Vadnais were sent to New York, while longtime Rangers Jean Ratelle and team captain Brad Park moved to Boston in return. (Esposito assumed the captaincy of the Rangers that was vacated by Park's departure.) The Bruins seemed to get the better of the deal while the underachieving New Yorkers continued to struggle. On January 7, 1976—ten days after their team played Central Red Army—both longtime general-manger Emile Francis and coach Ron Stewart were dismissed from their positions within the club.

Dick Irvin of *Hockey Night in Canada* pointed out to the large viewing audience that it was a groundbreaking night in another area: To the best of anyone's knowledge, it was the first international hockey game ever played in New York City at any level, which was a little bit surprising given the city's half century of NHL hockey. Undoubtedly, it would be the first time a referee from the Soviet Union had worked a hockey game at Madison Square Garden. Yuri Karandin was the man wearing the red armbands for the series' opening tilt. (Karandin became a figure of controversy before the first game of Super Series '76 had been played when it was learned he routinely travelled and worked out with the Central Red Army club. The Soviets had no idea why that was controversial; as a matter of convenience their sports officials routinely travelled with teams.) In the opener of Super Series '76, Karandin was supported by John D'Amico and Matt Pavelich, two veteran NHL linesmen from Canada. They were generally considered by the league's coaches and players to be among the best in the business.

Although the agreement for Super Series '76 stipulated that it would be governed wholly by NHL rules, apparently no one had bothered to tell the Soviet clubs that the allowable curve on a regulation NHL hockey stick in 1975 was a mere half inch. Clearly the blades on the Soviet players' sticks significantly exceeded that small amount. When this was brought to their attention, they responded with a brusque, "We don't play then." NHL poohbahs did not think excessively curved sticks were worth squabbling over and perhaps imperiling the series. An exception was made. The on-ice officials and the participating NHL clubs were quietly told that stick measurements would not be allowed.

A potentially embarrassing social faux pas was averted a few days before the game. The NHL expected that the common international hockey custom of players exchanging gifts with each other would be observed. Accordingly, the league and its participating clubs had gone to considerable expense to order special Lucite paperweights to present to the Soviets. Each one had the crest of the Soviet team and their NHL opponent for that game embedded inside it. They were quite attractive and more than just trinkets. Unfortunately, the Soviets did not expect gift exchanges to occur. They had brought nothing whatsoever to give the NHLers in return. Super Series '76 organizers quickly went into action to rectify the problem. A souvenir shop in Toronto was found that specialized in imports from the USSR. Luckily it was well stocked. Enough Russian dolls were acquired for the players from the USSR to present them as "gifts" to their NHL opponents during each game's opening ceremony.

On game night at Madison Square Garden, the 17,500-seat venue was officially sold out, but that did not mean every seat in the famous arena was occupied. Oddly, there were close to 1,000 no-shows, according to the estimation of Jack Dulmage of the *Windsor Star*.

The Rangers could not have asked for a better start. After the Red Army was whistled for an icing infraction, Phil Esposito won a faceoff to the left of goaltender Vladislav Tretiak. Seconds later, the puck found its way back to Esposito in the slot. He spotted teammate Steve Vickers, absolutely unguarded, to Tretiak's right. Esposito delivered an accurate pass to him. Vickers had an easy backhanded tap-in for the first goal of the game and of Super Series '76. It had taken all of 21 seconds for the underdog home team to assume a 1–0 lead over their feared visitors from Moscow. It turned out to be a total aberration. Soviet coach Konstantin Loktev later told the press he had expected the Rangers to score the game's first goal!

Of the Rangers' very positive start, Esposito later said, "We came out in the first four minutes [flying] and they [the Soviets] waited to see what was going to happen. We absolutely dazzled them."[7] That early stretch did not continue for long. It certainly was the high point of the game for the home team.

Harry Sinden, who was doing color commentary for *HNIC*, praised Esposito for his fine pass to Vickers. Dick Irvin reminded Sinden that in the 1972 Canada–Russia Series that Esposito's goal in Game #1 came after 30 seconds, but this one was even faster. Irvin, however, politely and tactfully neglected to mention to the TV viewers what that game's outcome eventually was.

Sinden's presence in the *HNIC* broadcast booth on December 28 was a bit of a surprise. He was the general-manager of the Boston Bruins. His club was playing a marquee game in Philadelphia against the defending Stanley Cup champions that very night (which the Bruins won, 4–2). Sinden, if he needed to do so, could justify his being in New York instead of Philadelphia by saying it was a special scouting trip. Boston would be hosting the Central Red Army club in the sixth game of Super Series '76, 11 days later, on January 8.

Shortly thereafter, referee Yuri Karandin got the attention of the vocal Ranger supporters by not calling two penalties against the visitors—which the fans figured should have been promptly whistled. He then issued an iffy hooking infraction against New York defenseman Doug Jarrett. During the delayed-penalty situation, Karandin neglected to stop play when the Rangers briefly but clearly controlled the puck. The Rangers momentarily froze, fully expecting the referee to blow his whistle. Fortunately for the Soviet referee, no goal was scored on the play. The Rangers did a magnificent job killing the penalty for the first 100 seconds, but a defensive breakdown eventually resulted in the first Central Red Army goal. A shot from the blue line got through to New York goalie John Davidson. He stopped it, but two Soviet players were somehow standing unguarded in front of him. Twenty-year-old Boris Alexandrov, the youngest player on the Central Red Army squad, slid a shot under the sprawling goaltender. The Soviet power-play goal at 4:04 leveled the game, 1–1.

After the Red Army tied the game, both Steve Vickers and Phil Esposito had very good scoring chances for New York that were both thwarted by Vladislav Tretiak. After Esposito failed to connect, the Soviets counterattacked and took the lead on a goal by Vladimir Vikulov. He finished off a pretty three-on-two passing play with a low wrist shot that beat Davidson. The time of the go-ahead marker for the visitors was 5:18. To that point in the game, Central Red Army had had three shots on net—and had put two goals on the board.

Central Red Army was now starting to roll—and they were greatly helped by young New York defenseman Ron Greschner. The 21-year-old from Goodsoil, Saskatchewan was whistled for three consecutive penalties, all of them quite justified. The Rangers managed to kill off the first two, but not the third one which came late in the first period. Valeri Kharlamov scored a beauty on an individual rush beginning at his own blue line. He deftly split two New York defenseman before beating Davidson with a wrist shot. Even the passionate Ranger fans elicited a collective gasp in astonishment at the wonderful skills shown by the talented Kharlamov on the play. They could sense which team was the better one. Harry Sinden was quick to praise the Soviet superstar. "You just won't see a better move through the middle of two defenseman,"[8] he said. The buzzer ended the first period soon afterward. The shots on goal were fairly even, 12–10 in favor of Central Red Army, but the comrades led 3–1 and were clearly in control of the game. The four penalties called by Yuri Karandin in the opening 20 minutes all went to New York. A smattering of boos rained down on the home team as the Rangers headed to their dressing room with glum faces, but there was a distinct buzz going through the Madison Square Garden crowd. Most of the patrons, new to international hockey, were very impressed by what the visitors had put forth. They had to be.

The dominance of Central Red Army continued into the second period. A two-on-one by the visitors was botched, then salvaged, as Valeri Kharlamov retrieved the puck behind the Rangers' goal and fed a perfect pass to Vladimir Petrov in the slot. His wrist shot at 1:26 cleanly beat Davidson on the stick side. The New York goalie was having a subpar night. It was now 4–1 for the Soviets. A few disillusioned Ranger fans began cheering the Soviet onslaught of goals. Perhaps it was out of admiration for the visitors or as a mocking insult to the overmatched home team; it was difficult to tell. Ranger coach Ron Stewart gave up on rotating four lines. He began giving 33-year-old Phil Esposito extra shifts in hope of reversing the game's momentum.

The Rangers finally got a chance to employ their power-play unit about a third of the way into the second period as referee Karandin twice called Red Army players for infractions. Vladimir Popov went off for charging and, just 48 seconds later, Alexander Gusev joined him in the visitors' penalty box for tripping. Thus, for 1:12, the Rangers enjoyed a two-man advantage. Nothing positive for New York came from it.

"Over-anxious New York passes went awry and shots went wide,"⁹ said the Associated Press. Phil Esposito had the best scoring opportunity for the NHL club, but Tretiak stoned him from close in front of the net.

After the Soviet penalties expired, the game was delayed for several minutes as a fight broke out in the stands, an occurrence not particularly unusual at New York Ranger home games. The battlers were quickly ejected, but at least one of them had tossed something onto the ice. It had splattered widely, causing a significant pause in the action. Both teams skated in circles around their own zones during the lull. *The New York Daily News* reported the next day that two male members of the Jewish Defense League, a 23-year-old and a 13-year-old, had tossed a number of rotten eggs onto the ice in front of Tretiak. They were apparently protesting the contentious Soviet emigration policy that prevented Jews in that country from relocating to Israel.

When play resumed, Central Red Army expanded their lead to 5–1 as Boris Alexandrov got his second goal of the game at 14:21 from a goalmouth scramble in front of John Davidson. With four Rangers positioned in front of their own net, Alexandrov still managed to jab at the loose puck and knock it fluttering into the goal. Not long afterward, Red Army captain Boris Mikhailov redirected a perfect pass from Valeri Kharlamov on a two-on-one situation past Davidson to make it 6–1 for the Soviets at 16:54. The game was now a rout. "Once again," noted Dick Irvin to the *HNIC* viewers, "Canadian hockey fans have to be impressed by the way the Soviets throw the puck around."¹⁰ There was no further scoring in the second period. Even though the Rangers had outshot Central Red Army in the middle period by a 14–9 margin, their fans were not a happy bunch. The boos for the home team were noticeably louder than they were after the first 20 minutes of play.

Central Red Army scored their seventh consecutive goal when Vladimir Petrov beat Davidson with a well-placed slapshot at 3:16 of the third period. It was his second goal of the game. (Dick Irvin accurately commented that the slapshot was seldom used by the Soviet players prior to the 1972 series, but they were now embracing it.) Under ordinary circumstances, John Davidson likely would have been replaced in the New York net. However, the Rangers' usual second-string goaltender, Dunc Wilson, was recovering from a bout with hepatitis and was not dressed for the game. Third-stringer, Doug Soetaert, was dressed. He was fresh out of junior hockey, and had the minuscule sum of 16 minutes of NHL play on his résumé. New York coach Ron Stewart decided that it was probably not in Soetaert's best interest if he were subjected to the Soviet juggernaut opponent in a mop-up role. Davidson was going to be in the Rangers' goal for the full 60 minutes regardless of how lopsided the score became.

With under five minutes to play in the game, Phil Esposito cleanly won a faceoff in the Red Army zone. The puck went back to Rod Gilbert. Stationed a stride inside the blue line, Gilbert quickly blasted a slapshot that whizzed by Vladislav Tretiak and into the Soviet net at 15:31. The score now stood at 7–2 for Central Red Army. (Gilbert and Esposito were the only two players on the Ranger roster who had played against Tretiak in 1972.) At 17:47 the Rangers added a third tally, converting on a power play. Again, Phil Esposito was involved, this time as the scorer. It was a typical Esposito goal. The Ranger captain fired a quick shot from the slot that beat Tretiak to the short side to make the score 7–3. Esposito had contributed to all three goals scored by the home team, but it was far from enough to make a difference in the game's one-sided outcome. In the next day's *Montréal Gazette*, Al Strachan wrote, "Phil Esposito is so talented there are some nights when he can singlehandedly defeat any NHL team. However, the Central Red Army team is not an NHL team."[11] Coach Ron Stewart said afterward it was easily the best game Esposito had played for New York since joining the club in early November.

There were no more goals scored in the game, but tempers and frustrations began to flare as the clock at Madison Square Garden wound down to zero. Defenseman Carol Vadnais, who was arguably the best New York player on the night, got an undisciplined five-minute butt-ending penalty in the final minute of play. Greg Polis brushed into referee Karandin—perhaps accidentally, perhaps not. Due to the uncertainty of the physical contact, Polis was issued only an unsportsmanlike conduct minor penalty rather than a game misconduct.

The Rangers had outshot Central Red Army 41–29 over the 60 minutes, but as Harry Sinden sarcastically said to the Canadian television viewers, it was goals that counted—not shots. It was confirmed as a thoroughly dominant performance by the visitors when three Soviet players swept the honors as the game's stars, as selected by *HNIC*: Valeri Kharlamov, Vladimir Vikulov and Boris Alexandrov.

The Associated Press duly reported,

> The precision-passing attack overwhelmed the Rangers who took a 1–0 lead after 21 seconds on a goal by Steve Vickers. The Rangers were outgunned in every department after the visitors recovered from some first-minute shakiness. The Red Army, winners of 19 Soviet championships in 29 seasons, breezed to victory with a clutching defense and a tireless offense. It was their ability to find the open man and take shots without stopping the puck that paved the victory....[12]

Similarly, Martin Lader of United Press International wrote, "[The] Soviet Army [hockey club] was highly impressive in opening its North American exhibition tour."[13] The *Boston Globe,* in its early edition the following day, featured a headline that read "Soviets trample Rangers." Its later edition called the Soviets' play "highly polished," said they had "swarmed" all over the Rangers at Madison Square Garden, and their victory was a triumph of "discipline over recklessness."[14]

Parton Keese of the *New York Times* commented,

> In the first game of an eight-game series between two Soviet teams and eight NHL clubs, the New York Rangers were routed last night by the Soviet [Red] Army, 7–3.
>
> Though the Rangers made the final count more respectable with two goals in the last five minutes, they did not prove quick enough, accurate enough, sharp enough, or tough enough to cope with the disciplined Soviet squad.
>
> The number-one Ranger line provided all the goals.[15]

"They outplayed us, no doubt about it," admitted humbled Ranger coach Ron Stewart in a postgame interview. "I like their system of skating and moving. I hope some of it rubs off. They skated for the whole 60 minutes—and we didn't."[16]

Wes Gaffer of the *New York Daily News* was completely impressed by the foreign victors and their appealing style of play. He wrote in his game report, "The Russians aren't coached. They're choreographed, whirling in elaborate circular patterns that utterly confused the Rangers and made the annual ice show a superfluous offering at the Garden."[17]

Red Army coach Konstantin Loktev explained the game's one-sided outcome quite nicely in the spirit of communism by saying, "The Rangers played individually, sometimes with two men working together. We play with all five skaters as a unit."[18]

Sports columnist Hal Walker of the *Calgary Herald* wrote,

> If Clarence Campbell ever had any serious doubts about the Russians being competitive enough to engage the clubs in the NHL, he got a quick answer on Sunday night in New York. The skaters from the steppes ran away and hid on the New York Rangers [who] were not very well prepared for the all-out offensive that the Soviets unleashed on a nice boy like John Davidson, the tall goaltender from Calgary.[19]

Walker, like many longtime hockey observers, had nothing but positive things to say about the winners. "It was refreshing to watch the highly skilled and disciplined Russians carry the puck to the New Yorkers," he continued, "with their excellent passing patterns and speedy skating. They've come a long way since the mid-fifties when the celebrated Penticton Vees, led by the Warwick brothers, gave them a thrashing."[20] (Interestingly, Walker and his colleagues at the *Calgary Herald* had another international hockey tour to cover in the own backyard, far away from

NHL cities: The Finnish national team was on a tour of western Canada, mostly playing university teams. Also, a junior club, the Czech Olympics, were on a nine-game tour of Canada, indicating the eagerness of Canadians to see other European clubs test their boys at all levels of hockey. International hockey was clearly in vogue in the Great White North.)

In the Rangers' dressing room, Phil Esposito glumly said, "We weren't prepared for this game. I was ready. I was prepared. So was Rod Gilbert. But some of these guys were shocked. They didn't know what to expect. You've got to be better prepared when you face the Russians—better prepared mentally." Esposito continued, "We were running around like stupid idiots instead of each man taking one of their men. I was yelling my brains out."[21]

According to the Ranger captain, the skills of the Soviets surprised many of the younger members of the home team. Pregame discussions and warnings seemed to make no impression. "They just couldn't understand what the Russians could really do," Esposito said. "Then, during the game, some of the players would come up to me and say, 'Those Russians can really shoot!'"[22]

Although defeated, Esposito had a slight smile on his face when he said he desired a rematch. "Jeez, I'd like to play these guys again. I think we could beat 'em. It's too bad they're not in our league. Now that's what I call a road trip."[23]

John Davidson was honest about his shaky performance in goal. "Our goaltending didn't come up real big," he said, as if he were analyzing someone else's play. "In other words, I didn't play that well. Yeah, I'd say that I was embarrassed. Any time I lose I'm embarrassed, especially when it's on TV all across Canada."[24]

In contrast to Davidson's subpar showing, Parton Keese of the *New York Times* declared, "As expected, Vladislav Tretiak, the 23-year-old Soviet goalie, excelled. Calmly and assuredly, he batted away the Rangers' shots, his rebounds too well handled to give New York second chances. Tretiak lived up to his advance notices."[25] Keese also noted that some disgruntled Ranger fans began chanting "Vlady! Vlady!" after each save by the Soviet netminder when the Red Army lead became insurmountable.

Keese surprisingly gave Davidson a passing grade which the Ranger netminder himself did not figure he deserved. "John Davidson played well in the Ranger net," Keese wrote. "However, the precise Soviet passing and quick execution left his defensemen in the lurch and he became the victim of three-on-one and four-on-one charges."[26]

Scribe Al Strachan firmly believed the Rangers were the authors of their own demise with their undisciplined, foolish penalties. Strachan singled out Ron Greschner for particularly heavy criticism. He wrote that the young Ranger defenseman "had watched far too many football games on the weekend as he tackled everybody who came within range."[27] "We took too many stupid penalties," agreed Carol Vadnais, who himself committed a pointless one with just 22 seconds left on the clock. "They wouldn't have changed the outcome of the game; they were just stupid penalties for no reason at all—and they killed us."[28]

Jack Dulmage of the *Windsor Star* brutally wrote, "One answer [to why the game was an easy win for Central Red Army] would be that the Rangers are a pretty lousy team, and that the Montréal Canadiens, Philadelphia Flyers, Buffalo Sabres, Boston Bruins and even the New York Islanders are considerably better. The Soviet Army team outclassed the Rangers from beginning to end."

Dulmage continued with his negative critique of the Rangers. He declared, "At times, the game degenerated to terrible mediocrity. The Soviets rapidly and consistently increased their lead, period by period, and even as early as the second period started playing under wraps with the outcome obviously clinched. The Rangers never got anything going in a sustained way."[29]

About a month after the team's bad loss to the Soviets, hockey journalist Stan Fischler described the 1975–76 New York Rangers as being "immune to improvement."[30] Considering the Rangers were on their way to missing the Stanley Cup playoffs for the first time in a decade, Fischler's comment was a cruelly accurate one. The Rangers' December 28 game versus Central Red Army was, in retrospect, a hopeless mismatch.

Soviet referee Yuri Karandin's performance definitely received mixed reviews. Most of the journalists at Madison Square Garden thought he had done at least a passable job, but that was far from a universal opinion. Somewhat surprisingly, Phil Esposito had few complaints. With justification, he favorably noted, "Compared to the [1972] series, it was so much better [tonight] that it was unbelievable."[31] Carol Vadnais severely disagreed with his fellow ex–Bruin teammate. "I thought the refereeing was terrible," he stated without hesitation. "I just hope one of our refs will do a nice job for us in one of the other games."[32]

On his way out of Madison Square Garden, a departing, frustrated Ranger fan vented to Strachan, "The referees [sic] were awful. They won't let you hit those guys. I hope Dave Schultz kills them in Philly."[33] Perhaps the most telling comment regarding Karandin's outing was a pithy one from embattled Ranger coach Ron Stewart. "I guess that referee learned from our referees," he suggested. "And they're all bad."[34]

Apparently, the Soviet style of hockey had quietly won a major convert. An impressed Bill Jennings, the president of the New York Rangers, told Mark Mulvoy of *Sports Illustrated*, "From now on we're doing our recruiting in Russia, not Canada."[35]

Jennings was not alone in his admiration of the visitors and their style of play. Another reporter from the *New York Times*, John S. Rodosta, was getting his first glimpse of Soviet hockey—and he was thoroughly impressed by what he saw. In a piece titled "Soviet Skaters Give Lesson in Hockey," Rodosta penned,

> [The NHL] could use is a lot more hockey of the type the Soviet Army team brought to Madison Square Garden. The visitors showed a razzle-dazzle of skating and passing that kept the New York Rangers off balance throughout the evening.
>
> The Russians seldom carry the puck very long—they pass it constantly—and defenders never get much chance to see who has it. On one occasion, in a combination of aplomb and chutzpah, a Soviet defenseman backpassed to his own goaltender.[36]

Parton Keese concluded his coverage of the game by taking a unique, optimistic view. He wrote, "Two good things in favor of the Rangers: the rest of their Patrick Division opponents in the NHL might look easier to beat after last night; they may have made the Russians a little overconfident for their next stop on the tour."[37] An unnamed employee of Madison Square Garden was considerably less optimistic. He said, "With our luck, the NHL may just put the Russians in the Patrick Division."[38]

"It was only one game and I don't like that," concluded Phil Esposito. "That's not an excuse, though. They played well and deserved to beat us tonight. But anybody could have beaten us tonight."[39]

Clarence Campbell seemed indifferent to the game's outcome. According to a Canadian Press story, Campbell rated the Rangers as only about the seventh- or eighth-best team in the NHL. He was confident that Boston, Montréal and Philadelphia would fare much better in their upcoming games versus the Soviet Elite League champions. In that same CP story, Phil Esposito, apparently unaware of what Dick Beddoes did in 1972, told reporters that he would eat the Soviets' uniforms in front of the Montréal Forum if they won all eight of their games versus the NHL teams.

Why was Esposito so confident that the Soviets would not sweep the NHL teams? He had noticed what he thought was a serious flaw in the visitors' style. "There's one lesson the other [NHL] teams should have learned," the Ranger captain said. "If you really start pushing them and forechecking them, they'll throw the puck away in their own zone."[40] That tidbit of information had indeed been noticed by two NHL coaches who were closely watching the game at home on their television sets: Scotty Bowman of the Montréal Canadiens and Fred Shero of the Philadelphia

Flyers. Both men intended to exploit it when they needed to do so over the next two weeks of the Soviets' tour.

Hockey players were often rated highly by North American journalists for their amiability and cooperation with the press. Therefore, media folks hoping to interview Soviet players were disappointed. What they saw was only what they got. No members of the media—especially foreign journalists—were granted access to the Red Army dressing room. No interviews were permitted elsewhere either. Without exception, all reporters' questions would be answered by coach Loktev or reps from the Soviet ice hockey delegation. Freedom of speech—even by its nation's star athletes—was an unknown concept in the USSR in 1975.

Not surprisingly, Konstantin Loktev was bombarded by reporters' questions following the game. He patiently and thoughtfully answered all of them, even if they did not directly pertain to hockey or what had just happened in that evening's contest. When asked about the rotten eggs being tossed onto the Madison Square Garden ice surface, the Central Red Army coach diplomatically said, "I guess there are a few bad people in every country, but I really admired the atmosphere of the people here."[41]

When asked to comment on what he thought of the Ranger players' average salary being $80,000 in 1975–76, Loktev did not quite know what to say. Such capitalist things were outside his scope of knowledge. Searching for an adequate reply, Loktev finally came up with, "I cannot answer. The NHL and other authorities have to rate them."[42]

Jack Dulmage of the *Windsor Star* reported that the Central Red Army club may have been on the shortest bus ride any hockey team ever had to endure to get to a game. The Soviets were staying at the Statler Hilton just across the street from Madison Square Garden. Yet, with all the festering anti–Soviet sentiment within New York City's large Jewish population, Frank Torpey, the head of NHL Security, deemed that it was unsafe for the Red Army players to simply make the brief walk to the Rangers' famous arena. Torpey told Dulmage a couple of hours before the opening faceoff, "This morning we let them walk across the street to practice, but not now. [There are] too many people around."[43]

Embattled Coach Ron Stewart summed up things as best he could. He noted, "We're the eighth-best team in the NHL—and we played the best."[44] [Authors' note: At the time of the Rangers–Red Army game, New York was tied with Toronto for the ninth-best record in the NHL with 34 points.]

It had been a horribly bad start for the NHL, quite similar to the first game of the 1972 Summit Series. Ironically, the 7-3 score in favor of the visitors from the Soviet Union was the same in both games. This time, however, there was no shock value attached to it.

Scoring Summary

Red Army 3+3+1 = 7
New York Rangers: 1+0+2 = 3

First period

1. New York Rangers: Vickers (Esposito, Gilbert) 0:21
2. Red Army: Alexandrov (Petrov, Gusev) 4:04
3. Red Army: Vikulov (Shluktov, Alexandrov) 5:19
4. Red Army: Kharlamov (Vasiliev, Petrov) 19:42

Second period

1. Red Army: Petrov (Kharlamov, Mikhailov) 1:26
2. Red Army: Vikulov (Shluktov, Alexandrov) 14:27
3. Red Army: Mikhailov (Kharlamov, Gusev) 16:54

Third period

1. Red Army: Petrov (Mikhailov, Kharlamov) 3:16
2. New York Rangers: Gilbert (Esposito) 15:31
3. New York Rangers: Esposito (Vickers, Sacharuk) 17:47 (pp)

8

Game #2

Soviet Wings vs. Pittsburgh Penguins

Monday, December 29, 1975
Pittsburgh Civic Arena

While Super Series '76 was dominating the hockey talk in most of the cities where the touring Soviets would be playing, Pittsburgh was a clear exception. A blasé attitude—typical of this NHL city that struggled at the gate each year—seemed to be the most dominant emotion. Only 10,000 of the 17,000 available tickets had been sold 24 hours prior to the Soviet Wings facing off against the hometown Penguins at the "Igloo"—the nickname given to the city's Civic Arena. Pittsburgh's 43-year-old coach, Marc Boileau, was not surprised at all by the less-than-overwhelming interest in the upcoming exhibition game in the city where he was employed to coach the local NHL club. He had a ready explanation.

"The series is a big thing in Canada," the native of Pointe Claire, Quebec explained to *Montréal Gazette* hockey reporter Al Strachan in a telephone interview conducted on December 28, "But it's not such a big thing in the United States. These are football fans here [in Pittsburgh]. Now, if you brought in a Russian football team and had them go against the Pittsburgh Steelers, the fans would go wild for that. But not for hockey."[1] The Steelers were currently the favorites to win the Super Bowl for a second straight time as the National Football League's playoffs were getting underway. Hockey games—any hockey games—would be a tough sell in Pittsburgh as 1976 approached and the Steelers were still winning.

One major problem in getting American fans excited about Super Series '76 was the lack of major television coverage of pro hockey in the United States at the time. The NHL had TV packages ready to sell to whatever stations were interested in acquiring them, but few did because the Soviets delayed in finalizing the Series. By the time the Series was confirmed to take place midway through November, many TV stations had already booked other programming for the same December and January nights and afternoons when the Super Series '76 games would be played. The hockey hotbed of Massachusetts was one example of a missed opportunity to grow the international game. The *Boston Globe* reported that only the Bruins–Red Army game on January 8 and the Buffalo–Soviet Wings game on January 4 would be available for TV viewers in the Hub. Fans located in the Boston area who were interested in watching the much-anticipated Montréal–Central Red Army game on television on New Year's Eve were simply out of luck.

When apprised of the TV situation in the USA, Phil Esposito, who was never shy about expressing his opinions on any topic, shrugged and said it was another example of how the NHL had bungled an opportunity. In 1975–76, the league no longer had a broadcasting deal with any of the three American TV networks. (Neither did the WHA.) NBC had opted out of its Sunday games after the 1974–75 season because of disappointing ratings. Esposito blamed the NHL for insisting that NBC's *Game of the Week* feature a wide variety of the teams instead of showcasing the marquee clubs on its telecasts that would likely have attracted considerably more viewers. (Espo had a valid point: The first Sunday game NBC aired after the NFL season ended in January 1975 was a tilt between the mediocre Chicago Blackhawks and the dismal California Golden Seals.)

Even Boileau was not outwardly excited about the novelty of his Penguins encountering a Soviet club in a mid-season exhibition tilt as part of Super Series '76. "I don't have any special feeling about this game," he honestly confessed. "It's not going to give us any points in the standings."[2]

Moreover, Boileau was unimpressed by Soviet hockey as a whole. "The Russians haven't proved anything to me yet," he declared. "I don't believe they're better than the Canadian players."[3]

He continued his rant. "If they're so good, why didn't they beat Team Canada '72 in eight straight games? They had their best players and I don't think we had ours. They had all the time in the world to get their team ready. We just threw ours together. Bobby Orr was injured and other good players weren't allowed on the team because they had jumped to the World Hockey Association."[4]

Boileau, who had been hired by the Penguins 52 games into the 1973–74 season, probably viewed his team's game versus the Soviet Wings as an unnecessary interruption in the regular season and a pointless distraction in a trying campaign for his club. Boileau was currently embattled with Penguins general-manager Wren Blair, whom he publicly accused of eroding his authority as the team's coach. Certainly, the timing of the Soviet Wings arrival in Pittsburgh was not the best for the home team.

Strachan noted that Blair, against the wishes of Boileau, was scheduled to address the team before the game versus the Soviets. "Perhaps he'll continue to do Boileau's job," quipped the veteran Montréal scribe, "and instill a positive attitude into the Penguins. They'll need it."[5] [Authors' note: Boileau would be fired after the Penguins' 43rd game of the 1975–76 season on January 15 with his team sporting an unimpressive 15–23–5 record.]

When Boileau was interviewed by Bob Whitley of the *Pittsburgh Post-Gazette* on the day of the game, he stressed that his team had not been especially focused on the Soviets—far from it, in fact. "I don't think the guys were thinking too much about this game before today," he commented. "They were more worried about regular-season games. But after coming out and seeing the Russians skate around, I think everyone is looking forward to the game. We'll be going all out to win. I can promise you that much."[6]

Boris Kulagin, the affable coach of the Soviet Wings, was also focused on the regular-season—not in the NHL but in the 10-team Soviet Championship League (SCL), also referred to as the Soviet Elite League by North American journalists. It had been completely shut down while the Super Series was being played. Presently his team was sitting in fourth place in that circuit. The previous season, the Wings were runners-up to Central Red Army in the SCL. That strong finish earned them the trip to North America. "Gentlemen, the national championship is not over," Kulagin insisted when asked if his Wings were hopelessly out of contention for top honors back home. "There is still plenty of time left."[7]

Kulagin had a chance to scout his team's first NHL opponents in action. He and the Soviet Wings were in attendance at Pittsburgh's Civic Arena when the Penguins edged the Atlanta Flames, 3–2, on December 27. That win give the Penguins a mediocre record of 14–17–4 after 35 NHL games in 1975–76. Kulagin told local media that he was impressed by the professionalism of the home team and that he was now scared of what the Penguins might do when his Wings confronted them on December 29. It was difficult to ascertain if Kulagin was serious or not.

One Penguin veteran, Lowell MacDonald, had experience playing against a Soviet team as a junior. Their fitness level left a lasting impression on him. "You wouldn't believe their conditioning," he told a reporter. MacDonald recalled with awe, "They got up in the morning and ran to the rink, three miles away. They skated for an hour, then ran back to their hotel and had their pregame meal. Then they played soccer in the afternoon and that night they ran to the game."[8] Unfortunately for MacDonald, he would be out of the Pittsburgh lineup when they faced the Soviet Wings in Game #2 of Super Series '76. The 34-year-old forward had a broken thumb that had not quite healed well enough for him to play on December 29.

Eventually, a push of late, local publicity about the game caused tickets sales to rise to a passable level, and 13,214 curious fans did pay their way into The Igloo four days after Christmas to watch the hometown Pens compete against the Soviet Wings. (It was not a sellout, but that figure was still about 1,800 more than the average attendance at the Civic Arena for Penguins home games during the 1975–76 NHL season.) What the fans saw that night may, unfortunately, be lost to history. There is no known surviving video of that game—at least it is not readily available to be viewed by contemporary fans. During the Red Army–Rangers game the evening before, Dick Irvin of *Hockey Night in Canada* made a point of saying the Pens–Soviet Wings game would not be televised in Canada. (Before the advent of all-sports specialty television channels, such was the sporadic reality of hockey broadcasting in much of the United States.) Thus, it seems that all that hockey fans have to remember this particular game with is raw statistics and the accounts of players and newspaper reporters who were on the scene that Monday night. Perhaps it is best forgotten by Pittsburgh Penguins supporters anyway. The game did not flatter their team in the slightest.

From all accounts, what they saw was very nearly a carbon copy of what Central Red Army inflicted on the New York Rangers 24 hours before. The Soviet Wings jumped out to a huge, early lead in the first period and coasted thereafter to a comfortable win over their gracious but overmatched hosts.

The Soviet Wings, much like Central Red Army, had borrowed a handful of players from another Soviet club to bolster their roster for Super Series '76. Joining the team were a talented threesome from Spartak Moscow: Vladimir Shadrin, Viktor Shalimov and Alexander Yakushev. They were the key players for the Wings in the opening period when the visitors absolutely dominated the hometown Penguins.

Robin Herman of the *New York Times* declared, "Using the same magic with which their Soviet Army comrades hypnotized the Rangers last night, the Wings of the Soviet beat the Pittsburgh Penguins, 7–4, tonight in the second game of an eight-game series with National Hockey League teams." Herman continued,

> The Russians' eccentric style, their weaving patterns that neutralize the traditional NHL wing-on-wing defense, and their quick passes from forehand or backhand, cast a spell on the Penguins so that they gave up four goals in the opening period. Michel Plasse was in goal for his first home loss as a Penguin. Although they caught on quickly to the foreign style and worked hard in the following two periods, the Penguins could not make up the deficit.[9]

The Canadian Press scribe at the Igloo, Ian MacLaine, agreed. He reported, "The Soviet Wings almost blew the NHL Penguins out onto nearby Center

Avenue in the first period, toying with their opposition and skating to a 4–0 lead." The visitors' lead was too great to overcome, even though the final 40 minutes was quite competitive. MacLaine, concurred. "It was an entirely different [Pittsburgh] club that came out for the last two periods,"[10] he penned.

Herman singled out one Wings player in particular for special praise: Alexander Yakushev, a familiar face to Canadians from his exploits in 1972. The *Times* correspondent stated,

> The Wings, a significant notch below the Soviet Army team in the proficiency of their passes and positioning, nevertheless played a superb fast-skating game and also showed that the Russians know how to check.
> Towering over the other Wings was Aleksandr Yakushev the left wing who, at a rangy 6 feet 4 inches, was the Russians' greatest physical threat on offense. His reach with a long sickle-shaped blade was astounding and he led his team through a marvelous first period.[11]

Vic Hadfield, the only player in a Pittsburgh uniform who played on Team Canada 1972—albeit sparingly in just two games before bolting—stated the obvious. "If we could have gotten past the first 10 minutes, we could have made it a pretty good hockey game,"[12] the veteran, 35-year-old forward said to the media. Hadfield termed his Penguin teammates as "watchers" in the game's early going—when its outcome was truly decided. United Press International scribe Pohla Smith wrote pretty much the same thing. "The Penguins spent the first period gawking at the visitors before they began earnest play,"[13] Smith stated.

Hadfield later admitted that the Penguins had liberally used their sticks on the Wings in an attempt to slow them down. He unapologetically noted,

> We gave them tough shots and ankle slaps. There was nothing could faze 'em. [It was] like they had iron legs or something. And once we found we couldn't hurt them, we started playing our game again. We took out the man instead. We went back to interference, skating, and checking. That's our game. If we were able to get, over those first 10 minutes we might have been able to do it.[14]

The visitors' attack on the home team's netminder was a relentless one. "The Wings skated swiftly and delivered short, unerring passes that drew them close enough to see the whites of goaltender Michel Plasse's eyes,"[15] declared Bill Heufelder of the *Pittsburgh Press*. Plasse was making his home debut for Pittsburgh after being acquired in a deal with the Kansas City Scouts. It was a difficult one for the 27-year-old native of Montréal.

Pittsburgh's Dave Burrows admitted he spent considerable time observing how the Soviet Wings operated. He did so with a growing sense of admiration. "We just kind of sat back and watched the way they played,"

Burrows admitted. "They kept switching positions all the time, like sending a basketball player into the key for three seconds, then getting him out so the next guy can go in. Unless you get used to that, it can burn you."

Burrows continued, "I don't want to take anything away from them," he explained, "They're good, but if they're in our league, we'd play them more than once and it would be a different story."[16] Burrows further admitted that he and many teammates were noticeably nervous and confused from the outset of the game. Their mindset had not improved after watching Red Army blow away the New York Rangers, 7–3, the night before at Madison Square Garden.

In outshooting the Penguins 15–5 in the opening 16 minutes, the Soviet Wings roared out to a daunting 4–0 lead on goals by Viacheslav Anisin on a high shot from 25 feet out at 1:45, Yuri Liapkin at 4:13 from a Vladimir Shadrin pass, Viktor Shalimov at 12:10 on a deflection, and Alexander Yakushev at 15:25, again on a pass from Shadrin. Ninety-nine seconds into the second period, Shadrin himself increased the Wings; lead to 5–0, virtually guaranteeing a victory for the visitors.

Somehow the Penguins turned things around. The first goal by the home team came off the stick of Pierre Larouche at 5:35 of the middle period. It was a power-play tally—the only one by either team—as the Wings had been penalized for having too many men on the ice. However, as soon as the red goal light flashed behind Soviet goaltender Alexander Sidelnikov, Larouche headed straight to the penalty box himself when he decided to give Russian referee Victor Dombrowski a piece of his mind not long after his teammates had congratulated him on his goal. Dombrowski promptly gave Larouche a 10-minute misconduct penalty for his unacceptable dissent. "I only pointed at my head and said that he should think about the game,"[17] Larouche later explained. He was complaining that a Soviet defender got away with high sticking him in the mouth. Few scribes could remember another incident—at any level of hockey—of a player being handed a misconduct immediately after scoring a goal.

Pittsburgh's considerably better showing in the final two periods impressed the Soviets—at least the man in charge of the team said so. "They learn fast," noted Wings coach Boris Kulagin, who was also the coach of the Soviet National team whenever that duty called. "They must have had some instruction from their coach after the first period and started to draw the necessary conclusions."[18] Those conclusions were that they stood no chance against the Wings if they did not alter the way they were playing the game.

"I'd give anything to play them again tomorrow night," insisted optimistic Pittsburgh coach Marc Boileau, sounding much like Phil Esposito did 24 hours earlier in New York City. "I don't know what happened to our guys in the first period. They were just out there skating around."[19]

Boileau told MacLaine that the Penguins' strategy was to skate with the Wings and check them closely to prevent them from initiating their attacks. It proved to be a dismal, disorganized failure. "Geez, we had three guys going in to take one of their men out of the play," said the Pittsburgh coach. "They were coming back at us three-on-two and two-on-one."[20]

Covering the game for Toronto's *Globe & Mail* was Peter White. He penned, "By the time Pittsburgh broke out of its coma in the second period, the club was behind, 5-0. But it demonstrated before it was over that the Russians, who looked nothing less than the perfect hockey machine early in the game, can be handled." White optimistically opined, "With their effort, Pittsburgh offered some hope that the eight-game exhibition series between Russian and National Hockey league clubs will not run to farce, though the NHL is behind, 2-0."[21]

The *Boston Globe* gave a harsh assessment of the Penguins' performance (and that of the New York Rangers too) by reporting, "The Russians continued to embarrass the National Hockey League last night when the Soviet Wings toppled the Pittsburgh Penguins, 7-4. It was the second time is as many games Russian teams have decisively beaten NHL clubs."[22]

Jack Dulmage of the *Windsor Star* opined that the first two NHL clubs to face the Soviets were simply bad teams in 1975-76. He accurately noted that the Los Angeles Kings and Atlanta Flames—two playoff-bound NHL clubs—had better records than both the Pittsburgh Penguins and the New York Rangers. How the Kings or Flames of 1975-76 would have fared against the Soviets will never be known, of course. One night after losing to the Soviet Wings, the Penguins rebounded to comfortably beat Los Angeles, 5-1, at the Igloo.

Over the final 40 minutes, the Penguins managed to outscore the Soviet Wings by a 4-3 margin and outshoot them, 25-20. The overall shot total was a 35-30 edge for the victors. Clearly only accentuating the positives was 20-year-old Pierre Larouche. The native of Taschereau, Quebec remarkably insisted to reporters after the game, "I don't think [the Wings] can say they beat us because we dominated them," Larouche explained. "We were nervous and throwing the puck away in the first period."[23]

Kulagin responded to accusations that the Wings were tired in the last two periods after expending so much energy against the Penguins during the first 20 minutes. He denied it emphatically. "We were not tired," he claimed. "I think our players were just satisfied with the first period and came down a little."[24]

Boileau insisted that some changes his Penguins made in strategy after the first period made it a closer affair, even if the game was already beyond the home team's grasp. "After we adjusted, we just took the play away from them. But I don't care what team you are playing against: When you are four goals down after the first period, it's tough to come back."[25]

Ron Schock, the NHL team's captain who notched the Penguins' second goal to cut the Wings' advantage to 6–2, thought other NHL teams on the Soviets' schedule would be wise to learn from the two games thus far contested in Super Series '76. Schock confidently predicted, "If the other [six NHL] teams benefit from what happened to us and the New York Rangers, they are capable of winning them all." The 32-year-old Schock admitted his team was "mesmerized" by the Soviet Wings during the first 20 minutes. "We could have had six goaltenders and it wouldn't have made any difference in that first period,"[26] he ruefully said.

Pittsburgh forward Stan Gilbertson, a 31-year-old American from Duluth, Minnesota, thought the Penguins were initially tentative because of the unknown quality of their adversaries. He stated, "We heard different theories [about Soviet hockey] at the start. No one knew what to expect."[27]

Vic Hadfield claimed that Pittsburgh's early-game physical tactics against the Soviets proved to be all wrong in the long run for the defeated Penguins. "Even a good ankle slap doesn't hurt them," Hadfield noted with just a touch of admiration. "If you can't hurt them by hitting them, you just have to interfere with them."[28]

The curious attendees at the Igloo, enthusiastic before the opening faceoff, were emotionally taken out of the game early. Peter White noted that there was no reaction whatsoever by the time Vladimir Shadrin of the Soviet Wings scored his team's fifth goal at 1:39 of the second period to make the score an unassailable 5–0. The Canadian scribe commented, "The crowd didn't know what to make of the game any more than the Penguins did."[29] Robin Herman wrote that the Soviets appeared to be playing "an ice version of monkey-in-the-middle"[30] with the befuddled home team until their shutout was broken.

Yuri Liapkin was probably the best player on the ice for either team. He scored two goals and added two assists in the one-sided affair. Ian MacLaine of Canadian Press certainly thought so. "Liapkin," he glowingly wrote, "was easily the best man on the ice at the Civic Centre. He scored two goals and [contributed] two assists while controlling the play like a Bobby Orr."[31]

Generally speaking, there were not too many complaints from either club about the Soviet referee who was surprisingly liberal in how he handled the game. "Russian referee Victor Dombrowski ruled with kid gloves in the first two periods," declared MacLaine, "with players from both sides taking runs at each other along the boards."[32] Wings coach Boris Kulagin said the roughness was not much different than his team would normally encounter in a league game back home.

Kulagin thought his team could have been better, however, despite winning the game fairly easily. Afterward Kulagin told a group of reporters, "I was not satisfied with everybody, but I am satisfied with the result."[33] He hoped his team would perform even better in the next game. It would be on Sunday, January 4 in Buffalo against the ascending Buffalo Sabres, who, as expected, were presently residing in first place in the NHL's Adams Division, just slightly ahead of the surging Boston Bruins as 1975 approached its end.

When asked if the physical play expected from the NHL clubs in his team's four games would be a detriment to the Wings, Kulagin had a ready answer that was a little bit on the abrasive and undiplomatic side. "If you remember the series of 1974," he said, "[the Canadians were a team] of tough and very rough players, but they could not beat us because we are deeply and firmly convinced that one can only win through skills."[34]

How little did Pittsburgh and its hockey fans care about the Super Series '76 game played in their fair city? The *Pittsburgh Post-Gazette*—one of the city's two major daily newspapers—amazingly provided no coverage whatsoever of the Wings-Pens game the following day! Zero. Zilch. Nada. A day later, the international hockey clash was briefly mentioned, almost as an afterthought, in the *Post-Gazette*'s discussion of the Penguins' upcoming NHL schedule. Clearly, hockey was still a niche sport in western Pennsylvania at the time, an underappreciated novelty lacking sustained mass fan support. It would take nearly two decades for that reality to change. Coach Marc Boileau was right. His hockey club played in a football city although the hometown NFL Steelers were only recently linked to gridiron success. In retrospect, Pittsburgh was the least-deserving of the eight NHL cities chosen to host this historic exhibition series. With the benefit of 20/20 hindsight, the game probably should have been played elsewhere. However, the other Super Series '76 game slated for Pennsylvania—Central Red Army versus the Stanley Cup champion Philadelphia Flyers on the afternoon of Sunday, January 11—would draw considerably more interest both locally and internationally.

Jack Dulmage of the *Windsor Star* alluded to the Flyers–Red Army game in his December 30 column. He wrote, "Six-eighths of the present series is relatively innocent. What is not harmless and is of definite consequence is the Game at Montréal on Wednesday and the closer at

Philadelphia on January 11. The Canadiens can be counted on to defend the honor of French Canada. The Flyers will rise to defend their stature as Stanley Cup champions. The Canadiens and Flyers don't have any choice in the matter. Their reputations are on the line."[35]

The *New York Times* reported that the day after the Penguins–Soviet Wings clash, Vladimir Shadrin had to make an unplanned visit to a Pittsburgh dentist. Shadrin had to have five cracked teeth repaired, all courtesy of a blow from an unnamed member of the home team.

In more esoteric matters, the *Times*, in its January 1, 1976, edition, noted three fun facts about the hockey-playing visitors from the USSR: Very few Soviet players wore traditional sweat socks during games or practices. Most simply wore everyday black street socks. Their advocates claimed their feet could feel the skates better with normal hosiery. The *Times* also said the typical beverage consumed by the visitors between periods was hot tea flavored with lemon. Finally, the Soviet players were conditioned to rise each day at 7 a.m. and do a regimen of calisthenics in their hotel rooms—with the TV on and the sound at full blast for some unexplained reason. Then they jog through the hallways to thoroughly limber up.

One thing the Soviets did not do compared to their NHL counterparts was launder their uniforms frequently. According to Rob Verdi of the *Chicago Tribune*, prior to the Wings–Penguins game, a group of Pittsburgh women hired to sew the Soviet Wings' players' surnames on the back of their jerseys (to align them with NHL standards) initially balked at the job. Apparently the stench from the garments was quite off-putting. Only when the jerseys were thoroughly laundered did the seamstresses get on with their task. Verdi sympathized with the women's task. "After all," he wrote, "those names are pretty long."[36]

Scoring Summary

Soviet Wings 4+2+1 = 7
Pittsburgh 0+3+1 = 4

First period

1. Soviet Wings: Anisin (Bodunov) 1:45
2. Soviet Wings: Liapkin (Shadrin, Shalimov) 4:13
3. Soviet Wings: Shallmov (Liapkin) 12:10
4. Soviet Wings: Yakushev (Shadrin, Turin) 15:25

Second period

1. Soviet Wings: Shadrin (Liapkin) 1:39
2. Pittsburgh: Larouche (Stackhouse, Faubert) 5:35 (PP)

3. Soviet Wings: Repnyev (Kapustin, Kalov) 6:02
4. Pittsburgh: Schock (Hadfield, Arnason) 6:53
5. Pittsburgh: Wilkins (Gilbertson, Pronovost) 14:52

Third period

1. Soviet Wings: Liapkin (Shalimov, Shadrin) 0:30
2. Pittsburgh: Morrison (Hadfield) 3:02

9

Game #3

Central Red Army vs. Montréal Canadiens

WEDNESDAY, DECEMBER 31, 1975
MONTRÉAL FORUM

There are people who witnessed the famous Central Red Army–Montréal Canadiens game on December 31, 1975, who maintain it was the greatest hockey game ever played. That is quite a bold statement. Are they just being overly nostalgic? Probably not. Here is what one esteemed Canadian journalist, Jim Coleman, wrote in the January 2, 1976, issue of the *Ottawa Citizen* about that truly memorable international hockey game:

> Thanks for the memory, Montréal Canadiens. The closing hours of the year 1975 always should be remembered gratefully by any Canadian who delights in watching hockey being played at the very peak of perfection. There are occasions when ice hockey, played at blinding speed, played with grace and technical brilliance, emerges as a veritable art form. New Year's Eve was one of those rare and precious occasions.

The 64-year-old Coleman continued issuing his lavish praise.

> The performance of the Montréal Canadiens on Wednesday night was, without question, the finest which has been given by an individual professional hockey team within the limits of my memory. It was superbly exciting entertainment. Les Canadiens and Soviet Central Red Army demonstrated conclusively that ice hockey, at the very height of excellence, is a game of speed and skill and stamina. Just give us those end-to-end rushes and the rocketing shots on net—and to hell with shoddy tactics such as intimidation, high-sticking and brawling.[1]

Years later, Red Army goaltender Vladislav Tretiak marveled at the fond memories of New Year's Eve 1975 at the Montréal Forum. He happily called the contest "technically beautiful" and "a joy to play."[2]

In March 2015, hockey journalist Gare Joyce wrote about the December 31 game, "Those of us old enough to remember those Montréal teams—Lafleur, Robinson and the rest—are also old enough to forget that the

Canadiens team that played the Red Army had been knocked out in the second round of the playoffs the previous spring by Buffalo and watched Philadelphia raise the Cup. That is to say, the dynasty hadn't quite started. The New Year's Eve game made a very good team great."[3]

Indeed, the Montréal Canadiens were not the defending Stanley Cup champions that night, but the Habs were in first place overall in the 18-team NHL and appeared to be the solid Cup favorites already for 1975–76. They had only lost one of their previous 17 games (and that was a fluke defeat to the woeful Kansas City Scouts on December 3). Six of the Canadiens had played for Team Canada in 1972. With Central Red Army being the perennial champions of the Soviet Elite League, in the minds of many fans the so-called "exhibition game" that night at the Montréal Forum was for the unofficial world club championship. All the combatants on both teams, on some level, probably sensed this was true.

More than three weeks before the hugely anticipated game, John Robertson [no relation to one of this book's co-authors], a prominent sports journalist for the *Montréal Gazette*, whimsically discussed its importance. He labeled it "a combination of the Super Bowl, the Grey Cup, the Stanley Cup all wrapped into one" and potentially the most meaningful hockey game the Canadiens had ever played. Accordingly, Robertson instructed hosts of New Year's Eve gatherings how to properly include the 8 o'clock encounter in their plans for that night's festivities in a handy list form.

1. Rent or borrow an extra color TV set, and put one in every room, if necessary.
2. Make sure you say on the invitations to arrive between 7 and 8 p.m.
3. Spell out clearly to [your guests] that they will have easy access to a TV so they can watch the game from start to finish....[4]

Clearly Montréal was not Pittsburgh. Unlike the disappointingly blasé atmosphere in the Pennsylvania city two days earlier for the Penguins–Soviet Wings contest, Montréal—the whole city—was geared up for the hockey game with the feared and formidable visitors from the Soviet Union's Central Red Army club against their beloved Habs. It was *the* topic of conversation throughout Montréal and beyond.

This sentiment was indeed shared by the Canadiens wholly. Jim Roberts said in a 2010 interview, "We were really looking forward to that game. The excitement around the team was right from the moment it was announced." Roberts was a 35-year-old, grizzled veteran in 1975. He had been in the NHL since 1958, but he could not think of any other game that brought with it the level of anticipation of the Montréal–Central Red Army clash. "There wasn't a player in that dressing room who wasn't at his best, ready for that game,"[5] he added.

In an interview with the *Montréal Gazette* on December 26, Don Awrey saw the New Year's Eve game as a chance for personal redemption. As a member of Team Canada 1972, he had been embarrassed in Game One of the Summit Series when Valeri Kharlamov blew by him to score a goal on Ken Dryden. Awrey, a competent but unspectacular defenseman, looked foolish on the play. Awrey only played in just one more game in that series after Game One. He hoped to make amends on December 31, 1975. "I've been thinking more and more lately about what I would do,"[6] he noted.

Just before Super Series '76 opened in New York City, Ken Dryden was interviewed by the Canadian Press where he expressed his thoughts about his Soviet counterpart, Vladislav Tretiak. Dryden was very complimentary toward the Central Red Army's netminder. "His biggest strength is his ability to move," Dryden noted. "On balance, I think that is the biggest strength of any goalie: to get into position to stop the puck and being in proper balance to do so. What that means is he can get all of himself into position—and all of himself is something considerable."[7]

The December 31 edition of the *Montréal Gazette* featured three full pages of analysis articles as the pregame excitement reached its apex. As it turned out, Al Strachan was the most prescient of the newspaper's prognosticators. He wrote, "No matter how well the Canadiens play tonight, they can't possibly hope to beat the Central Red Army team unless they come up with a big effort in goal. The pressure, therefore, falls squarely upon the shoulders of Ken Dryden."[8]

In another article that day, Montréal defenseman Serge Savard said that he had found himself rooting hard for the New York Rangers on December 28, but he was not surprised at all by the game's result. "They were just overpowered," he observed. Nevertheless, Savard felt that Central Red Army's one-sided victory over New York was going to inspire Montréal to raise their level of play. "If the Rangers had won 4–1," Savard explained, "everyone would be expecting us to really beat them badly. But I'm confident we can [win] because the guys have a lot of pride and they know that a lot of people are judging our whole league compared to theirs [based] on this one game."[9]

The Canadiens' six players who had faced the Soviet national team in the famous 1972 series were Serge Savard, Peter Mahovlich, Guy Lapointe, Yvan Cournoyer, Ken Dryden, and Don Awrey. (Awrey had been a member of the Boston Bruins in 1972.) It was going to be something of a reunion for those half dozen Habs. Ten members of Central Red Army had played in the 1972 Canada–Soviet series and 13 were presently on the Soviet national squad. "You have to remember we weren't too far removed from 1972," Dick Irvin explained to TV viewers in 2004 when *Hockey Night in*

Canada reran the game as alternate hockey programming when a labor stoppage halted the 2004–05 NHL season. "That was such a monumental event that there was going to be some emotional carry-over on New Year's Eve 1975."[10]

A festive but nervous atmosphere pervaded the venerable Montréal Forum on game night. Tickets were precious commodities. A packed house of 18,975 filled the arena. Jack Dulmage of the *Windsor Star* wrote, "There's nothing in the world of hockey quite like the Canadiens at home in the Forum in a game that means a good deal to them."[11] This contest certainly fit that description. Nobody—absolutely nobody—seated or among the standees inside the Forum on December 31, 1975, perceived this international friendly to be a meaningless game.

The atmosphere around the building was electric with anticipation. It was definitely an upscale crowd that packed the Forum. Many ticketholders were clad in their finery, suits for the gentlemen, full-length dresses for the ladies, in preparation for the festive New Year's Eve parties that would follow the hockey game. Among the celebrities scattered about the arena were bombastic Toronto Maple Leafs owner Harold Ballard and his faithful employee and companion King Clancy. Ballard grinned widely when he told a reporter it was the first time in 54 years that he would be rooting for the Montréal Canadiens to win a hockey game. Ballard, of course, would not permit a Soviet team to play in Maple Leaf Gardens, but, apparently, he was perfectly okay with travelling to Montréal to watch them play another NHL team in another building.

Media interest surpassed even most Stanley Cup playoff games. The Forum's press facilities could handle 140 reporters. More than 200 received credentials for the Habs–Red Army game. Simple arithmetic forced some of them to work from wherever they could find a vacant space in the building. There were not many such areas.

Numerous members of the Canadiens arrived at the Forum several hours earlier than they would have for an ordinary NHL contest. Peter Mahovlich was normally one of the most placid and unflappable Canadiens before most NHL tilts, but he was one of those six veterans of Team Canada 1972. In a remarkable sight, Mahovlich led the crowd in cheers 45 minutes before game time as a way of releasing his growing nervous tension. "I couldn't prepare for all our regular-season games like I did this one," Mahovlich later noted to a reporter. "I'd end up in a sanitarium."[12]

The *Hockey Night in Canada* broadcast began at 7 p.m. to an eager but anxious nation. In Moscow it was already 1976. It is 3 a.m. on New Year's Day. The game was shown live on Soviet television too—which was a first from any venue inside Canada. (During the 1972 and 1974 Canada–Soviet series, the games originating from North America aired in the USSR on a tape-delayed basis.) Danny Gallivan and his famously familiar voice called the play-by-play on CBC's English-language broadcast next to his usual analyst/color man Dick Irvin. Ex-Hab John Ferguson, the assistant coach from Team Canada 1972, was alongside the twosome as a guest announcer. Years later Irvin admitted, "I didn't originally feel much enthusiasm for the game. I had no experience with international hockey. I hadn't been involved in the 1972 series in any way. [The intensity] of the whole thing took me by surprise. Right from the start you could cut the tension with a knife."[13]

Howie Meeker and Dave Reynolds, clad in their powder blue *HNIC* blazers, co-hosted the broadcast. They quickly set the tone for the telecast: Objectivity would often be conspicuously absent. In his opening comments, Reynolds declared the game to be about more than the two excellent hockey clubs; it was about Canada. Meeker confidently assured the viewers that the Canadiens were better than Central Red Army in goaltending, defense, and offense. "So Canada," he concluded, "sit back, relax, enjoy yourselves, and have a ball. The Canadiens are going to win tonight."[14] Reynolds was noticeably surprised by his partner's optimism and unabashedly partisan perspective, but he could not contain himself, either. "I hope you're right,"[15] Reynolds succinctly added before turning over the broadcast to Gallivan.

Unlike in Madison Square Garden three days earlier, the Central Red Army players were sincerely applauded as they were individually introduced over the arena's public-address system by Claude Mouton. The visitors were clad in maroon jerseys. The crest on the front of each bore a hammer and sickle within a star atop a shield. Within that shield were the English alphabet letters UCKA in a downward diagonal slope. Valeri Kharlamov and Vladislav Tretiak each received more than polite hand-clapping; they were greeted with especially long, sincere ovations. The fans at the Forum that night were certainly a classy and knowledgeable bunch. They knew the Soviets' biggest stars quite well. Both players reputedly had received a tremendous amount of fan mail from Canada since 1972.

Red Army goaltender Tretiak entered the December 31 game believing he had reached the apex of his talents as a netminder. "Just before our departure to Canada," Tretiak wrote in his autobiography, "I finally reached my peak form. Until then, I'd had a few problems with my game, but everything fell into place. How perfect that it happened precisely in December."[16]

The expressions etched on the faces of the home team's players were telling. French-Canadian journalist Bertrand Raymond wrote, "I've never seen the Canadiens look as nervous as they were on Wednesday night.

9. Game #3

They were unable to remain still [during the pregame ceremonies]. Their skates shuffled back and forth as they stood. Peter Mahovlich looked like a caged lion, hammering his shin pads with his stick...."[17] The packed arena was equally edgy. Danny Gallivan commented, "I have never heard this crowd in such a frame of mind as they are tonight."[18]

Captains Yvan Cournoyer and Boris Mikhailov were summoned to center ice. Aging NHL president Clarence Campbell and Viacheslav Koloskov of the USSR's Sports Committee performed ceremonial faceoffs from a red carpet after the national anthems had been played. In 1975 "The Hymn of the Soviet Union" no longer had official words—they had been de-Stalinized by Nikita Khrushchev in the 1950s—so the tune was played on the arena's organ. Roger Doucet, a fixture at the Forum, sang his bilingual version of "O Canada" with his usual enthusiasm and panache. Shortly thereafter the puck was dropped for real by 40-year-old NHL referee Wally Harris. This was the third stop on the Soviets' North American tour, but for the first time in Super Series '76, an NHL referee was the chief official on the ice. Harris' linesmen were Claude Béchard of the NHL and Yuri Karandin of the Soviet Union. One of hockey history's greatest games had begun.

Trouble for the home team arrived early. Montréal forward Murray Wilson, who had been thwarted by Tretiak mere seconds into the game, took an undisciplined high-sticking penalty against Boris Mikhailov after just 38 seconds of play, generating fears that the contest might become as chippy as the December 28 game had been at Madison Square Garden. Fortunately, the 24-year-old Wilson's silly stick foul was an aberration.

A difference in hockey philosophies was displayed: Montréal sent out its penalty-killing unit. In 1975, the Soviets did not believe in employing specialized situational squads. Coach Konstantin Loktev just kept the same five men on the ice who had started the game. Twenty-year-old rookie Doug Jarvis, a skilled faceoff wizard with only 36 games on his NHL résumé, won the draw for the Habs. Montréal proceeded to control the play for a good portion of Central Red Army's power play. When the Soviets did win possession of the puck, they achieved nothing with it. Montréal killed off Wilson's minor penalty with great efficiency, effectively bottling up the Soviet attackers in the neutral zone. The visitors' man advantage failed to produce a single shot on Montréal goaltender Ken Dryden.

Back at full strength, with two and a half minutes gone in the first period, the Canadiens resumed their fast pace—which was expected from the talented team that would win the first of its four successive Stanley Cups in the spring of 1976. Montréal's 23-year-old Steve Shutt fired a high slapshot that sailed past Vladislav Tretiak's left shoulder and into the top corner of the net at 3:16 of the first period. Tretiak may have been slightly screened on the play by teammate Boris Mikhailov, but the puck that blew by him was a blur. Thirty-four years later, Shutt said, "To this day, when Tretiak meets me, he puts his glove hand up, waves it in the air and smiles at me."[19] Even though there were more than 56 minutes left to play, the Montréal bench emptied in great excitement to congratulate Shutt on his goal.

"Sometimes 1–0 leads don't mean much; the Rangers found that out,"[20] Dick Irvin coolly cautioned the millions of *Hockey Night in Canada* viewers tuned in to the broadcast from the Forum. But Montréal did something that New York did not do against the Soviets: They scored the second goal of the game, too. It came slightly more than four minutes after the first one from the stick of Yvon Lambert. He knocked home a rebound past Tretiak with a backhand at 7:25 to make it 2–0 for the hometown Habs. Emotions were running high. The entire home team again came onto the ice to congratulate Lambert on his tally—something rarely seen in NHL contests even once per game. The mighty Canadiens were up by a pair of goals while the visitors had yet to record a single shot on net. In the broadcast booth, John Ferguson said the Soviets "are playing a fired-up hockey club in these Montréal Canadiens. There's no doubt about it."[21] The Montréal Forum was a happy, rollicking place.

At 16:33, Yvan Cournoyer was whistled for a hooking penalty. To Wally Harris' great surprise, Cournoyer lost his composure over the correct call and angrily objected to it—something he seldom ever did in NHL play. Taken aback, Harris reminded the Montréal captain, "Yvan, it's only an exhibition game!" Cournoyer knew it was more than that, of course. "Yeah, but we have to beat these bastards!"[22] insisted the Montréal captain.

Again, the Canadiens killed off the shorthanded situation with ease. Again, Central Red Army did not get a single shot on Montréal goaltender Ken Dryden. The Habs' successful penalty kill included Jacques Lemaire willingly sacrificing himself to get in the way of a slapshot from the blue line launched by Valeri Vasiliev. "If you watch the Montréal Canadiens quite often, you don't see this too much—Jacques Lemaire sprawling to block a shot," noted Dick Irvin. "The Canadiens are very much fired up."[23] The period ended with the home team holding a 2–0 advantage. They were also 15 seconds into a power play thanks to an interference penalty assessed to Central Red Army's Viktor Shluktov at 19:45. The shots on goal after 20 minutes were 11–4 in favor of Montréal, a noteworthy edge.

Despite their two-goal lead, the Habs were not satisfied. They were fully aware that the success of Soviet hockey was largely based upon swift counterattacks and the exploitation of opponents' errors. Tretiak—who had been named the outstanding Soviet hockey player for two straight seasons—was singlehandedly keeping Central Red Army in the game with one dazzling save after another. Canadiens general manager Sam Pollock later speculated, "It could have been 7–0 after the first period."[24]

During the intermission, Central Red Army coach Konstantin Loktev kept things calm and simple in the visitors' dressing room. He urged his players to focus on fundamentals. The events of the first period where his team was clearly outplayed were not even mentioned. Loktev informed his troops that everything is bound to work out fine in the end. Meanwhile, *HNIC* viewers got to see a rare, prerecorded interview with Valeri Kharlamov. With the help of a translator, Kharlamov admitted to expressing his individual skills on the ice while doing his best to follow the instructions of his coaches. It was a very typical comment spoken carefully by a Soviet athlete.

Montréal took to the offensive with their man advantage to begin the second period. Three good chances by the Canadiens were all neatly turned aside by netminder Vladislav Tretiak. *HNIC* cameras caught contrasting images of the two teams' benches. Behind the Central Red Army players, Konstantin Loktev and his two assistant coaches were all frantically jotting down notes whenever there was a lull in the game. On the other side, Scotty Bowman of the Montréal Canadiens, who had no assistant coaches, remained utterly stoic. Author Todd Denault, who wrote an entire book about the 1975 Habs–Red Army game, said Bowman displayed a "glacial calm"[25] throughout the contest.

While Tretiak was constantly busy, his counterpart in the Montréal net, Ken Dryden, would face just 13 Red Army shots all night. He made a critical error on one of them early in the second period, though. On a three-on-two situation, Boris Mikhailov launched a wrist shot that struck the heel of Dryden's glove and deflected into the net at 3:54. It was the first shot the Soviets had mustered in the second period. The home team's lead had been tenuously reduced to 2–1. There was also a psychological aspect to Mikhailov's goal that weighed on the ticketholders. Montréal should have been well ahead on the scoreboard based on the run of play. Instead, Central Red Army was just one shot away from leveling the score. Each Soviet puck possession and attempted shot would henceforth be greeted by a tentative gasp from the sellout crowd.

With Central Red Army now on the scoreboard, the game's pace became more frantic. The on-edge crowd shouted with every Montréal rush. Doug Jarvis, having a terrific game, was hauled down by Vyacheslav Solodukhin at 7:38. Quite properly, a tripping penalty was whistled by referee Harris. Forty-five seconds later, Harris called another penalty, again for tripping, against Red Army's Alexander Gusev who illegally brought down Peter Mahovlich. There were still 75 seconds remaining on the first

Soviet penalty. Thus, Montréal would enjoy a two-man advantage for 1:15. To best exploit it, Scotty Bowman dispatched a five-man unit loaded with four future Hall of Famers: Guy Lafleur, Jacques Lemaire, Yan Cournoyer, and Guy Lapointe along with Peter Mahovlich.

Montréal applied tremendous pressure. It was rewarded when Yvan Cournoyer finally fired a low wrist shot through a crowd in front of the Soviet net at 9:39. Tretiak never saw the shot coming. Cournoyer's goal, which increased Montréal's lead to 3–1, occurred just as the first Red Army penalty, assessed to Vyacheslav Solodukhin, had expired. That meant that Alexander Gusev was also allowed out of the penalty box too. Dick Irvin correctly noted, "The last time Cournoyer scored against Tretiak was Game #8 in Moscow." Quite by chance, an *HNIC* shot of the excited crowd clearly showed a little-known Canadian politician named Brian Mulroney enthusiastically applauding Cournoyer's goal. Mulroney would be the country's prime minister for nearly a decade, from 1984 through 1993.

Prior to Cournoyer's goal, the Red Army bench had been displeased with the second penalty, whistled against Alexander Gusev for tripping Peter Mahovlich. It was a call that seemed wholly justified when the replay was shown on *HNIC*. Nevertheless, the visitors howled at referee Wally Harris. Dick Irvin commented that it was the first time Central Red Army had openly disputed an official's decision in their two games in North America. The Soviets' lobbying—if that is what it was—worked well: Montréal's Serge Savard was sent off for an iffy hooking penalty shortly after play resumed.

Nothing came of the subsequent Central Red Army power play, however. For the third straight time, they failed to get a shot on the Montréal net while enjoying a man advantage. "The Soviets have been unable to get on track with their power play tonight," stated Danny Gallivan. "The tenacity of the checking of the Canadiens has been a thing of beauty."[26]

However, despite the two-goal deficit, the visitors' renowned patience and discipline paid off before the second stanza concluded. Montréal was doing a good job stifling the Soviet attacks, but they faltered late in the second period. A terrific pass from Vladimir Petrov to Valeri Kharlamov gave the talented forward a brief opening. He exploited it well. Kharlamov's backhand along the ice eluded Dryden and found the mark just inside the left goalpost. It was just the seventh shot on goal for Central Red Army. (Remarkably, only two Soviet players had recorded shots on Dryden thus far in the game: Kharlamov had three of them and Mikhailov had the other four.) Kharlamov's goal narrowed their deficit to 3–2 at 16:21. The highly competitive second period ended that way, with the home team holding a slim one-goal edge.

Tretiak completely stole the show in the third period. Despite constant pressure, the Habs could not put another puck by him. He made 16 saves, several of the spectacular variety. By the time the third period had ended, Tretiak would face a total of 38 Montréal shots—a great many of them clear-cut scoring chances. That sum was nearly three times what Ken Dryden would be called upon to handle from Central Red Army's shooters.

Early in the third period, Tretiak's stalwart goalkeeping was rewarded by his teammates. Against the run of play, the two youngest Red Army players combined for a pretty goal. Viktor Shluktov fed Boris Alexandrov with a lovely pass. The latter, who was just 20 years old and only 5'9" tall, finished off a Soviet counter-attack at 4:04 to even matters. Like Red Army's first goal, Alexandrov's shot was partially stopped by Dryden, but it agonizingly trickled into the net behind him and the Forum faithful groaned. "These fellows are just amazing," marveled Dick Irvin. "That was a two-on-one break with Don Awrey trapped on the play. You just don't give them a chance!"[27]

Dryden was clearly rattled—and the crowd sensed it. There was a keen sense of impending doom. It was not lost on Dick Irvin, either. He told the *HNIC* viewing audience, "There are 19,000 people collectively holding their breath every time the Soviets get inside the Canadiens' blue line."[28]

Alexandrov's goal was the final scoring play in a 3–3 tie as Tretiak stifled every subsequent Hab attack. In contrast, Ken Dryden was mockingly cheered over the remaining 16 minutes when he made the most routine of plays. Montréal was also victimized by two glaringly bad calls by Yuri Karandin, the lone Soviet official, who was working as a linesman. After one disputed icing call against the Canadiens, a program was angrily flung onto the ice by a disgruntled Forum patron. Karandin too was ruthlessly jeered by the ticketholders until the final buzzer sounded.

Montréal had several decent opportunities to score a fourth goal, most notably when Steve Shutt had a chance to direct a pass into a gaping net only to have the puck strike a rut in the ice and fly over the blade of his stick. It was a horribly unlucky break for the Canadiens. During the postgame handshake, Shutt could not control his emotions over the heroic opportunity that got away from him. He broke into tears over his misfortune—something seldom seen in typical NHL play.

Remarkably, the Soviets nearly stole the game when Vladimir Popov knocked a puck out of midair that beat Dryden but rattled high off the goalpost. With 87 seconds left in the third period, Dick Irvin said what many fans undoubtedly thought, "This game has lived up to its advance billing right up to the hilt. It's a credit to both teams."[29]

In the final 65 seconds of play, Jacques Lemaire was brilliantly stopped twice by Tretiak from point-blank range. "Thievery of that magnitude gets people sent up the Volga,"[30] wrote Red Fisher in his game report. At the other end of the ice, Boris Mikhailov put a puck between Dryden's arm and his torso, but it skittered wide of the Montréal net.

Not long afterward, the sound of the horn wafted through the Forum, no doubt to the relief of the shaky Dryden. The game was over. Final Score: Central Red Army 3, Montréal Canadiens 3. (Excluding playoff games, ties were not broken in the NHL in 1975 nor in the Soviet Elite League. They were simply ties. Nobody thought of playing overtime or using a godawful shootout to determine a winner.) In a way, the inconclusive result was perfect for everyone involved. Tretiak jumped for joy when the clock hit zero despite his team not winning. In contrast, Dryden looked thoroughly dejected when he met his teammates filing off the home team's bench even though the Canadiens had not lost. More than a few hockey historians have called it "the greatest tie game ever played," for whatever that is worth. Other scholars say the same thing—but choose to omit the word "tie." That statement is much more meaningful.

"I don't think we're being anything but fair to say that the Soviets were completely outplayed tonight," opined Dick Irvin as the teams shook hands, "but we've just seen one of the greatest displays of goaltending you could ever see." Irvin added, "It has been a fine hockey game. There was nothing untoward that happened."[31]

Forty years after the historic match, Montréal's Doug Risebrough recalled, "We outshot them 38 to 13 and that was pretty indicative of the way the game went. Vladislav Tretiak stole the game. He was just great. But the final score didn't matter. Whether we won, lost or tied the game, we knew we had something special."[32]

At the final buzzer, the partisan Forum fans wholeheartedly voiced their approval with a lengthy standing ovation for both exhausted teams. They knew they indeed had witnessed a classic, perhaps something that might not be repeated for a very long time. It had been, as Gare Joyce called it, "a tie for the ages."[33] Larry Robinson would later say, "We only made four mistakes the whole game. They scored on three of them. On the fourth one they hit the inside of the crossbar."[34]

The major difference in the game, of course, was the play of Red Army goaltender Vladislav Tretiak who was given a huge, sustained ovation by the Montréal Forum fans at the end of the game when he was rightfully named its first star. (Several writers noticed that hardly any fans had left the building at the final buzzer. They had all wanted to stick around to applaud Tretiak's outstanding individual performance.) Tretiak had become the most popular of the Soviet players among Canadian hockey fans. This was news to him. He seemed completed startled and on the verge of tears by the outpouring of appreciation and affection he received from the huge Montréal crowd. Jim Coleman would glowingly write with a touch of hyperbole, "Goalie Vladislav Tretiak deserves selection to hockey's Hall of Fame for holding Les Canadiens to fewer than eight goals."[35]

There were contrasting moods after the traditional handshakes, however. Peter Mahovlich, angry that the Canadiens' terrific effort had not been rewarded with a victory, took out his frustrations by bashing his stick on a discarded popcorn box. The 29-year-old Mahovlich was also rightly named one of the game's three stars along with Yvan Cournoyer. The two Canadiens' admiration for the Soviet goaltender's play was obvious. Mahovlich hugged Tretiak and playfully mussed his hair, which the latter found amusing. All three men happily posed for group photos at center ice, varying versions of which were featured on the front pages of many Canadian newspapers on their January 1 edition (if they had one) or January 2 (if they did not). The photos were undeniably symbolic. "In a time of the Cold War, it is a stunning statement of athletic solidarity,"[36] wrote author Todd Denault.

It was later revealed that if the Canadiens had won the game, Roger Doucet would have returned to the ice for a special encore of "O Canada"—certainly something that would have been emotionally stirring. However, it was not to be.

Shortly afterward, during an extraordinary postgame interview on *Hockey Night in Canada*, a sweat-soaked Mahovlich rushed into the studio and promptly apologized to the country for not winning—a remarkable statement that startled co-hosts, Howie Meeker and Dave Reynolds. They both insisted there was no need to apologize for anything about that night's game. It had been a superb display of hockey by any measurement.

"They're not supermen," Meeker said about the Soviets. "They can be beaten." As an aside, Meeker stated, "This is the greatest entertainment in the world today played by the greatest people."[37] That was something that Canadian hockey fans already knew and understood quite well.

However, Canadians were now more accepting of hockey results versus the Soviet Union that were not outright victories. A telling caption that appeared on the front page of the January 2 edition of the *Ottawa Citizen* under a photo of the game began, "Well, at least we didn't lose."

Mahovlich had obviously enjoyed the terrific game despite its inconclusive result. "It reminded me of my kid days," he glowingly said during the postgame *HNIC* interview, "when playing on a pond was nothing but fun and you didn't have to worry about [receiving] a stick across the ear. That's the way hockey should be."[38]

The official *HNIC* viewership of the game (in both French and English) was tallied to be five million. Years later, Ralph Mellanby, who produced the anglophone telecast, still believed that number was incorrect. He figured the count was underreported or badly miscalculated due to all the people watching the game at New Year's Eve parties. Mellanby supposed eight million viewers was a better guesstimate. Canada had a population of 23 million at the end of 1975, so whatever the true number was, a huge chunk of the country was tuned into the high drama at the Forum via CBC television. Mellanby was later informed that the crime rate in Canada that New Year's Eve was about half what it had been the previous December 31. He found that oddball statistic to be very amusing. Mellanby liked to joke that even Canada's criminals had interrupted their lawless misdeeds for a few hours on December 31, 1975, to watch the Montréal Canadiens play hockey against Central Red Army.

The Soviet television broadcast had a celebratory aspect to it. At the conclusion of its postgame show, the host signed off by saying, "Hurray! It's a tie! Happy new year!"[39] He then gleefully dumped a container of confetti over his own head. The rare display of zaniness certainly went against the stereotype of Soviet television announcers being humorless, state-controlled automatons.

In the Montréal dressing room, defenseman Serge Savard figured the Canadiens deserved a win based on how well they had played over the full 60 minutes. "Of one thing I am sure: God was a Russian tonight," he said bitterly to a group of reporters within earshot. "If he is not, how do you explain a tie when we outplayed them so much?"[40]

Savard would later make this thoughtful comment about what had occurred at the Forum: "[The game was] a victory for hockey. I hope this era of intimidation and violence that is hurting our national sport is coming to an end. Young people have seen that a team can play electrifying, fascinating hockey while still behaving like gentlemen."[41]

Montréal coach Scotty Bowman was thoroughly blunt in his postgame assessment. He stated, "We totally outclassed them in every department—except goaltending."[42] Similarly, Alan Eagleson opined, "Montréal won everywhere but on the scoreboard. The Canadiens were, by far, the better team tonight, but they just couldn't put the puck in the net."[43]

Steve Shutt said basically the same thing, noting, "We made three mistakes and they scored on all three."[44] Scribe Robin Herman from the *New York Times* fully backed up Shutt's opinion. "His assessment was accurate. Montréal could not have played a more superb game."[45]

Similarly, veteran *Montréal Star* hockey scribe Red Fisher waited patiently for the crowd of reporters asking Dryden questions to disperse. He then approached Montréal's acclaimed goaltender and said, "Happy new year, Ken…. You screwed up."[46] Dryden agreed that Fisher's comments were undeniably true.

Forty-five years later, Pat Hickey, in writing a retrospective piece for the *Montréal Gazette*, succinctly stated, "Tretiak was outstanding and Dryden wasn't."[47] Accepting the obvious, Ken Dryden added, "I remember everyone playing at the top of their game. Except me. It is my biggest regret in hockey."[48]

Thirty-nine years later, in 2014, Red Fisher once again assessed Dryden's New Year's Eve 1975 performance and had not changed his opinion one iota. He penned,

> If he had played like the Dryden who had [entered] the game with a remarkable 1.79 goals-against average in his first 31 games of the NHL season, he would not have been beaten three times on 13 shots. If he had been vintage Dryden, he would not have allowed the only goal of the third period, during which the Canadiens outshot the Soviets 16–6 in a mismatch that had [Montréal] holding a 2–0 lead fewer than eight minutes into the game....[49]

"We played a great game," Bowman recalled years later. "We played a dominating game, and an exciting game, and in an atmosphere that was just electric. The game gave us an awful lot of confidence. The team was building up an awful lot of confidence. To play a game like that against a team as good as the Russians were, that was pretty dominating."[50]

Steve Shutt, who had emotionally pulled himself together in the privacy of the Habs' dressing room before the media arrived, said the digits showing a tie game on the Forum's massive clock did not really matter. "We had fun out there," he declared. "We beat them. Maybe not on the scoreboard, but we beat them. We outplayed them for 60 minutes."[51]

Robin Herman knew, like everyone else who watched the enthralling game, why the Canadiens had not defeated Central Red Army. She wrote, "Montréal was stymied by the poised goaltending of [Vladislav] Tretiak, who turned away all sorts of shots from the slot without flopping to the ice. Singlehandedly, he stifled a Montréal power play early in the third period, kicking away a flurry of three shots and then smothering a stuffing attempt by Guy Lafleur."[52]

The much-maligned Dryden offered his opinions on what made Tretiak so good in the Central Red Army net. "Tretiak always has his balance," said the Montréal goalie, repeating what he had already said in an earlier interview, "and he always has proper position."[53] Dryden then offered this opinion to Mark Mulvoy of *Sports Illustrated*:

> It's easier [for a goaltender] to play against NHL teams than Soviet or European clubs because we have no deception. A player lifts his stick and shoots the puck. Tretiak sees that and has plenty of time to get ready. Once European and Russian goaltenders get over the initial shock of the force of our shots—and the shock of seeing our players shoot from everywhere on the ice—then their jobs are very simple. Our system is not that challenging to Tretiak.[54]

In Jim Coleman's report on the thrilling game, he doubted that neither of the two NHL opponents left on Central Red Army's schedule, Boston and Philadelphia, would be able to find a way to win if the Canadiens could not manage the feat. Neither the Bruins nor the Flyers, he wrote, played with the free-flowing style of the Habs that gave the Soviets so much trouble on New Year's Eve.

Journalist Jack Dulmage of the *Windsor Star* wrote in his January 2 column, "During the great 1972 Team Canada–Russia series, the Canadian side did not, in any of the eight games, play as well as the Montréal Canadiens did on New Year's Eve. The 3–3 tie notwithstanding, the Canadiens proved they can handle the Russians—artfully, industriously, and thoroughly. Now it remains to be seen if anyone else can."

Dulmage continued,

> The Canadiens lived up to their best notices and would have won easily if Dryden had been as hot as Tretiak. [Not many] of us thought we'd live to see the day when a Russian goalkeeper would [outplay] our best. Dryden could have shut out the Russians without [being named] one the three stars. He didn't face a shot in the first seven minutes. Maybe that was the trouble. No team of Canadian players had ever outplayed the modern Soviets so convincingly.

Dulmage also added a remarkably prescient but dire afterthought near the end of his column. "The Montréal game was wonderful," he declared. "The one at Philadelphia could be an international incident."[55]

Montréal's Doug Risebrough, who was just 21 years old at the time, believes the New Year's Eve match played a pivotal role in the sustained success that his club achieved over the rest of the decade. He said,

> The Red Army game was one of the two best our team ever played. The only one up there with it would be Game Five against the Rangers in the final in '79. When you get down to it, [the latter contest] was the last game of the run that we had in Montréal. Everything that came before was predicated on that Red Army game. If things had turned out differently, if we hadn't performed, everything that came after might have [turned out] differently.[56]

Montréal Canadiens general-manager Sam Pollock marveled at the brilliant display of clean hockey and at the happy, satisfied faces of the patrons leaving the Forum on their way to ring in the new year. "Are the Russians doing anything tomorrow?" he joked with the media. "Maybe we should play another game."[57]

In Central Red Army's dressing room, head coach Konstantin Loktev accepted the 3–3 draw philosophically and realistically. "A tie is a tie. It is better to have one dollar in your pocket than to have nothing at all," he explained with a strangely capitalistic analogy. Loktev, praiseful of the home team's performance, continued,

I'm very happy with the tie. Our team could have played better against the Canadiens. This was certainly not our best game, but Montréal was very strong defensively, holding us to only 13 shots and allowing us seven in the first two periods. Most of our problems came as a result of Montréal's style of play. Their checking was very effective, they played their positions well, and they worked very hard. Montréal played a very fine hockey game.[58]

Loktev would later tell journalist Glenn Cole almost the same thing: "To a great extent, [our club's] many mistakes were due to the very good game played by the Canadiens. The Canadiens play their positions very well. They stick to their positions."[59]

Steve Shutt, while being interviewed by Scott Abbott of the *Winnipeg Free Press*, noted that the Soviets had a glaring weak spot—at least in his opinion. "They're terrible defensively," Shutt insisted. "Tretiak made a lot of saves, but he made a lot of lucky ones too."[60]

Robin Herman of the *New York Times* also thought the indecisive result was a perfect ending—for political reasons. She wrote, "Whatever deity watched the splendid New Year's Eve contest between the Canadiens and the Soviet Army team was also a diplomat, for the representatives of the world's two hockey powers played to a 3–3 draw tonight."[61]

Refreshingly, there were few complaints from either side about the officiating of Wally Harris. Under tremendous scrutiny and pressure, he had refereed a fine game. It was a major highlight of his distinguished, 17-season career in the NHL. Harris would later serve as the league's supervisor of officials for another 16 years.

Was the Habs–Red Army contest the best hockey game ever played anywhere at any time? That is a totally subjective question, of course, so it can never be answered with absolute certainty, but December 31, 1975, gets plenty of votes from those who witnessed it and were around hockey for decades. Danny Gallivan, the longtime English-language voice of the Montréal Canadiens remembered it fondly. He said, "The New Year's Eve game is etched in my memory forever."[62]

In recalling the famous tie game in his 1987 autobiography, Vladislav Tretiak fondly wrote, "As far as I'm concerned, this is what the game of hockey is all about; fast, full of combinations, rough (but not rude), with an exciting plot. I would love to play it all over again."[63]

The game had been such a monumental contest, packed with thrills, that it merited a front-page editorial in the *Montréal Star*. It declared, "For Canadians from coast to coast, 1975 went out like a lion as they were treated to the finest hockey spectacle in memory by the Canadiens and the Soviet Union's Red Army team."[64]

Proving there is truth in the adage that one can never please all the people all the time, there was not universal happiness about the thoroughly compelling hockey game. At least two people found reasons to be negative in its tremendous wake. Bill Hunter, the outspoken owner of the Edmonton Oilers of the World Hockey Association, stated that the NHL had led itself into disaster because the excellent play of the Soviets had exposed the fact that fans in North America were getting substandard entertainment, or, as he put it, "customers ... have been paying elite prices for second-rate games."[65]

The second wet blanket was the only disappointed face outside the Forum. It belonged to a prominent, longtime ticket scalper who realized the quality of the Montréal–Central Red Army game would rarely be repeated. "After what I saw tonight," the man said sadly, "people won't want to buy tickets to watch the California Golden Seals."[66]

Speaking of the California Golden Seals—a lackluster, unloved bunch who were perennial doormats in the NHL—they were supposed to play in Toronto at Maple Leaf Gardens at precisely the same time the Habs–Central Red Army game was being contested in Montréal on the evening of Wednesday, December 31. Although Leaf home games had routinely been sellouts for 30 years—and this one was too—Toronto management was worried. They quite reasonably feared that, under the circumstances, thousands of ticketholders would choose to stay home and watch the important action from the Montréal Forum on television instead of attending the Seals–Maple Leafs game in person. A half-filled arena would be an embarrassment to the club. Therefore, the poohbahs did what they considered to be a very sensible thing: With the NHL's permission, the California-Toronto game was postponed 18 hours until the

NHL referee Wally Harris had an excellent game on December 31, 1975, in the tension-packed Montréal Forum (Toronto Star Photograph Archive, Courtesy of Toronto Public Library).

following afternoon on New Year's Day. The Leafs won it easily, 5–1, before the usual enthusiastic full house at Maple Leaf Gardens. A headline in the sports section of the January 1 *Boston Globe* declared, "In Toronto, fans don't miss a thing."

Scoring Summary

Red Army 0+2+1 = 3
Montréal 2+1+0 = 3

First period

1. Montréal: Shutt (Mahovlich) 3:16
2. Montréal: Lambert (Risebrough, Savard) 7:25

Second period

1. Red Army: Mikhailov (Vasiliev) 3:54
2. Montréal: Cournoyer (Lafleur, Lemaire) 9:39 (pp)
3. Red Army: Kharlamov (Petrov, Mikhailov) 16:21

Third period
4. Red Army: Alexandrov (Shluktov, Tsygankov) 4:04

10

Game #4

Soviet Wings vs. Buffalo Sabres

SUNDAY, JANUARY 4, 1976
BUFFALO MEMORIAL AUDITORIUM

On Thursday, January 1, the Buffalo Sabres hosted the Los Angeles Kings at Memorial Auditorium. The Sabres looked dreadful, losing 9–6, in a game where both teams' defenses went completely out the window. Observing the contest from the stands was a group of VIP guests: the Soviet Wings. They would play the Sabres three days later in a memorable Sunday afternoon clash. Based on what they saw the Sabres do (or not do) against the Kings, the touring team did not think much of their upcoming opponents.

"When our guys watched the Sabres play that night," admitted Wings coach Boris Kulagin on January 4, "our players thought it was an easy team to beat. They were mistaken."[1]

It turned out they were more than just mistaken—they were badly mistaken. The Sabres rolled past the Soviet Wings, 12–6, in a wild game that would have been one of the highest-scoring in NHL history had it been a league game and counted in its statistics. Finally, after four games of Super Series '76, an NHL team recorded a victory over a Soviet opponent. Furthermore, it was a spectacular one.

There was an international incident before the game started. It was a snub toward Canada. At Buffalo home games, Canadian hockey fans typically comprise a huge chunk of the attendance. The Sabres recognize and value this obvious fact by playing the Canadian national anthem as well as the "Star-Spangled Banner" before their home games regardless of which NHL teams are playing. It has been the case since the team began play in the NHL in the 1970–71 season. However, in accordance with the IIHF's international hockey protocols, only the anthems of the participating teams could be played. During the opening ceremonies, the fans were

10. Game #4

apprised by the public-address announcer that "O Canada" would not be played that afternoon. They were a displeased bunch and loudly booed the omission. Typical of the demographics of the NHL in 1976, Buffalo had just one American on its roster, defenseman Lee Fogolin, who was born in Chicago. All the other Sabres were Canadians.

There were obviously many knowledgeable Canadian hockey fans in attendance at the Aud, as usual. When the Wings of the Soviet were introduced individually, the familiar names from the 1972 Canada–Soviet series—particularly Alexander Yakushev—received extended applause.

Emotions were running noticeably high in the Sabres' antiquated and undersized arena. Even without the anthem controversy, the air was thick with anticipation and passion. "The tension is really building here at the Aud as the teams get ready for the first period,"[2] noted play-by-play man Bill Hewitt. A significant snowstorm in the Buffalo area—hardly a rarity in western New York in January—did not keep anyone away from the sold-out arena. Hockey fans were keenly interested in seeing how the high-flying Buffalo Sabres would fare against the Soviet visitors. Beyond the Memorial Auditorium would be an estimated worldwide TV audience of 200 million people. The bulk of the viewership would be in the Soviet Union and Canada, but the game was also being televised in West Germany and Japan.

Buffalo was playing without their captain, Jim Schoenfeld. He was ill. There was a fear that he had contracted mononucleosis, but tests for that disease came back negative. It was a less serious infection. Buffalo general-manager George (Punch) Imlach, who was making a onetime appearance as a color commentator for *Hockey Night in Canada*, said the Sabres would be without Schoenfeld's services for about ten days.

Perhaps two of Buffalo's best players had something extra to prove against the Soviets that Sunday afternoon. Both Gilbert Perreault and Rick Martin had been two of the disgruntled players who opted to leave Team Canada partway through the 1972 Summit Series because they were not getting enough ice time. When the Series was over, they caught hell for their decision from many unsympathetic Canadian hockey fans for not toughing it out.

Prior to the opening faceoff, the organist at Buffalo Memorial Auditorium entertained the capacity crowd with some Russian-themed music: "Somewhere, My Love" from *Doctor Zhivago*. There was not much love to be had, however, once the puck was dropped by NHL referee Ron Wicks.

Thirty-six seconds into the game there were offsetting penalties to each team for stick fouls, but more critical to Buffalo was the loss of Don Luce. He injured his leg after taking a solid and legal body check from Yuri Liapkin. Luce hobbled off the ice with the assistance of a trainer. He would miss the remainder of the first period, but Luce would be back on the ice for the faceoff to start the second stanza.

Jim Coleman wrote in the next day's edition of the *Ottawa Citizen*,

> Personally, if I had been prepared to bet even a plugged nickel on Buffalo, my gambling instincts were throttled in the first 36 seconds of the game when center Don Luce suffered a cracked knee after he was tripped by Yuri Liapkin. As I watched trainer Frankie Christie escort Luce to the infirmary, I opened my briefcase and took out a crying towel.
>
> Then, miraculously, the Sabres took complete charge of the proceedings....

Indeed, Buffalo dominated the action immediately and missed on a few quality scoring opportunities. However, the home team did open the scoring—and the floodgates—with a slapshot goal by Jocelyn Guevremont that got by Wings goalie Alexander Sidelnikov who appeared to be screened on the play. Punch Imlach noted that the goal, scored at 6:10, must have been especially sweet for the 24-year-old Guevremont because he had been part of Team Canada 1972 but he did not play in any of the eight games in that famous series. Guevremont had been chosen third overall in the NHL's 1971 amateur draft by Vancouver.

Not long afterward, Gilbert Perreault accepted a pass from Jerry Korab and advanced toward the net on the left wing. Sidelnikov moved out of his goal crease to challenge him. The Buffalo superstar fired a slapshot through the small opening between the Soviet goalie's pads. Exactly one minute after their first goal, the Sabres had jumped out to a 2–0 lead over the Soviet Wings. "This arena has erupted,"[3] declared *HNIC*'s Brain McFarlane above the deafening clamor. There was a clear sense that this game would be different than the first three clashed between the touring Soviet clubs and the NHL.

Slightly more than four minutes later, Buffalo's lead rose to 3–0 when Richard Martin took advantage of some sloppy Soviet defensive play and slid the puck along the ice and into an open net. Goalie Sidelnikov was way out of position as the puck crossed the goal line.

Goals came quickly thereafter. The Soviet Wings got onto the scoreboard at 13:45 with a power play goal while Buffalo's Jerry Korab was sitting out a charging penalty. The Sabres had done a good job killing it until Vladimir Repniev beat Gerry Desjardins, the Buffalo netminder, not long after the Wings had fired a puck off the goalpost. The score did not remain 3–1 for very long. Rick Martin got an unassisted goal for the home team on a scrambly play at 14:23. Martin picked the top corner of the goal above Sidelnikov's left shoulder to restore the Buffalo lead to three goals. However, the Wings got that one back in the final minute of the first period. At 19:16, Sergei Kapustin nicely finished off a two-on-one attack. Desjardins was helpless on the play and was beaten by a well-placed wrist shot. The two teams went to their dressing rooms with Buffalo ahead, 4–2. A defensive battle it was not.

Buffalo got their fifth goal on a power play at 4:32 of the second period while Sergei Kapustin was sitting out a hooking penalty. Danny Gare fired a low wrist shot at Sidelnikov. The crouching goalie knocked the puck down with his glove, but the rebound was swiftly knocked home by the opportunistic Jim Lorentz, a 28-year-old who played 68 games for the Boston Bruins in their Stanley Cup season of 1969–70. Lorentz had seen precious little ice time in the game before notching his goal. The scoring play prompted Wings coach Boris Kulagin to make a goaltending switch. Alexander Sidelnikov was replaced by another Alexander. His surname was Kulikov.

Kulikov did not start well. Exactly one minute into his stint, the first shot Kulikov faced was from René Robert from close in. It beat him through the legs at the 5:32 mark—and Buffalo was flying with an impressive 6–2 lead early in the second period. Thus far in the one-sided game, Buffalo had badly outshot the Soviet Wings by a 21–10 margin.

Buffalo's Gerry Desjardins allowed six goals to the Soviet Wings, but the Sabres' offense bailed him out by scoring twice as many (Toronto Star Photograph Archive, Courtesy of Toronto Public Library).

Seemingly unfazed by the four-goal deficit, the Wings responded immediately with a goal of their own. Vladimir Repniev got his second tally of the game, accepting an accurate, long pass from Sergei Kapustin, and beating Gerry Desjardins with a rising slapshot. The score was now 6–3 in favor of the Sabres. The Wings were showing they were still a dangerous foe despite trailing on the scoreboard.

Buffalo regained its four-goal advantage by capitalizing on a power play. Defenseman Jerry Korab scored on a shot from the point. The new Wings goaltender, Kulikov, did not look especially sharp on the play. Korab's goal came at 8:26. Fourteen seconds later, the Sabres made the worst blunder of Super Series '76 when they embarrassingly put the puck into their own net. Buffalo goalie Gerry Desjardins mishandled the puck to the side of his net. When it trickled in front of the goal, Jocelyn Guevremont panicked and tried to knock the puck aside. Instead, he put it directly in the open net to make the score 7–4. The Wings' Viktor Shalimov properly got credit for the goal as he was the last member of his team to touch the puck. Brian McFarlane summed up the debacle in two words: "A gift."[4]

Remarkably, Alexander Sidelnikov unexpectedly returned to the Wings net with 8:56 left in the second period. It was an odd strategic maneuver, to say the least. Sidelnikov looked bad when Danny Gare scored on a low wrist shot at 11:44 from a tough angle. Buffalo was back in front by four goals with an 8–4 lead. In the *HNIC* booth, Brian McFarlane stated the obvious when he said the Montréal Canadiens would have fared better on New Year's Eve if they had faced either one of the two Wings goaltenders rather than Vladislav Tretiak.

At 13:17, Peter McNab upped the score to 9–4 by finishing off a nifty three-way passing play for the home team. One assist went to Brian Spencer. Another went to Rick Martin who was "having a whale of a game"[5] according to Brian McFarlane. The final 6:43 of the middle period featured no goals—a rare offensive dry spell in this wide-open game. The Sabres efficiently killed off a minor penalty assessed to Jerry Korab and went to the dressing room holding a five-goal advantage. After 40 minutes, Buffalo had soundly outshot the Soviet Wings, 34–16.

During the second intermission when he showed clips of the porous Soviet defense, analyst Howie Meeker was asked by *HNIC* host Dave Hodge if Buffalo should be satisfied with their nine goals and rein in their attack in the third period. "Golly, no," Meeker promptly replied. "That's the worst thing they could do. I think the fans across the country want to see 10, 11, or 12 [goals]. As long as they keep firing, they're going to get it."[6]

However, it was the Soviet Wings who scored first in the third period. Sent in all alone on a fine pass from teammate Sergei Kotov, Sergei Kapustin split the Buffalo defense and beat Gerry Desjardins with a wrist shot at

10. Game #4

3:28. In the *HNIC* broadcast booth, Punch Imlach was displeased with his team's defensive blunder in allowing a breakaway while holding a five-goal lead. The scoring play drew a round of sincere applause from the spectators who recognized the skill level it took to execute it.

Buffalo got that goal back six and a half minutes later when a Rick Martin slapshot from the slot literally ripped the catching glove off goaltender Sidelnikov. The puck retained enough momentum to dribble toward the goal line where it was tapped over the line by Fred Stanfield for the easiest of goals. (At first Martin was credited with the goal, but the television replay showed that Stanfield had knocked the puck the final few inches over the goal line. A correction was quickly made.) Buffalo had hit double digits and now held a 10–5 lead.

Again, the Soviet Wings responded. Their sixth goal came at 11:32 when Gerry Desjardins, who was not having a particularly stellar game in the Buffalo net, had trouble handling a high shot from Vladimir Krikunov. The rebound dropped in front of him where it was alertly smacked home by 24-year-old forward Yuri Lebedev. The Soviet Wings had lessened their deficit to 10–6. They would get no closer, however. One Montréal sportswriter, after the game, noted that the Wings' six goals would have been enough to win 95 percent of NHL games.

Danny Gare scored his second goal of the game, and Buffalo's eleventh, at 14:04. This one was a backhand deflection from a Fred Stanfield pass. It came on a total defensive collapse by the Wings as first Stanfield stood unguarded near Sidelnikov, then Gare was similarly left all by himself to the right of the Soviet goalie. The Buffalo fans were thoroughly enjoying themselves and their club's offensive explosion. They wanted more, though, and began rhythmically chanting, "We want twelve!"

Buffalo obliged at 18:02. On the power play, with Yuri Turin sitting out an elbowing penalty, Brian Spencer, who had played an effective game for the Sabres, was justly rewarded for his fine efforts with a goal. It was a give-and-go play orchestrated with Peter McNab. Spencer redirected the puck into the net past Sidelnikov who was no doubt tired and discouraged at this point of the game. It was the tenth goal he had allowed; his partner Alexander Kulikov had allowed two during his brief relief appearance in the second period. There was no further scoring; the game ended 12–6 for the home side with ten different Buffalo players scoring goals. They had come at such a swift pace that a few Sabres, during postgame interviews, were not quite certain what the final tally was.

The well-spoken Peter McNab had notched a goal and two assists in the rout. The 23-year-old was all smiles when he was interviewed outside the Sabres' dressing room by Dave Reynolds of *Hockey Night in Canada*. He said, "Today was for the National Hockey League, and it was for all of

Canada and the United States, to show the people we have the best league in the world. We proved we are the best."

McNab said he and his teammates learned a lot by studying the films from the Soviet Wings–Pittsburgh game from December 29. McNab said that the Sabres' aggressive checking disrupted the Wings' attack. It caused the visitors to depart from their usual offensive strategy and just dump the puck into the Buffalo zone and chase it, rather than try to carry or pass it in. "Against Pittsburgh," McNab claimed, "they only threw the puck in four times. Today they must have done it at least ten times in the third period alone."[7]

Later, when being interviewed by Robin Herman of the *New York Times*, McNab would characterize the Wings as robotic whose personalities were nearly impossible to gauge. "They showed no emotion at all," he noted, "They never smiled, even when they scored."[8] This was McNab's third and final season with the Sabres. He would be traded to Boston after the 1975–76 season for André Savard where he would blossom into a superb scorer for the Bruins. At the time of McNab's death, at age 70 in November 2022, he was in eleventh spot among Boston players in all-time regular-season goals with 263.

Peter White of the Toronto *Globe & Mail*, saw the Sabres victory as a much-needed boost for the entire NHL. He wrote, "The pendulum that hangs over hockey supremacy has begun to move, but who could have expected it to swing as wildly as it did here yesterday afternoon? Buffalo forced some humility on the touring Russians with a 12–6 victory of the Wings of the Soviet."[9]

Through an interpreter, Boris Kulagin aired some complaints about both the refereeing of Ron Wicks and the unusual dimensions at the Buffalo Memorial Auditorium. (The ice surface in Buffalo was 196 feet long, four feet shorter than a typical NHL rink. It was the NHL standard 85 feet wide—but that is 15 feet narrower than a standard IIHF rink.) "In this game I didn't understand many of the penalties called on my players,"[10] Kulagin said. He further opined that the refereeing in Montréal on New Year's Eve had been excellent—certainly a backhanded jab at Ron Wicks' work on January 4 in which the Soviet Wings had gotten eight out of the 15 total penalties, four of which came in the third period. Kulagin also added, "We are not accustomed to playing on such a small rink. For our players, the rink was somewhat unusual."[11]

When asked about his team's strategy and why it failed so miserably versus Buffalo, the amiable Kulagin managed a smile. The Soviet coach, who had just turned 51 years old on December 31, told reporters, "I am never asked such questions when our team wins. We do appreciate some of the techniques and tricks the professionals use, but we play a purely European style."[12]

10. Game #4

Kulagin did generously heap praise on Buffalo's three most noteworthy star players: the dominant French Connection line of Rick Martin, Gilbert Perreault and René Robert. "In my opinion," the Wings coach gushed, "they are the best players I have ever seen in my life in professional hockey."[13]

Hal Walker of the *Calgary Herald* wrote that the Buffalo triumph was largely due to Soviet netminding that was "deplorably bad" along with heavy checking from the Sabres which, to use an American football term, he claimed made the visitors "hear footsteps."[14]

Buffalo coach Floyd Smith thought that immediately neutralizing Alexander Yakushev had been a key to Buffalo's easy victory. Twice in the early part of the game Jerry (King Kong) Korab leveled the Wings' big winger with clean bodychecks. Smith noted, "After that, you didn't see him [Yakushev] doing much."[15] Korab was named the game's second star. Yakushev concurred that Korab was an outstanding Sabre in an afternoon when there were many outstanding Sabres. "Korab kharasho," Yakushev told a reporter. A translator told reporters it meant "Korab is good."[16]

Robin Herman, covering the Sunday afternoon game for the *New York Times*, concurred. She wrote, "[Jerry] Korab was chiefly responsible for shutting out the best Soviet line of Yakushev, Shadrin and Shulimov—additions from the Moscow Spartak club. Every time Yakushev went weaving down the left side or tried to traverse Buffalo's zone for one of his shovel shots, Korab bounced the 6'3" Russian against the boards."

Korab told Herman it was his deliberate strategy to focus on Yakushev. "I thought about it before," the Buffalo defenseman noted. "He was about the only guy [on the Soviet Wings] I knew of, and I figured if I could stop a guy like him, I can slow down the whole team."[17]

In 2018, 71-year-old Alexander Yakushev, still a tall and imposing figure, was interviewed by a reporter from the *Buffalo News*. Proving he had a good sense of humor, Yakushev amusingly feigned horror when the scribe, Mike Harrington, identified that he was employed by a Buffalo newspaper. "I remember that game very well," the retired Soviet star stated. "We were smashed by your team. They were really tough. They played really well. It was very surprising the game went that way. There were four [exhibition] games that year [for the Wings] and the only game we lost was in Buffalo."[18]

Floyd Smith continued with his dissection of Soviet hockey. He said, "They have one style: Play, play, play around for the break. We set the style for the other clubs. I think the Islanders, Bruins and Chicago will know what to do now."[19]

Mark Mulvoy of *Sports Illustrated* focused on the contrast in styles between the NHL teams and the visitors. He wrote of the two touring Soviet clubs,

... Both Soviet teams generally played textbook hockey. They baffled most of their NHL rivals with perfect execution of the game's most subtle tactics. They passed the puck accurately, artfully and often—maybe too often. They trapped adventurous forecheckers and neatly removed them from the action. They patiently advanced on the power play until their extra man suddenly had the puck at point-blank range. They took some theatrical falls to invite the officials' attention to the naughtier NHL men.[20]

Soviet Wings defenseman Yuri Liapkin did not have a particularly impressive game, although he was often referred to in his own country as "the Bobby Orr of Soviet hockey." Brian McFarlane thought the comparison was laughable. "I'll take Bobby Orr seven days a week and twice on Sundays,"[21] the *HNIC* analyst bluntly said when the camera focused on Liapkin during a lull in the action in the second period. His two broadcast partners, Bill Hewitt and Punch Imlach, speedily concurred.

The odd Soviet maneuver of returning their starting goaltender back into the game after he had been yanked was causing considerable discussion among hockey scribes. Few North American journalists reporting on Super Series '76 could ever recall seeing that happen at any level of hockey in their lifetimes. Robin Herman, covering the game for the *New York Times* had an explanation, however. She wrote, "Early in the second period with Buffalo ahead, 5–2, Boris Kulagin, the Wings' storied coach, removed Alexander Sidelnikov as goaltender 'to give him a chance to relax and think it over.' In the next seven minutes, the Sabres scored twice on the backup netminder and Sidelnikov was returned."[22]

Rick Martin, who was rightly named the game's first star, reflected on the four series games thus far played as a whole. He told reporters he thought Montréal should have beaten Central Red Army on New Year's Eve, but, "by the same token, I'm glad we were the first NHL team to beat [one of the touring Soviet teams]. We've proven that we can beat them. Let's hope they give us credit for showing that they can be beaten."[23]

The Sabres, of course, were celebrated across the NHL and by North American hockey fans for their overwhelming victory. They had only been in the NHL since 1970–71. Now in their sixth season, the club had quietly become a formidable force in the league. The Sabres were Stanley Cup finalists in 1975 and, in hindsight, probably should have played the stronger Central Red Army club instead of the lesser Soviet Wings in Super Series '76. Remarkably, the 12 goals were not the highest scoring output for Buffalo in the 1975–76 season. They had accrued 14 goals against the lowly Washington Capitals in a merciless 14–2 rout at Memorial Auditorium on December 21. It was the third-highest goal total ever recorded by an NHL team in a single game—and the highest total accrued since the

Second World War. The Sabres scored eight third-period goals in that shellacking. Over the course of the game, Buffalo recorded 50 shots on net.

Floyd Smith, who had played on the Buffalo defense as a player-coach for the Sabres as late as 1972, conceded that the Wings' netminding was blatantly poor over the course of the game. Smith stated the obvious, "No, the Soviets did not have good goaltending." Smith was quick to add, "But they did have super goaltending in Montréal."[24]

Later during Super Series '76, a member of the Soviet delegation, Vyacheslav Koloskov, surprisingly asserted that Alexander Sidelnikov was thought by some hockey executives in the Soviet Union to be superior in skill to Vladislav Tretiak! In broken English, Koloskov told Robin Herman of the *New York Times*, "Sidelnikov number one in Moscow. In America, no good. Nervous."[25]

Smith preferred to focus on the achievements of his own team rather than the porous defensive play of the Wings. He said, "This was the first time we played up to our potential in a long time. It was a great, all-round team effort. We've been working hard for the last ten days. I think we've finally broken out of our slump."[26]

Smith also said the game played at the Forum on New Year's Eve had been a helpful teaching aide for him. "We knew from watching the Montréal[–Red Army] game that we had to check them down the center. We did it for most of the game and we made fewer mistakes than we have in a long time."[27]

Two esteemed spectators were shown on the *HNIC* telecast at least three times over the course of the game. They were Harold Ballard, the controversial 72-year-old owner of the Toronto Maple Leafs; and his jovial 73-year-old sidekick, King Clancy. The latter was a former star player, Leafs coach, and NHL referee who now held a largely ceremonial upper management position with the Toronto club. This was the second fan road trip by Ballard and Clancy, having attended the New Year's Eve contest in Montréal. There was no Super Series '76 game featuring the Maple Leafs because Ballard would have none of it. A strident anti-communist, Ballard liked to denounce any and all Soviets as "a bunch of bastards." (Be that as it may, one Leaf fan in attendance held up a small, crudely made cardboard sign to a cameraman that said, "The Leafs need Yakushev.") Accordingly, Ballard had no intention of paying the Soviet hockey authorities their going rate of $25,000 to play a game at Maple Leaf Gardens. Yet, the two septuagenarians were prominently seated within the Buffalo Memorial Auditorium beside Punch Imlach's wife, Dorothy, who answered to the nickname "Dodo." Both Clancy and Ballard sported oversized Buffalo Sabres buttons on their suit jackets to show their support for one of their usual NHL rivals. In the *HNIC* broadcast booth, Punch Imlach chuckled when he quickly confirmed that Ballard and Clancy had bought their own tickets—and the buttons—just like all the other typical fans at the Aud had that Sunday afternoon.

Forty-four years later Jim Lorentz remembered the Sabres' mindset before the game. "When we played the Soviets, it was like the seventh game of the Stanley Cup [finals]," he recalled in a 2020 interview for the Sabres' website. "That's the way we approached it. There was a genuine hatred for the Russian team, I think. We wanted to win. We wanted to win big. And we did."[28]

In 2004, *Hockey Night in Canada*'s Dick Irvin recalled a truly remarkable incident involving the Sabres when they showed up at the Montréal Forum to play the Canadiens the very next night, Monday, January 5, in a regular-season tilt. It illustrated how seriously hockey fans in Canada had embraced Super Series '76 and what every victory meant to them and their sport. "The Buffalo players came onto the ice for their pregame warm-up and were greeted with some applause," Irvin remembered. "It did not stop. It kept steadily building and building. It kept growing until the Buffalo Sabres were receiving a standing ovation at the Montréal Forum."[29] Perhaps inspired by the unexpected outpouring of love by rival fans, Buffalo upset the formidable Canadiens that night, 4–2.

Unfortunately for the Soviet Wings, timing is everything. Their being on the wrong end of a horrible 12–6 score to the Buffalo Sabres was how they would be entirely remembered by hockey fans in Canada. None of their three wins they achieved in Super Series '76 was televised by *Hockey Night in Canada*.

Even though the Soviet Wings were hammered, and were left like "inanimate pieces of beluga caviar"[30] according to journalist Jim Coleman, the Wings coach made a pragmatic statement to journalists. He said, "I want to add that this series of games are not over," said Kulagin of the Wings' schedule. "Our score is one to one."[31]

Scoring Summary

Soviet Wings 2+2+2 = 6
Buffalo 4+5+3 = 12

First period

1. Buffalo: Guevremont (Spencer, Hajt) 6:10
2. Buffalo: Perreault (Korab) 7:10
3. Buffalo: Martin (Stanfield) 11:32
4. Soviet Wings: Repnyev (Shalimov, Yakushev) 13:45
5. Buffalo: Martin (unassisted) 14:23
6. Soviet Wings: Kapustin (Kotov) 19:16

Second period

1. Buffalo: Lorentz (Gare, Guevremont) 4:32
2. Buffalo: Robert (McNab) 5:32
3. Soviet Wings: Repnyev (Kapustin, Kuznetsov) 5:59
4. Buffalo: Korab (Martin, Perreault) 8:26
5. Soviet Wings: Shalimov (unassisted) 8:40
6. Buffalo: Gare (Stanfield, Korab) 11:44
7. Buffalo: McNab (Martin, Spencer) 13:17

Third period

1. Soviet Wings: Kapustin (Kotov, Kuznetsov) 3:28
2. Buffalo: Stanfield (Martin, Perreault) 9:41
3. Soviet Wings: Yuri Lebedev (Krikunov, Budonov) 11:32
4. Buffalo: Gare (Stanfield, Ramsay) 14:04
5. Buffalo: Spencer (McNab, Robert) 18:02

11

Game #5

Soviet Wings vs. Chicago Black Hawks

Wednesday, January 7, 1976
Chicago Stadium

"When that Russian referee gets home, they'll probably give him a medal,"[1] said an exasperated Billy Reay. The longtime coach of the Chicago Black Hawks was more than a little bit upset after his team lost to the visiting Soviet Wings by a pair of goals on Wednesday, January 7, 1976, before a packed house at venerable Chicago Stadium.

Reay had a handy conspiracy theory ready to explain his club's loss to the Wings of the Soviet. He figured the questionable officiating was some sort of payback for the Buffalo Sabres throttling the Wings 12–6 three days earlier in front of a large television audience. "Take a look at the penalties," Reay insisted. "It looks as though they had a meeting after the Sunday game [in Buffalo] and decided to make this one all Russian."[2]

"We got it in the nose from a Soviet hose," Dennis Hull rhymingly told reporters after the game. "Hey, we tied them 1–1 in even-strength goals."[3]

"The score was 4–2," wrote Bob Verdi is his game report for the *Chicago Tribune*, "the opponents were the Soviet Wings, and the cause for it all rests in the eyes of the beholder. Wednesday night's most important pair belonged to referee Yuri Karandin."[4]

Defenseman Dick Redmond was thoroughly miffed after the game, too, about the quality of officiating he and his teammates had endured at the hands of the Soviet official with the red arm bands. "To say we got hosed it to be nice about it," Redmond insisted. "They gave us the lumber all night, hooking and kicking us, high-sticking us. Nothing was called. It was brutal out there."[5]

Pit Martin tried to be philosophical about the subpar officiating. "I didn't think we played that badly," the veteran Hawk told Rob Verdi of the *Chicago Tribune*. When you get the kind of refereeing that we saw tonight, after a while you just say to yourself, "'What the hell's the use?' It's a shame the game had to turn into that, but it did."[6]

Not surprisingly, Wings coach Boris Kulagin had a distinctly different view about Karandin's handling of the game. "If you play rough against a Russian team," he noted, "you will not win. Because there was not a single bad injury or bad fight, I think the officiating was quite good."[7]

Verdi could at least say, "I told you so." The day of the game, in previewing the Wings–Black Hawks clash for the *Tribune*, Verdi had penned, "The nuances of Soviet referee Yuri Karandin's whistle may or may not affect Wednesday's match."[8]

Dennis Hull was one of four Chicago Blackhawks on their 1975–76 roster who had also been on Team Canada 1972 (Toronto Star Photograph Archive, Courtesy of Toronto Public Library).

In preparing his preview piece, Verdi discovered that the Hawks and their coach seemed to be awestruck by the visitors' reputation, preoccupied by what the Soviet Wings might do to one of the NHL's touchstone franchises. "We have to think defensively," Dennis Hull firmly stated. "We can't expect to score 12 goals like Buffalo did."[9]

Veteran center Pit Martin stated he was quite eager to play the Soviets—as were all his Chicago teammates. "This is just an exhibition," he noted. "Other than a chunk of the proceeds going to the pension fund, we don't get paid for it, but there's no question we'll be excited." Then the 32-year-old warned, "Our biggest problem could be getting too excited. We have to relax and keep our heads. They're too good."[10]

Chicago coach Billy Reay fully realized the Soviets possessed excellent skills—especially the basics. He said the day before the game, "The thing they do best is the thing we've let slip in our hockey—skating. They have come a long way since I saw them in Prague in 1959. Until Sunday, I didn't think it was possible to skate with them. But after seeing them lose to Buffalo, I believe we can win."[11]

Verdi himself piled on the plaudits for the visitors in advance of the game. He noted, "They're the most professional-looking amateurs you've ever seen." The Chicago scribe continued, "They possess the grace of Nureyev, they pack more thrills than The Brothers Karamazov, and they are as determined as Nikita Khrushchev when he served up filet of sole at the United Nations' round table during a bygone tirade. They are the Wings of the Soviet."[12]

The most maddening part of the string of penalties handed to the home team was that Chicago was typically a pacifistic bunch, sitting dead last in the 18-team NHL in penalty minutes at the time of their tilt with the Soviet Wings. Verdi noted in his game summary, "The Black Hawks sometimes play as though they crave the Nobel Peace Prize. Normally a cool, calm, and collected lot, [they] were none of the above on Wednesday. At evening's end, [the sellout crowd] was seeing red."[13]

In all, the Black Hawks were assessed 12 minor penalties by referee Yuri Karandin. The majority were retaliatory in nature. In contrast, the Soviet Wings had just six of their men sent to the sin bin. The Hawks clearly were trying to get even with the Wings for various infractions the visitors committed that had been overlooked by the Soviet official. Dennis Passa, covering the game for Canadian Press, seemed to agree there was some selective enforcement of the rules by Karandin. He noted,

> Dick Redmond, who along with Dennis Hull scored the Chicago goals, was called for elbowing and cross-checking. Dale Tallon went off for slashing. Grant Mulvey had elbowing and cross-checking penalties. Even Stan Mikita, the usually mild-mannered captain of the Hawks, was driven to near fisticuffs on a number of occasions.[14]

At times, the overflow crowd of 18,500 fans became so upset with the quality of Karandin's officiating that he was pelted with empty beer cups thrown by the angry Chicago partisans. That attendance figure was almost certainly low. Rob Verdi figured 20,000 attendees was a better guess. This mathematical chicanery was nothing out of the ordinary at Chicago Stadium. For as long as anyone could remember, fudging the turnstile count was a long-accepted practice to keep the "official" crowd number at Black Hawks home games within the city's fire code.

In his report, Passa described the Wings-Hawks game as the hardest-hitting affair of the five so far contested in Super Series '76. He had seen the previous four matches played by both the Wings and Central Red Army.

The Hawks featured four players who had played for Team Canada

11. Game #5

in the famous 1972 clash with the Soviet Union's national team: Tony Esposito, Dennis Hull, Stan Mikita, and Bill White. (Dale Tallon was technically number five. He was a member of that 1972 squad as a 21-year-old but he saw no action whatsoever versus the Soviets. Tallon only played in the anticlimactic post-series exhibition game in Prague.) Mikita saw only limited ice time, but Hull and White both made significant contributions to the Canadian victory three years before. White, in fact, scored an important goal for Canada in Game Eight in Moscow. Esposito split the netminding duties with Ken Dryden, but Phil Esposito's younger brother was unquestionably better than Dryden overall during the historic eight games. His masked face was a familiar one to several players on the Soviet Wings.

The Hawks came into the game versus the Soviet Wings as a first-place club—but that statistic was a misleading one. They had 45 points in 39 games, an eight-point lead over second-place Vancouver in the Smythe Division. But the Smythe Division was clearly a weak collection of teams in 1975–76. Chicago's 45 points would have put them in fourth place in the much more competitive Patrick Division.

To their credit, the Soviet Wings did not let the dozen goals the Buffalo Sabres scored against them on January 4 affect their collective psyches for very long. Their next contest, three nights later versus the Black Hawks, at Chicago Stadium, saw the visiting club's fortunes change dramatically. Their defense was much improved. Wings coach Boris Kulagin said this was especially true of his goaltender Alexander Sidelnikov. "He did not play so well in Buffalo," Kulagin told reporters the obvious through an interpreter. "After that game he drew the necessary conclusions from himself and improved."[15]

Unlike in Buffalo, Sidelnikov had a very easy night in the Wings' goal. He only had to face 18 Chicago shots throughout the entire 60 minutes. His only egregious error was when Dick Redmond's long shot eluded him on his right side. His counterpart, Tony Esposito, had a much busier night in goal, facing 30 shots from the Wings. Three of the four goals he allowed were power-play tallies, scored from close to the net after some brilliant passing plays got the Soviets within point-blank range of the Hawks star netminder. Esposito had little chance on any of them.

A wire service story in the *Boston Globe* reported the following day, "The Soviet Wings exploded with second-period goals by Sergei Kapustin, Victor Shlalimov, and Yuri Liapkin last night to trounce the penalty-prone Black Hawks, 4–2, and rack up the third victory for the two touring Russian hockey teams in five games against National Hockey League teams."

The *Globe* continued, "It was the second victory in three games for the Wings, runners-up to the other touring Soviet team, the Army, in the

Russian amateur championships. The Wings beat the Pittsburgh Penguins and [lost to] the Buffalo Sabres in their only defeat thus far in the United States."[16]

The first goal of the game came when Chicago's Darcy Rota was in the home team's penalty box for cross-checking, the first of two such penalties he would receive during the game. The Blacks Hawks trailed 1–0 after a 60-foot slapshot from the Chicago blue line was launched by Yuri Tyherin of the Soviet Wings. It found its way through a jumble of players from both teams stationed haphazardly in front of a harried Tony Esposito. (Afterward, Esposito said he was partially screened on the play.) Dick Redmond's goal for the Black Hawks, which tied the game at one goal apiece just 15 seconds after the Soviets had opened the scoring, was also a 60-foot bomb from the blue line. It eluded a surprised Alexander Sidelnikov who was tending the Wings' goal.

The only goal recorded by the Soviet Wings when both teams were playing at full strength went to Sergei Kapustin about four minutes into the second period. Kapustin collected a pass from Vladimir Rasko about 15 feet in front of Esposito. His wrist shot nicked part of the Chicago netminder. Nevertheless, the puck bounced through Esposito's legs and into the net. The goal put the visitors ahead, 2–1. It was a lead they would not relinquish in the final 36 minutes of play.

Viktor Shalimov's goal with his club holding a man advantage made the score 3–1 for the Soviet visitors. About 8½ minutes later, Yuri Liapkin increased the Soviet Wings' advantage to 4–1 over the Black Hawks with another timely power-play marker. It was an accurate 30-foot shot at 17:13 that sent the visitors into their dressing room with the luxury of a three-goal cushion over the Black Hawks.

The only goal of the third period went Chicago's way. Dennis Hull scored at 7:44 on a 25-foot shot that was well placed into the far corner of the Soviet net behind Sidelnikov. Despite conceding the only goal of the final stanza, the Wings were clearly the better team in the last 20 minutes and never looked to be in danger of surrendering their lead to the Hawks. A United Press International writer declared, "In the last period, the Wings were obviously faster and used their quickness to pick up almost every loose puck and stymie the Hawks repeatedly, except for Hull's goal."[17] That was the end of the night's scoring. The Soviet Wings left the arena a happy bunch with a 4–2 win. It raised their record to 2–1 versus the three NHL clubs they had faced so far in Super Series '76. They had one contest left on their schedule: Saturday, January 10 versus the New York Islanders at the Nassau Coliseum.

The *Boston Globe* correspondent also thought the main, contentious story of the Black Hawks–Wings game was the suspect refereeing of Yuri

11. Game #5

Karandin of the Soviet Union. The scribe believed Karandin impacted the game's outcome more than he should have. Karandin certainly was a conspicuous fellow throughout the spirited contest. "Three of the Wings' four goals came on power plays, one when the Hawks were short two men while the Soviets were at full strength," declared the hockey writer who merited no byline in the *Globe*.

"The Hawks were facing a span of 96 seconds with two men in the penalty box midway through the second period when Shalimov took a pass from Yuri Tyerhin," the reporter continued, "and whacked a 20-footer past Tony Esposito, only 44 seconds after the second penalty was called on Chicago."[18]

Stan Mikita, who knew a smattering of Russian because of his Slovak ancestry, gave referee Karandin an earful in his own language in a corridor at the end of the game. Mikita declined to provide a precise English translation to curious reporters who wanted to know what he had said.

Chicago defenseman Dick Redmond complained about the officiating long into the night, calling it "one of the most frustrating experiences of my life," suggesting that the quality of the Soviet officials was so substandard that it compromised the entire series of games. "The Russian players knew they could get away with murder with their own referee, and they sure did."[19] Redmond had uncharacteristically been whistled for four minor penalties in the game. During the entire 1975–76 regular season, in which he played 53 games, Redmond would accrue just 25 penalty minutes.

Another hockey writer, Brodie Snyder of the *Montréal Gazette*, chose to put the blame for Chicago's defeat squarely on the shoulders of the home team. He wrote, "[The Soviet Wings] won because they were tremendously improved defensively, and because the Black Hawks played one period about as stupidly as is possible to play against a Soviet hockey team."

Snyder explained his observation further. "The Hawks had done what everyone in the western world knows you have to do against the Soviets throughout a good first period—forechecking them, clogging up the middle, and coming back to knock them off the puck—and they had a 1-1 tie at that point. In the third period the Hawks scored the only goal and controlled a good deal of the play."[20]

Chicago's John Marks made similar comments. "Let's face it," he said dejectedly in the Hawks' dressing room. "We didn't play a very smart game. We are last in the league in penalty minutes. We average about 11 per game. So, all of a sudden, we go out there and spend 24 minutes in the box against a team that is tough enough to skate with when you are at even strength. It didn't work for the Rangers, or Pittsburgh, or us."[21]

One of the harshest critics of the Black Hawks was also the most powerful man in the NHL—70-year-old league president Clarence Campbell. When Super Series '76 ended on January 11, Campbell summed up his feelings about the eight games to a scrum of hockey reporters. Among Campbell's critiques was this gem: "The Black Hawks were pathetic. There was no excuse for their dismal game."[22]

Prior to the fifth game of Super Series '76, Robin Herman of the *New York Times* wrote an eye-opening article about how Soviet hockey teams—including the two clubs on tour—heavily relied on foreign-made equipment as the necessities of playing elite hockey were very scarce in the USSR. Capitalist countries were their major suppliers, of course. Victor Kuznetsov of the Soviet Wings was cited as a prime example. Herman wrote,

> Like all his teammates, Victor Kuznetsov was outfitted in truly international style. A red helmet, manufactured by Jofa, a Swedish company, protected his head. His blue Czechoslovakian-made jersey with the white letters KC for Kyrili Soviet, (Wings of the Soviet) fell over baggy blue shorts made in the Soviet Union. On his feet, in striking green and gold, were skates that once belonged to Charlie Finley and the California Golden Seals.[23]

Chicago Black Hawks general-manager Tommy Ivan recalled, "When the Russians first came here in 1972, I sneaked a look into their locker room to see their equipment. They had almost nothing."[24]

It was the same story for the Soviet goaltenders on both touring clubs. Vladislav Tretiak and Alexander Sidelnikov used the Cooper Legends line of equipment. (Tretiak, however, did use a Soviet-made stick which, curiously, was called a Montréal Special.) His bird-cage style of goalie mask was made in Canada. Few Canadian goaltenders had embraced it—yet.

Both the Soviet Wings and Central Red Army were about to get some very welcome and much-needed upgrades, however. Herman penned,

> Coming from a country where the manufacturing of hockey helmets is low on a list of national priorities, the two Soviet hockey teams continue to scrounge for equipment.
>
> Recent trips to North America have been equipment boons to the Russians. When the Soviet players arrived in Montréal two weeks ago, Bauer salesmen measured them for complimentary skates. The players have been waiting anxiously the arrival of their gifts plus other equipment promised them by the Cooper Company.[25]

Viacheslav Kilosokov, the head of the Soviet Ice Hockey Federation delegation, admitted that most of their equipment had to be imported from beyond the borders of the communist nation. Kilosokov noted, "The Central Red Army team wears Cooper pants that they got on one of their other trips here."[26]

Fortunately for the visitors, the host NHL teams were a generous and helpful bunch when it came to providing them with ample hockey basics.

11. Game #5

For example, the Buffalo Sabres allowed the Wings of the Soviet to liberally help themselves to small items prior to their January 4 game. The Sabres' equipment manager reported, "[Alexander] Yakushev took rolls and rolls of tape. He took almost all of it—and none of the other players said a word to him."[27]

Herman mentioned that the Soviets did arrive for Super Series '76 with plenty of Soviet-made hockey sticks but they were seldom employed in their games. "[The Russians] seem to use them exclusively as trade items for gifts to North Americans they meet,"[28] she wrote.

The *Chicago Tribune* did something a little bit different with its coverage of the Hawks-Wings game. It hired an interpreter to listen to the account of the game provided by Soviet broadcaster Nikolai Ozerov and take notes. Ozerov was garnering quite a bit of attention because he curiously called the games from the Soviet team's bench rather than from a usual broadcast facility. (Why? He simply preferred to witness the action at ice level.) During the game, Ozerov combined the description of the hockey action with pro-communist propaganda—which was entirely expected. He referred to the Hawks as "true professionals" which was akin to an insult because the Soviets were "pure amateurs." He did compliment the skills of Chicago's Pit Martin, Stan Mikita and Bill White, although he did chastise White's occasional rough play by saying, "An experienced master is nervous." Ozerov also praised the pair of NHL linesmen who worked the game, Matt Pavelich and Neil Armstrong, for being "exact and just" in their officiating. The Soviet broadcaster claimed, "The American and Canadian players are trying hard to defend the honor of their uniforms," but "the Hawks just cannot restrain our young players."[29] Ozerov even offered some atypical criticism of Soviet referee Karandin by noting that when Bill White was high-sticked by Sergei Kapustin, the Soviet player should have received a five-minute penalty rather than just the two-minute sentence that was dished out by the official.

Rob Verdi happily gave the Wings their due, however. He wrote, "If you can forget about all the political implications, prides and prejudices, it is well to appreciate the Soviets' brilliant skating, their splendid password [sic], and their ability to motor nonstop for 60 minutes."[30]

Scoring Summary

Soviet Wings 1+3+0 = 4
Chicago 1+0+1 = 2

First period

Soviet Wings: Tyerhin (Yakushev, Risqunov) 8:46 (pp)
Chicago: Redmond (Mulvey) 9:11

Second period

Soviet Wings: Kapustin (Rasko, Kuznetsov) 4:03
Soviet Wings: Shalimov (Tyerhim, Liapkin) 8:41 (pp)
Soviet Wings: Liapkin (Turin, Yakushev) 17:13 (pp)

Third period

Chicago: Hull (Mikita, Mulvey) 7:44

12

Game #6

Central Red Army vs. Boston Bruins

THURSDAY, JANUARY 8, 1976
BOSTON GARDEN

If media interest was the sole criterion by which to judge overall interest, the sixth game of Super Series '76 was still peaking. More than 170 media representatives had been granted press passes for the game between Central Red Army and the Boston Bruins at Boston Garden on Thursday, January 8, 1976. Somehow Boston hockey writer Tom Fitzgerald tried to downplay its importance. He wrote, "The thing to remember is this is not one of those battles of the century. It really doesn't have all that much to do with lifestyles, or political philosophies, or anything along that cosmic order. Purely and simply, it will be a game of hockey, played with stick and puck by superbly conditioned and strong-skating athletes."[1]

"We are here to learn," insisted Konstantin Loktev, Central Red Army's head coach. It was an old refrain, one first heard in September 1972. This time Loktev added an extra sentence when he spoke to the aforementioned Tom Fitzgerald: "We hope our opponents can learn from us too."[2] This teaching opportunity was the first one Loktev's club would have in 1976. They had not played a game since tying the Montréal Canadiens on New Year's Eve.

This was a new-look Bruins outfit for most fans outside of Boston. Phil Esposito and Carol Vadnais had been traded in a blockbuster deal to the New York Rangers in early November for Brad Park and Jean Ratelle. For an all-too-brief time Bobby Orr and Park were defense partners—arguably the most lethal blueline combination ever seen in the NHL. The club won nine of ten games with that tandem controlling the play. Then came the umpteenth knee injury to Bobby Orr. It was not even a glorious one occurring in the heat of battle. Instead, Orr's knee just gave out on him while he was simply walking down a ramp to board a team bus that was carrying the Bruins to an airport. His return date to the Bruins' lineup was unknown. Some skeptics thought the correct answer might be never. Orr told the *Boston Globe* on January 6 that he was looking forward to finally playing against the Soviets in September when a special six-nation tournament (soon to be called the Canada Cup) would be contested.

Orr had missed out in playing in the 1972 Canada–Soviet Series because he was recuperating from a knee surgery then. It seemed especially cruel that Orr would miss yet another chance to face off against the Soviets for the very same reason three years later. "God, I'm disappointed," Orr told an interviewer from the *Globe & Mail*. "I missed them in '72. The last time I played them I was 16. All I've been doing is watching, and from that I think they are a hell of a club. Now they are here and I am not [available]."³

Central Red Army wanted to see Orr in action too—just to see if the stories of his vast skills were legitimate. They had seen him only in NHL highlight films. Soviet coach Loktev said, "It is unfortunate that every time we're over here he is injured or has some other misfortune. We wish him a quick recovery."⁴ Boris Mikhailov said he had been looking forward to playing against Orr and was disappointed that he would not get the opportunity.

Prior to their game versus the Bruins, the Central Red Army Club was given a guided tour of the Bruins' facilities at Boston Garden. Even though the home of the Bruins was becoming archaic by NHL standards in 1976, the visitors were impressed with the luxuries it had compared to the starkly spartan facilities of Soviet arenas. Frank Torpey of NHL security, who led the tour, noticed the Red Army players were absolutely awestruck when they saw Orr's jersey and equipment in his cubicle. One by one they individually approached it and gently ran their fingers over it. "They just kept on touching everything that was his," Torpey said. "It was very strange."⁵

That day's *Boston Globe* featured a picture of Orr, but it was far from an action shot. He was posing for a publicity photograph for the local March of Dimes campaign, holding six-year-old Tammy Patterson in his arms. Tammy was certainly a typical Bostonian. One could easily tell from her wistful gaze at the Boston superstar that she loved Orr, who was identified as the charity's "special events chairman." The newspaper also carried a more dire story for Boston hockey fans: Orr was now openly talking about where he might be headed if he could not make a deal with the Bruins after the 1975–76 season had concluded. That was when his contract with his present club expired. It was an awkward and uncertain time for the Bruins organization.

With Orr sidelined indefinitely and Esposito playing for a

12. Game #6

disappointing New York Rangers club, it was no longer the familiar Boston Bruins of old that television viewers across Canada would see. The Bruins were still a talented, rough-and-tumble bunch under the leadership of colorful second-year coach Don Cherry. Excluding Orr (whose tenure in Boston was over, but nobody knew it yet), Boston only had four members of their 1971–72 Stanley Cup team still with the club just three and a half years later: Don Marcotte, Wayne Cashman, Johnny Bucyk and Ken Hodge. Quite coincidentally, three members of the 1972 New York Rangers, whom the Bruins vanquished in the Cup finals, were now wearing Boston jerseys: Gary Doak, Jean Ratelle, and Brad Park.

Park, who was immensely disliked in Boston when he was a New York Ranger, was now slowly becoming a fan favorite at Boston Garden. "Brad is playing like a captain, skating with confidence," wrote Stan Fischler in the January 10, 1976, issue of *The Sporting News*. "He is winning the heart of Bruin fans, compensating for the loss of Bobby Orr. Park's presence has unified the entire Bruins' defensive unit which had seemed lost. Even Gary Doak has been looking sharp."[6]

There was a different approach to Bruins hockey now. Boston no longer bludgeoned too many teams with lopsided scores. The Bruins outworked them instead, and regularly left the ice with 4–2 and 5–3 victories. Wins were still plentiful. In fact, Boston had just returned home from a highly successful five-game road trip with four wins and a tie. They were the hottest team in the NHL, currently riding a 12-game undefeated streak. On January 8, 1976, the Bruins were sitting in first place in the Adams Division, two points ahead of the Buffalo Sabres, whom they had just overtaken in the standings, when Central Red Army came to town for their Super Series '76 game at Boston Garden. The Thursday night affair was, of course, a sellout despite very frigid temperatures that had descended upon the Hub.

The Bruins had watched the films from the New Year's Eve game at the Montréal Forum. They became convinced that a solid dose of forechecking—a typical staple of Bruin hockey—could disrupt the flow of the visitors' attacks. Coach Don Cherry told Tom Fitzgerald on January 7 that would be his club's game plan against the touring Soviets. The next day's *Boston Globe* featured an ursine cartoon showing a stereotypical Russian bear with a hockey stick facing off against a similarly equipped bruin—a Boston Bruin, of course.

Boston general-manager Harry Sinden had witnessed Central Red Army's previous two games in Super Series '76 and was thoroughly impressed by the visitors. "We've got a hell of a job on our hands on Thursday, I'll tell you that" he told the Associated Press. "If anything, this Russian team is better than the one in 1972—and that's hard to imagine. I saw the tie in Montréal. In my ten years in the NHL, I've never seen the Canadiens higher for a game. Yet all they got was a tie even though they outshot the Russians 38–13." Sinden continued with his praise of Soviet hockey. "The Russians actually scare me they are so good. The Russian goalie, Vladislav Tretiak, is sensational. [He is] certainly as good if not better than anybody we've got in the NHL."[7]

A novelty for those who were tuned into the *Hockey Night in Canada* telecast was the addition of Phil Esposito as an analyst alongside Brian McFarlane and play-by-play man Danny Gallivan. With his Rangers having no game that night, Esposito was invited by *HNIC* to see the Boston–Red Army game and offer his insights and observations. He accepted with alacrity. Of course, Esposito was the outstanding player of the Canada–Soviet Series in 1972. (Throughout the broadcast, Esposito comically had trouble pronouncing the surname of old rival Valeri Kharlamov. He frequently transposed the L and the M so it came out sounding like "Harm-a-lov." Danny Gallivan occasionally had that same difficulty.) It had been two months since Esposito had been shockingly traded from Boston to the New York Rangers. (It was his second trip back to Boston. The first one occurred on December 11 when his Rangers had beaten the Bruins, 5–1. The Bruin fans fittingly and appreciatively gave him a long ovation the first time he stepped on the ice. Esposito got one assist for New York in that game.) His presence at Boston Garden on January 8 not as a player for either the Rangers or the Bruins had to have been very odd indeed for both Espo and his old fans. While he was in Boston, Esposito learned that New York Rangers coach Ron Stewart had been dismissed. Stewart was replaced by John Ferguson, who, like Esposito, had been a special commentator during Super Series '76. Ferguson had been an analyst for the thrilling December 31 game in Montréal.

Central Red Army were a well-rested group. They had not played in the eight days since their memorable and much-discussed 3–3 tie versus the Canadiens in Montréal on New Year's Eve. The Bruins featured three players who participated in the 1972 Canada–Soviet Series: Cashman, Ratelle and Park. The all-important position of referee was assigned to Victor Dombrowski of the Soviet Union who had previously worn the red armband for the Soviet Wings' games versus Pittsburgh and Buffalo. He had the capable Canadian NHL duo of Leon Stickle and John D'Amico as his linesmen.

The game opened positively for the home team with the Bruins carrying most of the play. Their best scoring chance came in the first minute but a scramble for a loose puck in front of goaltender Vladislav Tretiak amounted to nothing. Against the run of play, Valeri Kharlamov was sent in on a breakaway, but Boston goalie Gilles Gilbert stood firm and made a big save on the Soviet sniper to keep the game scoreless. Less than a minute later, Kharlamov had another fine chance to put Central Red Army in front. Again, he was thwarted by Gilbert. The crowd roared its appreciation. It had been an entertaining and exciting start to the highly anticipated game.

The contest remained goalless and free of penalties past the midway mark of the first period, but there was still plenty of action to enjoy. Gilles Gilbert made a few sparkling saves. From in close, Wayne Cashman fired a wrist shot that beat Tretiak but clanged off the goalpost behind him. On the rebound, Cashman thought he had scored, but somehow Tretiak kept the puck from crossing the goal line, "Tretiak is picking up where he left off in Montréal,"[8] commented Brian McFarlane. About 13 minutes into the period, Gregg Sheppard's shot hit the goalpost too and stayed out. Brian McFarlane, who must have been rehearsing his one-liners, noted, "The goalposts are painted the right color tonight." By rule, all NHL goalposts are painted a bright shade of red.

Soviet referee Victor Dombrowski refereed with a liberal mindset in the first period, issuing just two penalties in the opening 20 minutes, winning praise from *HNIC* analyst Phil Esposito for not over-officiating. One minor penalty went to Boston's Dallas Smith for holding. The other, about a minute later, went to Central Red Army's Boris Alexandrov for roughing. Neither team capitalized on their abridged power plays. The period ended as it began, 0–0. Brian McFarlane correctly noted it was the first scoreless period of any game of Super Series '76. It was initially announced that the Bruins outshot Central Red Army by a 19–9 count. That was later amended to an even wider margin of 19–8. Boston probably deserved to hold the lead based on the run of play. However, goaltender Vladislav Tretiak was clearly the star of the first period, making a few improbable saves. Bobby Schmautz and Jean Ratelle led the Bruins in shots on goal, each with four. Four of the eight shots from Central Red Army came off the stick of one player: Valeri Kharlamov.

Longtime Bruin forward Ken Hodge did not get much ice team in the opening 20 minutes as he was in coach Don Cherry's doghouse. In previous weeks, many Boston Garden patrons had been riding Hodge for his apparent lack of willingness to engage in rough play. By the time he was given a shift, the first period was more than half over. When Hodge did play, he played well.

The first break of the game—and its first goal—went the way of the home team at 2:54 of the second stanza. Dave Forbes intercepted a Red Army pass in the neutral zone. He crossed the visitors' blue line and launched what looked to be a routine shot toward the net. It ought to have been a very ordinary save for Tretiak but he reacted late on it. Looking surprised, Tretiak may have been momentarily screened by one of his Red Army defensemen. The puck went through the Soviet goaltender's pads and trickled across the goal line to the surprise—and delight—of the Boston Garden crowd. "Maybe [Tretiak] sleeps a bit like some of the goalies in the NHL do," suggested Phil Esposito in the *HNIC* broadcast booth. "Maybe he *is* human."[9] Forbes' unassisted goal, out of nowhere, gave Boston a 1–0 lead. For the third consecutive outing in Super Series '76, Central Red Army had surrendered the game's first goal.

The Bruins' edge on the scoreboard did not last very long. Bobby Schmautz was penalized for hooking by referee Victor Dombrowski. (Phil Esposito labeled it a "rotten call."[10]) The Bruins killed the first minute of the minor penalty efficiently. However, Central Red Army recovered the puck after Alexander Maltsev lost a faceoff to Jean Ratelle at the left of Gilles Gilbert. Boston defensemen Al Sims and Brad Park both failed to control the puck. Maltsev capitalized on the defensive confusion and quickly sent an accurate pass to Valeri Kharlamov. He backhanded the puck along the ice and into the net past the surprised Bruin netminder—and the game was tied at one goal apiece 4:41 into the second period.

In the minutes following the tying goal, Central Red Army frequently ragged the puck, retreating to their own zone and making numerous passes without being overly pressured by the Bruins. The Boston fans—a worldly bunch, apparently—began derisively whistling at the visitors. "The Russian raspberry!"[11] exclaimed Esposito.

There was more whistling when Valeri Kharlamov scored his second goal of the game from the slot at the 11-minute mark after receiving a pass from Alexander Maltsev. The main focus was not on the go-ahead goal by Central Red Army's Kharlamov, but what occurred behind the Boston net immediately afterward. Wayne Cashman and Boris Mikhailov got tangled up. Cashman ended up giving Mikhailov a hefty two-handed slash across his ribs. The Soviet star seemed to have a delayed reaction before crumpling dramatically to the ice. Mikhailov had to be assisted to the Central Red Army bench. Cashman was fortunate to escape with just a minor penalty for the stick foul and not an ejection for an attempt to injure Mikhailov. Phil Esposito explained that Cashman was enforcing hockey's version of frontier justice. He was merely paying Mikhailov back for spearing him in Toronto during Game #2 of the 1972 Canada–Soviet series. During the second intermission, Esposito stated, "Cash owed him one. Let's put it that way."[12] When the *HNIC* announcers' attention did return to Central Red Army's second goal, Esposito readily conceded that "Kharlamov is one of the best goal-scorers I've ever seen."[13] Danny Gallivan agreed.

Furthermore, replays of the scoring play showed that Mikhailov had briefly become entangled with Gilbert at the side of the Boston net just before Kharlamov scored. Gilbert lost his stick on the play. Most observers thought Mikhailov's collision with Gilbert was planned, including John Powers who was covering the game for the *Boston Globe*. He described it as a "deliberate interference ploy."[14] Gilbert kidded about it after the game. "It was like I was hit by a Zamboni," he told Powers. "I didn't think you could be that dirty in the crease, but it was a good thing for him to do." Gilbert gave more details of his encounter with Mikhailov to Tim Burke of the *Montréal Gazette*. According to the Boston netminder, "First [Mikhalov] kicked me, then he cross-checked me, then he elbowed me. Finally, he punched the stick out of my hands."[15] Burke labeled Mikhailov as "the meanest critter east of the Polish corridor."[16]

The general opinion among the patrons of Boston Garden and the *HNIC* crew was that Mikhailov was greatly embellishing his discomfort from Cashman's slash. This belief had some merit. Boston coach Don Cherry compared Mikhailov's performance to that of a famous Oscar winner. "George C. Scott had better watch out," he quipped. "I thought we'd never see him again."[17] Brian McFarlane jokingly alluded to a popular TV doctor several minutes later: "For a while I thought it might take Marcus Welby's magic hands to revive that young man, but suddenly a few seconds later he was back on [the ice]."[18] Cashman told reporters a similar version, "Gee, [Mikhailov] got out of the hospital and back on the ice quickly," he said. "It took about 32 seconds, I think."[19] Cashman later told Mark Mulvoy of *Sports Illustrated*, "Hell, I hit my kids harder on their rears than I hit him."[20] Cashman later told the media that he was simply applying the NHL's unwritten law of the jungle that says that any opposing player who runs a goalie will face consequences.

The Bruins killed off Cashman's minor penalty, but just seconds later, Valeri Vasiliev sent a beautiful pass to Alexander Maltsev through the center ice area. Maltsev easily eluded the check of Darryl Edestrand and then beat Gilbert on the partial breakaway that the long pass had created. "I'd never seen that play before," Boston coach Don Cherry later said as a compliment to the Soviet visitors. "The guy just came around [his own] net and just zipped it right up there. It was a lovely pass."[21] Central Red Army now held a 3–1 lead over Boston. (Sadly, it appears that no video of the Red Army's third goal exists. There were technical difficulties with the TV broadcast from Boston Garden that began just after Kharlamov's second goal—first audio, then visual. These issues were not resolved for several minutes. Maltsev's goal occurred at 13:19 of the second period when the picture was temporarily on the fritz.)

Boston narrowed the Red Army's lead to 3–2 when Jean Ratelle scored on a power play goal at 17:31 of the second period. The home team's goal came on the Boston man advantage with Viktor Shluktov in the penalty box for hooking. Ken Hodge fired a shot on goal that Tretiak stopped, but Ratelle beat the Soviet goaltender and defenseman Valeri Vasiliev to the juicy rebound sitting in front of the net. Ratelle's wrist shot dented the twine behind Tretiak. The game score was now a slim 3–2 for Central Red Army with plenty of time remaining in the contest. The Ratelle goal seemed to enliven and energize the Bruins for the remainder of the second period, but there was no further scoring in the middle frame. After a goalless first 20 minutes, the next 20 had produced five goals. As was becoming the norm in this series, the Soviet teams were getting the most from their limited shots. Central Red Army scored three goals on just five shots on the Boston net that period. The Bruins fared decently too, scoring twice from their eight shots at Tretiak. Heading into the third period, Boston had badly outshot the visitors by a 27–13 margin but, nevertheless, trailed the Soviets by a goal.

The third period began with a flurry of action. Bobby Schmautz had a good chance for Boston, but he fired a hard shot wide of the left goalpost. Not long afterward, Brad Park made an individual rush up the ice and sent a low wrist shot on Tretiak. The Red Army goalie coolly made the stop with his left pad on the Bruin defenseman. On the return rush, Central Red Army got their fourth goal. Gennady Tsygankov beat Gilbert with an accurate slapshot from the blue line after Boris Alexandrov and Vladimir Vikulov exchanged passes near the Bruins' net. (Mark Mulvoy of *Sports Illustrated* noted in a joking fashion that Soviet hockey players "employ slapshots only about once a month."[22]) The visitors' quick strike came just 42 seconds into the third period, the first shot on goal by the Soviets since play resumed. "Every time they get a shot, they make it count,"[23] said Phil Esposito on the *HNIC* telecast with a tone of exasperation in his voice. One could sense the energy and hope leaving from both the Boston Garden crowd and the Bruins themselves.

Still, the Bruins persisted. Ken Hodge—who was now playing a regular shift for the first time in a few weeks—got two good chances on Tretiak but he came up empty each time. After one stoppage of play, the *HNIC* coverage briefly focused on the sidelined Bobby Orr. Clad in a garish blue plaid blazer, he was seated near the Bruins bench, urging his teammates to keep working hard as they came off the ice.

Orr's exhortations did not pay dividends, however. An egregious giveaway by young Boston defenseman Al Sims resulted in a fifth Central Red Army goal that essentially salted the game away for the Soviets. Sims, who was splitting the 1975–76 season between the Bruins' AHL affiliate in Rochester and the parent club, carelessly coughed up the puck inside the Boston zone when he whiffed on a backward pass to Brad Park. Within a matter of seconds, the puck was seized by advancing Red Army winger

Shluktov, who quickly fed a one-handed pass to Boris Alexandrov who was moving into the slot. Alexandrov moved in on goaltender Gilles Gilbert, deftly deked him out of position, and calmly slid the puck into the gaping, vacated net. The time of the goal was 8:58 of the third period. The score was now a daunting 5–2 for the visitors.

"You can't give that little fellow, number 11, Alexandrov, an opportunity like that!"[24] declared Danny Gallivan. "Let's give credit where credit is due," insisted Brian McFarlane. "Alexandrov has just been sensational."[25]

Phil Esposito was blunt and sympathetic at the same time with his opinion of Sims' blatant error. "Al just made a mistake. Here's a kid who hasn't been playing regular [sic]. He's out there on the ice against the Russians. He's nervous. He makes a mistake, and they score a goal."[26]

Frustration began to overtake some Bruins. When play resumed, Boston's Bobby Schmautz gave Gennady Tsygankov a scary crosscheck to the head behind the Red Army net, which resulted in just a two-minute penalty—not a five-minute major. (In today's NHL it would have been a major penalty followed, almost certainly, by a fine and a suspension.) The foul was so blatant that Tretiak gave Schmautz a lecture about it. Central Red Army did not score with the man advantage. Kharlamov was thwarted from a possible hattrick by Gilbert, who made his best save of the game to do it. At one point during the Soviet power play, Boston's Darryl Edestrand clearly tripped Boris Mikhailov at the Bruins' blue line, but the Soviet star embellished the foul so much that even referee Victor Dombrowski had had enough of Mikhailov's thespian efforts. He did not call the obvious penalty.

Nothing too significant occurred in the final nine minutes of the third period. The final score favored Central Red Army, 5–2. The victory clinched Super Series '76 for the two touring Soviet teams as they held an insurmountable 4–1–1 edge with just two games left. The 15,003 fans—or at least those who stuck around until the conclusion of the third period—gave both teams a warm reception during the postgame handshake ritual. "Bruins Lose Their Turn at Russian Roulette," declared a headline in the next day's *Ottawa Citizen*.

As for the Soviet teams now guaranteed of having a superior record over the NHL clubs in Super Series '76, Boston coach Don Cherry seemed unconcerned. "I don't think about the series," Cherry commented. "I'm just disappointed that we lost. I thought we were going to win after the first period. I thought we'd come out smoking."[27]

The major hero for Central Red Army was once again goaltender Vladislav Tretiak. (The Bruins had outshot the visitors 40–19—almost as badly as Montréal had on New Year's Eve. Boston had gotten as many shots in the first period as Central Red Army launched in the whole game.) He was named the first star of the game. In fact, Central Red Army swept all three stars, as Valeri Kharlamov and Boris Alexandrov were the other two. To coach Konstantin Loktev, Tretiak's strong outing was nothing out of the ordinary for the young man wearing #20 on his jersey. "We expect a goalie to stop 90 of 100 shots," he coolly told the media. "Our goaltender played his normal, regular game tonight."[28]

Of the wide edge the Bruins held in shots, Don Cherry noted, "Outshooting a team like that doesn't mean much. They're just good opportunists and they don't shoot [the puck] until they can put it in."[29]

Boston's Brad Park insisted that an NHL team's one-game outing versus a Soviet team was an insufficient sample size. "I would like to have them in our league and play them every few days," Park said. "I think in the NHL, the 80-game season, the travelling, the body contact, would wear them down. I don't really know. I would like to see them there."[30]

United Press International reporter Gil Peters glowingly praised the skills of the visitors when he wrote, "What the Soviet Red Army team did to the Boston Bruins needed no translation. Russia's top hockey team used superior conditioning, magnificent shot selection, and peerless goaltending to down the Bruins, 5–2...."[31]

In recapping the action, Tim Burke of the *Montréal Gazette* penned that the first period, despite being scoreless, was filled with "wondrous hockey in which the inspired Bruins had mustered the best bombardment of the three games against the Red Army only to have Tretiak thwart them with save after save that boggled the imagination."[32]

The following day's *Boston Globe* was filled with rave reviews of the visitors and their refreshing style of hockey. "They performed like some wondrous red swallows, dipping and swooping around the Boston Garden ice" wrote Ernie Roberts. "They never stopped. You knew you had seen the purest form of this often maligned and sometimes vicious sport."[33]

Roberts' *Globe* colleague, John Powers, readily concurred. "We had not seen that kind of hockey on this continent for quite a while," Powers penned. "Last night, for two hours, we became connoisseurs again. And as we filed out into the cold night air onto Causeway Street, we had to admit we enjoyed it."[34]

Powers' admiration for the Soviet style of hockey was obvious. He wrote,

> While the NHL has been hung up on raw macho and superstar chic, the Russians have put the game under a microscope and sliced away its excess. What is productive they have kept and incorporated into their system. What is not—cheap elbows, shots on glass, hired goons—has been forbidden or ignored. Statistics are meaningless. They will gladly let Boston outshoot them 40–19. That is why there is a Vladislav Tretiak.[35]

12. Game #6

The man in charge of the Bruins' personnel seemed impressed too. "Sure, they skate well, they pass well," Boston general-manager Harry Sinden said of the Central Red Army players. "But a point overlooked is that they may be better goal-scorers than we are. Every good shot they got, they scored on. The same chances we had, we missed." Sinden continued, "Except for the first period, when Gilbert stoned them twice, I've never seen them miss one-on-one versus a goaltender."[36]

Another similar Sinden quote appeared in the January 19 edition of *Sports Illustrated* in which he opined about the offensive prowess of Soviet hockey, "What has never been said before is that from certain ranges, these guys are much better goal-scorers than we are. They never waste their opportunities. They seem to be saying, 'Hey, what's the rush?' Then zing! The puck is in the net."[37]

Boston coach Don Cherry further added, "I don't know how any Olympic team is going to beat them [the Soviets]. They made a believer out of me."[38]

Red Fisher of the *Montréal Star* rated the performance of Central Red Army against Boston as the best of their three games thus far versus NHL opposition. "The New York game was a joke," Fisher said. "At Montréal they didn't play well, but maybe that was because the Canadiens wouldn't let them. Tonight they took everything the Bruins could throw at them in the first period and then just took over."[39]

Journalist Robin Herman of the *New York Times* disagreed. She thought Central Red Army had played their best game in the 3–3 stalemate at the Forum on December 31. "[They were] not as good as they were in Montréal," Herman insisted. "Maybe they were tired. Maybe it was because the Bruins were hitting them very hard."[40]

Central Red Army head coach Konstantin Loktev sided with Red Fisher in the debate. "I thought we were greatly improved over the play in our first two games," he announced through an interpreter. "At the beginning we played better than we normally do early in the game. And you are aware our competition is getting stronger and stronger with each game. It is nice to win against the strongest players."[41] Loktev's implication that Boston was a better team than Montréal in 1975–76 would be overwhelmingly disputed by even the most ardent of Bruin fans. True, Boston had a strong team that season, but Montréal was in a class by itself, pretty much cruising to the Stanley Cup that spring after finishing in first place overall in the NHL standings. The Bruins, however, were markedly improved the following year when the club acquired Rick Middleton from the New York Rangers for the much-maligned Ken Hodge in May 1976 and Peter McNab from Buffalo for André Savard in June. Don Cherry's gritty, "lunch pail" Bruins would be a force to contend with for the rest of the decade.

During the *HNIC* brief postgame show, Dave Hodge and Howie Meeker agreed that the Boston Bruins did not play like a potential Stanley Cup contender they were alleged to be. Still, Hodge optimistically pointed out that the four NHL teams that had appeared in the 1975 Cup semifinals seven months earlier had so far in Super Series '76 produced a win (Buffalo), a tie (Montréal) with the New York Islanders and Philadelphia Flyers yet to play their games against the touring Soviet teams. Meeker cynically said the NHL players had shown they were skilled "woodchoppers"[42] with their stick fouls but they needed to learn to contain their emotions if they wanted to compete against the Soviet teams. Hodge agreed with his colleague, stating, "The lesson is there to be learned."[43]

Don Cherry was not much of a scholar on Soviet hockey techniques. He honestly told Tim Burke of the *Montréal Gazette*, "I've never read any of their books on hockey, nor have I studied their system to any extent. In fact, I never saw a Russian in my life until yesterday."[44]

Hodge also gave special praise to the excellent play of 20-year-old Boris Alexandrov. The *HNIC* host noted that Alexandrov's plentiful skills had first caught his eye at the unofficial 1975 World Junior Hockey championship which had been held in Winnipeg a year earlier. (The Soviets won that event with a perfect 5–0 record; Canada was second with a 4–1 mark. The 19-year-old Alexandrov was named one of the tourney's top stars.) Hodge boldly suggested that one day in the not-too-distant future that Alexandrov could overtake both Valeri Kharlamov and Vladislav Tretiak in greatness and popularity. The youthful Alexandrov seemed absolutely delighted at being named one of the three stars of the game at Boston Garden. When he returned to the ice, he smiled widely and waved warmly to the Boston crowd. Not expecting such a display of outright joy from an emotionless Soviet "robot," the Garden patrons promptly increased the volume of their polite applause considerably.

"It will be no problem putting the Russian game behind us because we never put it in front of us," insisted Boston forward Gregg Sheppard. "It was an exhibition game."[45]

Two days Later, *Boston Globe* columnist Ernie Roberts reported, "Despite the Bruins' defeat, that Soviet game was a great stimulant to hockey interest in the Boston area. [It was] celebrity night in the Garden seats and the TV audience was tremendous." Roberts also noticed that, for one night at least, the Bruins fans had mimicked their counterparts in Europe by whistling at tactics, calls or non-calls that bothered them. Roberts did not like it at all. "I never realized how ear-shattering group whistling can be until the Garden crowd took up that method of indicating disapproval. Bring back the booing!"[46]

Leigh Montville, also of the *Boston Globe*, wrote a very flattering column about the quality of Soviet hockey in the Sunday, January 11 edition of his newspaper. He penned, "The longer you think about it, the scarier the result becomes: the Russians beat the Bruins at Boston Garden. They skated onto the Garden ice and into the Garden corners and beat the Boston Bruins. Here. Beat 'em bad. This was a cultural shockwave that was stronger than the first 1957 sighting of Sputnik circling the globe."

Montville continued, "The Russians have shown that they can start from nowhere—virtually being taught the rules in 1945—and in 30 years dominate a sport. They can attack it much more scientifically than we can in North America. They can be so single-minded. They can cut out the frills and the agents and the rock-and-roll star qualities. They can, let's face it, work better and probably harder, in their system. They don't have the same pop-art distractions."[47]

Mark Mulvoy reported that the Soviet players from both teams were very much typical tourists wherever they ventured and that "they had thoroughly enjoyed themselves immensely in North America" during the time they spent away from the ice. Mulvoy documented their various travels. "Tretiak and his Red Army comrades," he penned, "saw a porno flick in Montréal, danced the hustle at Lucifer's in Boston, battled the bargain hunters in Filene's basement, and discovered that Kentucky Fried Chicken really is finger-lickin' good." Meanwhile their compatriots on the Wings went to a screening of *Jaws* at a Buffalo movie theater. (The Red Army players did the same thing while in Philadelphia.) They were also thoroughly engrossed with buying western goods that were not readily available to them in the USSR. Mulvoy wrote, "Yakushev and the Soviet Wings maintained a lower profile, but did raid New York's Orchard Street discount shops, buying everything from baby rattles to Levi's for their wives, to Elton John records for their stereos and Beach Boys tapes for their Volga decks."[48]

"We got some very good deals,"[49] a smiling Yakushev happily stated.

Scoring Summary

Red Army 0+3+2 = 5
Boston 0+2+0 = 2

First period

No scoring

Second period

Boston: Forbes (unassisted) 2:54
Red Army: Kharlamov (Maltsev) 4:41
Red Army: Kharlamov (Maltsev) 11:00

Red Army: Maltsev (Vasiliev) 13:19
Boston: Ratelle (Hodge) 17:31

Third period

Red Army: Tsygankov (Alexandrov, Vikulov) 0:42
Red Army: Alexandrov (Shluktov) 8:58

13

Game #7

Soviet Wings vs. New York Islanders

SATURDAY, JANUARY 10, 1976
NASSAU COUNTY COLISEUM

"I haven't even mentioned Russia to them."[1] That is what New York Islanders coach Al Arbour claimed when asked on January 8 if his team was adequately prepared to face the Soviet Wings two days hence on their home ice at the Nassau County Coliseum in Uniondale, New York. Apparently, Arbour was serious.

The 43-year-old Arbour was asked about the upcoming international game not long after his club had lost at home, 5–3, to Toronto on January 8. Arbour quickly discounted the notion that his team had overlooked the Maple Leafs and was instead fixated on the game versus the Soviet club on January 10. He did, however, freely admit, "If we're going to beat [the Soviet Wings], we'll have to do a better job than we did tonight. A whole lot better. We were out of it from the start. We were just plain terrible. It was the worst game of the season by a country mile."[2] [Authors' note: That was a bit of an exaggeration by Arbour—or he had very high standards for his club. In that loss to Toronto, the Islanders held a 3–2 lead over the Leafs going into the third period and did not give up their advantage until the 8:31 mark of the final stanza. Furthermore, the Islanders had lost a game, 5–1, back on November 12, to the lowly California Golden Seals in Oakland. Surely they must have played worse that night!]

Of the eight NHL teams to play in Super Series '76, the Islanders had the briefest history. They had only been around since the 1972–73 season when they entered the league the same time as the Atlanta Flames did. That first season was a dismal one on Long Island with the Islanders winning just 12 of 78 games. However, steady improvement based upon solid draft picks made the Islanders a playoff team by 1974–75. That year they became the NHL's darlings by beating the New York Rangers two games to one in a preliminary round of the postseason. Next, they rallied to upend Pittsburgh in a best-of-seven quarterfinal four games to three—after dropping the first three games of the series to the Penguins. (It was only the second time such a huge comeback had been achieved in the long history of the Stanley Cup playoffs.) Then the Isles fell behind three games to none in a semifinal round versus Philadelphia and promptly won the next three games to even that series! Philadelphia easily prevailed 4–1 in the seventh game—but the Islanders accrued a huge number of fans with their undeniable pluck and never-say-die attitude. They had won eight do-or-die playoff games before falling in the ninth one. "The New York Islanders pressed the miracle button one more time. It didn't function. Finally, the battery was dead,"[3] wrote Jim McKay of the *Windsor Star* after Game Seven. Even NHL president Clarence Campbell heaped praised the NHL's exciting Cinderella team when they finally succumbed to the reigning champs. Accordingly, it was thought that the Islanders would represent the NHL quite well in their encounter with the Wings of the Soviet.

By the time Super Series '76 was approaching, Islanders general manager Bill Torrey was aware of the positive perception of his club by hockey fans in general. It pleased him. On the day of the game versus the Wings of the Soviet, Torrey spoke to Robin Herman of the *New York Times*. He said,

> It seems to be the consensus around the league that our team has the physical ability and the system to beat [the Soviet Wings]. The question is, how good has [our NHL] goaltending been? I'm told Gilles Gilbert played pretty well in Boston. I don't think Michel Plasse [of Pittsburgh] can be happy with himself, and the Ranger goaltending was inconsistent. I'm fairly worried. They score on a high percentage of their shots. You can't totally eliminate them from shooting.[4]

Arbour did start to take his team's upcoming matchup versus the Soviet Wings seriously after their loss to Toronto. On Friday, January 9, one day before the game, the Islanders practiced in secret after holding a workout that was open to the public. In contrast, the Soviets held their practice in the open, free for anyone who wanted to watch. Some wags joked that, in this case, the Islanders were the ones who had constructed an Iron Curtain.

Hockey journalist Robin Herman was pleased with what she saw on Saturday, January 10, 1976, at the Nassau County Coliseum. She wrote in the *New York Times* the following day, "[It was] the most evenly matched, exhilarating and competitive contest thus far in the series between NHL clubs and two Russian teams...."[5] It certainly was high praise to rank it as a better game than the Habs–Red Army tilt on New Year's Eve.

In a closely fought contest—the tightest-checking affair in all of Super Series '76—the Soviet Wings edged the hometown Islanders, 2–1.

All the scoring plays occurred in the second period. Viktor Shalimov and Vyacheslav Anisin each scored unassisted goals for the visitors. Shalimov's marker, which had a fluky aspect, was scored while the Wings were shorthanded. Anisin's came with just 14 seconds left in the stanza. Sandwiched between the two Wings goals was Bryan Trottier's power-play tally for the home team at 14:59. It came just five seconds after Sergei Babinov was assessed a minor penalty for interference, the second time the 20-year-old Wings defenseman had been banished to the penalty box in that period.

Viktor Shalimov's goal for the Wings came when Islander all-star goaltender Glenn (Chico) Resch was playing with a broken stick. Resch had not even damaged it during play. While the Islanders were controlling the puck on a power play at the other end of the ice, Resch leaned too heavily on his stick which caused its blade to shatter. Not long afterward, the 24-year-old Shalimov stole the puck and beat the pursuing Islander defenseman. Moving in alone on the home team's goal, Shalimov then fired the puck past Resch—and his partial stick—for a shorthanded marker that opened the game's scoring.

Islander coach Al Arbour said he had never seen such an unfortunate thing happen to a goaltender before in all his years in hockey. He ruefully noted, "Resch often leans on his stick, trying to bow it and give it some snap for when he next shoots the puck. This time it didn't come out of the bow. It just went crunch."[6]

Resch himself elaborated on what exactly happened with his goalie stick on Shalimov's goal when he spoke to reporter Robin Herman. "Before the game I got a new batch of light sticks, a different make [than usual]. I leaned on it a little to clear a puck and it snapped right off."[7]

Herman wrote in the *New York Times*, "With only the jagged handle in his hand, Resch rushed out of the net to poke the puck away, but the Wings' Viktor Shalimov picked it up and shot it into an empty net." Herman humorously added that "the company manufacturing Resch's sticks ought to get an assist"[8] on Shalimov's goal.

Wings coach Boris Kulagin admitted his team had benefited by Resch's unusual and untimely goalie stick mishap, but he insisted that such unforeseen misfortunes are just part of the game. Kulagin said he preferred to focus on the positive aspect of the play—Shalimov's superb goal in which he controlled the puck well and did not hurry his shot. In the end, Kulagin, philosophized, hockey is a game of breaks—both literally and figuratively in this case. "Every hockey game consists of mistakes. The team that makes more mistakes loses."[9]

The tying goal for New York came about 8½ minutes later when 19-year-old Bryan Trottier tucked home a rebound from a Denis Potvin shot on a successful Islander power play. Sidelnikov had stopped Denis

Potvin's slapshot from the point but, as Herman noted in her game report, "Trottier swooped in, picked the puck off the goalie's pads and sent it around Sidelnikov's leg with a backhanded shot."[10]

However, Vyacheslav Anisin's 45-foot slapshot from the slot in the period's dying seconds restored the Soviet Wings' one-goal lead. The time of the go-ahead goal was 19:46. The score stayed the same, 2–1, throughout the third period. (Of course, several punny journalists referred to the 24-year-old Anisin as a "headache" for the home team.)

"Each team adjusted to the other's style, creating a grand tug-of-war," Herman declared. She continued,

> Flaws in the Wings' previous games were mended. Sidelnikov, who had played poorly in other games, was in good form tonight. His teammates displayed their best forechecking work of the past two weeks.
> The Islanders, meanwhile, got excellent goaltending from Resch. [They] made a fine defensive showing, clogging the Wings' favorite center lane, and showed plenty of stamina. Some other NHL clubs had failed to keep pace with the Russians. The sellout crowd of 14,865 responded enthusiastically to the fast-paced game.[11]

Arbour believed the loss stemmed from his young team being overly nervous about playing a Soviet club. It was, of course, a new experience for them. "We've got so many kids, they just couldn't loosen up. We couldn't get our offense going on all four cylinders. We were just working on two or one-and-a-half."[12]

Losing goaltender Glenn Resch confirmed there was an air of apprehension in the home team's dressing room prior to the game. He said, "Bobby Nystrom, André St. Laurent and Garry Howatt were saying they were very nervous. Denis Potvin did not have much of an offensive game because he was worried about making a mistake and looking bad."[13]

Stan Fischler summarized in *The Sporting News* that the Islanders lost to the Soviet Wings "by the margin of a broken goalie stick."[14]

Writing for Canadian Press, Al Colletti noted, "The Islanders played their usual strong defensive game, but they were unable to generate much on offense, especially with their vaunted power play which did produce their lone goal by rookie Bryan Trottier."[15]

Unfortunately, the game was interrupted twice in the second period when political activists tossed objects onto the ice to protest the presence of the Soviet Wings. It nearly resulted in Wings coach Boris Kulagin pulling his team off the ice for their safety.

The culprits were allegedly linked to the same group, the Jewish Defense League, that tossed eggs onto the ice at Madison Square Garden on December 28 when Central Red Army was playing the New York Rangers. Unlike that incident, in this case it appeared the object-tossers were deliberately aiming their throws at Wings players. Kulagin warned the referee that a third such disruption would compel him to pull his team from the ice. Thankfully, it never came to that. After the second incident, an announcement was made over the PA system that the NHL was "embarrassed by the actions of a few individuals."[16] The announcement was loudly cheered by the majority of the 14,685 ticketholders and applauded by the players on both teams. After the game, Kulagin condemned the dangerous incidents as "acts of barbarians."[17] Kulagin insisted things such as that would never happen in the Soviet Union. He was pleased by the supportive reactions of the Islanders players and fans, however.

As for the fate of miscreants, Elizabeth Redly, a 22-year-old woman from Queens Village, was apprehended by arena security for throwing a bag containing red dye and marbles that just missed the head of a Wings player about four minutes into the second period. Two minutes later, three other suspects were apprehended for throwing smaller bags onto the ice. According to police, their names were Johnathan and Sharon Silver of Bayside and Jill Bedrick of Woodmere. Their ages were not given. Nassau County Police Department said charges would be laid against the foursome, although those specific charges were not immediately made public.

Islander coach Al Arbour was equally displeased by the object-tossers' hostile and dangerous actions. He said, "We are trying to create good relations with other countries through sports, but something like that certainly dampens the event."[18]

Billy Harris of the Islanders was nearly hit twice by the paint-bombers. He told Robin Herman, "I felt like jumping into the stands to get them. It bothered me, the fact that it takes away from a great game—and it was a great game."[19]

After the close game was in the win column for the visitors, Wings coach Boris Kulagin happily shared his observations about the entire series with reporters. He said to the media that he hoped that touring Soviet teams would continue to be an attraction at NHL rinks in future years—perhaps annually. Kulagin also informed the North American writers that, before leaving the Soviet Union, he told hockey writers in the Soviet Union that he thought his Wings club would split their four Super Series games versus NHL opposition. Stating the obvious, Kulagin added, "But, you know, the score of 3–1 is better than 2–2."[20]

The Wings' 2–1 triumph concluded their portion of the Soviet teams' NHL tour. Boris Kulagin deemed it to have been a success on many levels. He praised the NHL for promoting the tour in such a way that seven of the eight exhibition games played by the two Soviet clubs were sellouts.

When asked if the results proved that Soviet hockey was superior to the NHL brand, Kulagin was very diplomatic with his thoughtful answer.

"I decline to make such comparisons," he said to the reporters in the Wings' dressing room. "I have too much respect for those great hockey players you have in North America and for the NHL."

Kulagin exposited, "We did not duplicate the style of play of your players, but we tried to learn various things that are good in your hockey. I heard that the professionals also learned something from us. That sort of exchange of cooperation is very important. It does really matter. If we can learn from each other more, then it would contribute substantially to the development of hockey."[21]

Truer words were never spoken.

The Islanders managed to quickly put this narrow defeat to the Soviet Wings behind them and embark on an impressive ten-game undefeated streak that extended into the first week of February. Over that stretch, with six home contests and four on the road, the Islanders won seven games and tied three. Two of the wins were shutouts, one for Billy Smith and one for Chico Resch. The latter experienced no broken goalie sticks in any of the games.

Scoring Summary

Soviet Wings 0+2+0 = 2
New York Islanders 0+1+0 = 1

First period

No scoring

Second period

Soviet Wings: Shalimov (unassisted) 6:31 (sh)
New York Islanders: Trottier (Potvin, Gillies) 14:59 (pp)
Soviet Wings: Anisin (unassisted) 19:46

Third period

No Scoring

14

Game #8

Central Red Army
vs. Philadelphia Flyers

Sunday, January 11, 1976
The Philadelphia Spectrum

Lloyd Gilmour was not supposed to referee the Philadelphia Flyers–Central Red Army game on the afternoon of Sunday, January 11, 1976. It had originally been assigned to Bruce Hood. However, Hood suffered a broken jaw in a New York Rangers–St. Louis Blues game on January 6 when he violently collided with Chuck Lefley of St. Louis, five days before the climactic international clash at the Spectrum in Philadelphia. The NHL penciled in Lloyd Gilmour to take Hood's place. In a remarkable coincidence, Gilmour was from Penticton, British Columbia—the small town the 1955 IIHF champions proudly represented.

It was a huge disappointment for the 39-year-old Hood; he was eagerly anticipating being the chief official for the final and most anticipated game of Super Series '76. With his jaw wired shut, it was now impossible for him to blow his whistle. The desperate Hood even suggested he be allowed to ref the game using an old-fashioned cowbell—which went out of style at just about every level of hockey in the 1930s. There was no way around it: Hood would not be at the Philadelphia Spectrum on January 11; Lloyd Gilmour would instead be the man wearing the striped shirt with the red armbands. It would be the game for which Gilmour would be most remembered. When he died just short of his 83rd birthday in 2010, the Flyers–Red Army game was mentioned in virtually every one of Gilmour's obituaries.

Like many NHL officials, the 48-year-old Gilmour had hoped to make the NHL as a player. He was a young prospect in the New York Rangers' organization before a logging injury at age 19 ended his playing career. Wanting to stay involved in hockey, Gilmour turned to officiating. He was good at it, advancing swiftly through the amateur and low professional ranks. Gilmour spent 19 years as an NHL official before retiring in 1976. *Sports Illustrated* once appraised his performance as a referee by noting, "The 42-year-old Gilmour is the NHL's best official because he is virtually an invisible man on the ice."[1] However, there were those in the NHL fraternity who believed Gilmour was overly lenient in his handling of games. Compared to Hood's somewhat intrusive style of calling marginal penalties to keep games from getting too chippy, there were questions about whether Gilmour, despite his lofty status as perhaps the NHL's best on-ice official, might be a bad choice as Hood's replacement for the Red Army–Flyers tilt on January 11. One concerned and unnamed NHL insider told Al Strachan of the *Montréal Gazette* that Gilmour "will probably start World War Three."[2] Prior to the Red Army–Flyers game, Gilmour's most famous NHL assignment had come less than a year before. It was a surreal Stanley Cup finals game, played in foggy conditions because unseasonable May heat clashed with the ice surface in the aging Buffalo Memorial Auditorium which had no air conditioning.

Of the four NHL clubs that would face Central Red Army, the Philadelphia Flyers had the briefest history by far. While New York, Boston and Montréal all had at least half a century of top-level hockey behind them, the 1975–76 season was just the Flyers' ninth. They were easily the most successful of the six hopeful outfits that had joined the NHL brotherhood in 1967. Albeit a short one, the Philadelphia Flyers had a very interesting history.

"In any great drama, you need heroes and villains. The Flyers were both."[3] That is the opening line of a 58-minute documentary titled *The Broad Street Bullies*—the apt nickname acquired by the Philadelphia Flyers of the mid–1970s, a club that ascended to the top of the NHL by both fair means and foul. It was mostly foul, the fans of the other NHL teams in 1975 would have said had they been polled about Fred Shero's aggressive bunch. "They were despicable—a disgrace to hockey,"[4] bluntly declared Howie Meeker of *Hockey Night in Canada*, a frequent and outspoken critic of the Flyers' brand of play.

The Flyers were slow to evolve into a team of rowdy, belligerent, tough customers. They were one of the six expansion teams that entered the NHL in 1967–68 when the league aggressively doubled in size from six to 12 teams. For their first two NHL seasons, they were mostly a finesse club. However, in both those years, they were ousted from the Stanley Cup playoffs by a much more physical St. Louis Blues team that featured terrorizing players such as Noel Picard and the Plager brothers, Bob and Barclay. In one infamous incident during the 1968 playoffs, Philadelphia's speedy Claude Laforge, who was 31 years old, 5'8" tall, and weighed just 160 pounds, was coldcocked from behind by Picard during a bench-clearing

14. Game #8

skirmish, separating him from his senses and a few teeth. Laforge also suffered a damaged eye socket. He was generally a bloody mess. Laforge's only crime was being the closest player to Picard when the mayhem began. Laforge was out of the Flyers' lineup for the rest of the quarterfinal series—which Philadelphia lost to St. Louis in seven games—and only played two more NHL games after receiving Picard's vicious and unprovoked wallop. According to Flyers lore, owner Ed Snider witnessed what had happened to Laforge and vowed that no Flyer would ever be manhandled in such a manner again. Acquiring large, physical players who could take care of themselves against the meanest and toughest of the NHL's pugilists was henceforth going to be a top priority in Philadelphia. Thus, the likes of Don Saleski, André Dupont and, most noteworthy of all, Dave Schultz were each drafted by the Flyers.

Teammate Bill Clement accurately called Dave Schultz "the baddest animal in the hockey jungle."[5] In retrospect, it is difficult to fathom that Schultz seldom had a hockey fight until he played professionally. "I was a goal-scorer, believe it or not, before the Flyers sent me to the Eastern Hockey League after training camp," Schultz recalled decades later in the documentary film *The Broad Street Bullies*. "I got into a fight in my first game. I got into a fight in my second game—and, all of a sudden, I was Sergeant Schultz. What was I to do except to come to Philadelphia and continue my ways? I became this guy who fought like crazy."[6] Indeed, after he had totaled more than 1,100 penalty minutes in three seasons in the minor leagues, the NHL was about to experience the fearsome presence of Dave (The Hammer) Schultz.

Schultz and his heavy fists conducted a personal reign of terror on the rest of the NHL, beating up those players who used to regularly beat up the Flyers, setting new NHL records for fights and penalty minutes along the way. Philadelphia's fortunes began to swiftly turn around. Owner Ed Snider figured if one enforcer was working well, why not employ several? Accordingly, Bob (Battleship) Kelly joined the team. He enjoyed the mayhem. One of Kelly's other nicknames was Machine Gun for the rapid way he delivered punches on his foes. Kelly explained his philosophy of hockey this way: "I always had lots of energy and I liked to expend it. There's nothing like driving somebody's head through the boards to make you feel good."[7]

Stu Hackel, a onetime director of broadcasting for the NHL, explained what had set the Flyers of the mid–1970s apart from any other team in the league's history. He said,

> The game had been played a long time with fighting as a major element of the game. It never really was thought of as anything unusual. But things were different for the Flyers. What the Flyers did, that no other team had previously

done, was win through intimidation. They really made fighting a tactic. People knew right away that this was something different.[8]

It succeeded. Midway through the 1972–73 season, with fights a routine part of each Philadelphia game, the Flyers were dubbed the Broad Street Bullies by local media. (Jack Chevalier of the *Philadelphia Daily News* is credited with creating the term.) It was a well-deserved moniker. They accrued 600 more penalty minutes than the second-most penalized NHL club. It was all part of the plan, though. The Flyers went from missing the Stanley Cup playoffs in 1971–72 to winning the Stanley Cup two springs later against the favored Boston Bruins. (One telling moment from the Flyers' victory over the New York Rangers in the 1974 semifinals was Schultz's extended pummeling of pacifist Ranger Dale Rolfe without one teammate coming to Rolfe's aid. That fear spoke volumes about both the Flyers and the Rangers.) Philadelphia then repeated their triumph the following season by beating the Buffalo Sabres in the Cup finals. (It is perhaps noteworthy that he 1974–75 Flyers were the last Stanley Cup championship outfit to feature an all–Canadian roster.) The team's transition from pushovers to aggressors was complete. Goon hockey clearly had its rewards in the mid–1970s.

It was also beneficial inside the Philadelphia Spectrum at the turnstiles. Flyer captain Bobby Clarke bluntly told *Sports Illustrated* in 1975, "Let's face it: More people come out to see Dave Schultz than Bobby Orr. It's a reflection of our society. People want to see violence."[9] In that same damning *SI* article, NHL president Clarence Campbell said he was not totally opposed to the violence in his sport, but he pensively noted, "I sometimes wonder when I see the Russian and Olympic teams with their emphasis on teamwork, finesse and passing, why it is necessary to get into needless fights."[10]

Of course, Philadelphia had the offensive talent to produce wins. That was still a requirement for success in the NHL in the 1970s regardless of the peripheral mayhem. Bobby Clarke, Reg Leach, Rick MacLeish and Bill Barber were all terrific players, but they were largely permitted to operate without opponents' harassment because of the Flyers' numerous enforcers who throttled anyone who dared touch the team's scoring stars, or practically anyone else on the ice wearing Flyer colors.

Philadelphia also had an excellent goaltender, Bernie Parent, a former Boston Bruin, who was the Flyers' first pick in that 1967 NHL expansion draft. Parent was traded to Toronto in 1971. He jumped to the Philadelphia Blazers of the WHA in 1972 and then rejoined the Flyers in 1973–74. That season, Parent played in all but five of the Flyers' 78 games—an incomprehensible feat by today's NHL standards for teams frequently resting goaltenders. Leaving Parent unprotected back in 1967 was a decision the Bruins would rue in 1974, as it was Boston who lost to Philadelphia in the Stanley Cup finals. Parent won the Conn Smythe Trophy as the MVP of that spring's playoffs.

With Central Red Army having two wins and a draw in their three previous contests in Super Series '76, their final game symbolically took on a whole new meaning. This would not be just an exhibition game at the Spectrum. Philadelphia coach Fred (The Fog) Shero had been planning for the game all season. "If we win, I'm going to be sky high. If we lose, it will be worse than dying,"[11] he famously said in a brief introductory snippet leading off the *Hockey Night in Canada* telecast that afternoon. One could tell by the look on Shero's face and the tone of his voice that he definitely was not kidding.

The 49-year-old Shero, the introverted, scholarly son of Russian immigrants, had done his homework well. He figured he had read Anatoli Tarasov's book on Soviet hockey philosophy, *The Road to Olympus*, a hundred times at least. During Shero's trips abroad, he studied the Soviet style of hockey in depth, even traveling to the Soviet Union prior to the 1974–75 NHL season to attend a coaching seminar hosted by the Soviet Ice Hockey Federation. Of about 40 North American hockey coaches who opted to attend the event, Shero was the only NHL coach among them. There Shero met Anatoli Tarasov, listened to long, technical lectures about what tactics made the Soviet teams successful, and cultivated an unlikely friendship with the foremost hockey authority in the USSR. Fully realizing that the Soviets had made some worthwhile innovations to the sport, Shero readily implemented some of their style and drills into his own system, altering them ever so slightly to better fit his club. For example, the Flyer forwards were told never to turn their backs to the puck. To avoid costly turnovers, blind centering passes in the offensive zone were forbidden, as were long diagonal passes in the defensive zone. Of course, Philadelphia hockey doctrine preferred bodily contact to relieve opponents of the puck—a lot of it—while the Soviet style of the sport emphasized sweep checks.

After the Central Red Army–Boston game on January 8, Brad Park was asked if he thought the Flyers played hockey like Soviet teams do. "Yes and no," the Boston defenseman replied. "Philadelphia does some of the same things, but the Russians don't run around hammering people like the Flyers do."[12] One Soviet tactic that Shero did employ was a rotating box of defenders when killing a penalty instead of having his players basically stay almost stationary in one position. "Nobody else in the NHL does that,"[13] Shero commented.

Armed with this knowledge of Soviet hockey, Shero devised a game plan specially designed to thwart Central Red Army on January 11. He concluded that the Soviet style of hockey involved making excessive passes often to spots where a player had just vacated. Shero cleverly instructed the Flyers not to futilely chase the puck, but rather to hold their positions. "Why chase them?"[14] he later told Mark Mulvoy of *Sports Illustrated*. While in the offensive zone, the Flyer forwards were to hold onto the puck as much as possible. They were not to take hopeless long shots at Vladislav Tretiak or make any risky passes or lose possession of the puck too easily. This was all done to avoid the Soviets' often deadly and demoralizing counterattacks that had frequently gotten them goals seemingly out of nowhere in their games versus New York, Boston and Montréal. The Flyers were also going to clog their own blue line to prevent Central Red Army from having easy access to their defensive zone. Bobby Clarke later explained, "You can have the puck between the blue lines all night long, but it won't do you any good if you can't get in."[15]

With no other team being able to defeat the best Soviet club in three attempts, the finale of Super Series '76 took on greater importance in the minds of many NHL fans and the hockey writers who covered the league. John Powers of the *Boston Globe* wrote after the Bruins' loss on January 8, "You and I may think of all this as just a bit of mid-winter athletic détente. But if Loktev and his boys beat Philly at the Spectrum on Sunday, they [Central Red Army] will essentially have won the Stanley Cup."[16] Indeed, the two touring Soviet teams had yet to lose to a current NHL division leader. Boston and Chicago had both lost. The vaunted Montréal Canadiens had at least managed to secure a tie. For likely the only time in history, the vast majority of NHL fans were rooting for the Stanley Cup champion Philadelphia Flyers—easily the most hated team in the league—to beat the Soviets by any means necessary to salvage some pride in the elite level of North American professional hockey. Even Clarence Campbell, who was no fan of the Flyers' roughhousing, made a special visit to their dressing room before the puck was dropped on January 11 to remind them, quite unnecessarily, that they were responsible for upholding the prestige of the National Hockey League.

"It was Us against Them,"[17] recalled Rod Smith of the Sports Network in Canada on the 40th anniversary of the game in 2016. It had come down to a hive mentality among hockey fans in the United States and Canada. It was highly out of the ordinary that the entire NHL depended upon the circuit's detested champs, the terrifying Philadelphia Flyers, to restore the league's dignity. It mattered little that on any other day of the season, fans of the other 17 NHL clubs likened the Flyers as something akin to wild beasts. Fred Shero's team was generally despised by every other team in the NHL because they had found a way to turn goon hockey into a highly successful artform. It had turned them into winners—feared winners.

"The Flyers were at the height of their reign as the 'Broad Street Bullies.' [They] had battled all comers with their elbows, sticks and fists in winning back-to-back Stanley Cups,"[18] wrote Brad Kurtzberg in a 2104 retrospective piece about the famous game.

The irony of the Flyers now becoming the standard-bearers for the NHL was not lost on Shero. "All year long people keep telling us that we're bad for hockey, bad for the NHL, and bad for Canada because we're too rough," Shero said before the highly anticipated showdown. "Now we're supposed to save the game for the NHL, for Canada, for everyone. Hah! For the first time, we're the good guys."[19]

Similarly, Joe Watson recalled the last regular-season game Philadelphia played before their matchup with Central Red Army. "We were in Toronto for our last road game before we came back to play the Soviets," he said. "Remember, the fans in Toronto hated us. We won that game [7–3], and we got our usual reception from the crowd. But as we left, those same fans were cheering for us to beat the Russians."[20]

Based on his experience in Moscow in 1972, Flyer captain Bobby Clarke may have uttered the most amusing quip of the series. He joked before the game, "They [the Soviets] are always trying to play with our minds," he told a reporter. "But that won't work with our club. We've got 20 guys with no brains."[21]

The NHL hosted a social event for both teams the evening before the game. Not much socializing occurred. Writing about the awkward pregame party nearly 40 years later, John Kreiser of the *Philadelphia Inquirer* noted, "The get-together was chillier than the coldest Philadelphia winter." Red Army coach Konstatin Loktev and Fred Shero shook hands without speaking or even making eye contact. The players did not mingle at all. "They stared at us, and we looked right back at them,"[22] Bill Barber said years later. "They didn't like us. We didn't like them. We were ready for a war."[23] Likewise, Bobby Clarke pulled no punches. "I hate the SOBs,"[24] he bluntly told *Sports Illustrated*. Flyers owner Ed Snider had memorized a few polite Russian phrases for an after-dinner speech, but seeing the tension and dislike etched onto the players' faces at the banquet, he could not bring himself to wish good luck to the Soviets, even insincerely. Vladislav Tretiak said in his 1987 autobiography that the Flyers' unwavering coldness surprised everyone on the Red Army team, considering how friendly and accommodating the Montréal Canadiens and Boston Bruins had both been to them in their earlier tour stops.

Hockey Night in Canada was there, of course, to broadcast the Sunday afternoon game to an eager and huge TV audience north of the border. Bob Cole would call the play-by-play with the steady and stately Dick Irvin alongside as an analyst. Denis Potvin, the terrific 22-year-old New York

Islanders defenseman, also had a place in the *HNIC* broadcast booth as a special guest announcer. He had been rushed from Long Island to Philadelphia after his team had narrowly lost to the Soviet Wings, 2-1, the night before in the penultimate game of Super Series '76.

The Spectrum had been sold out well in advance, naturally. However, the Soviet Union's best hockey team was not welcomed by all Philadelphians. Hundreds of protesters picketed the venue, demanding that Soviet Jews be allowed to immigrate to Israel. Upon entering the arena, Soviet team officials were appalled to see perhaps four dozen politically charged, anti-communist banners, printed in Russian, hanging from the Spectrum's rafters—which would have been clearly visible to the enormous television audience in the Soviet Union, projected to be about 100 million people. Another 100 million people elsewhere in Europe and North America were expected to watch. In accordance with international sports protocols, Ed Snider—who had initially okayed the banner to appease Jewish activists in Philadelphia—reluctantly ordered the banners be removed and impounded by Spectrum ushers before the puck was dropped. However, Philadelphia's famous Sign Man, a 27-year-old teacher and season-ticket holder from New Jersey named Dave Leonardi who brought his own elaborate hand-held sign collection to every Flyer home game, could not be stopped from doing his thing. Leonardi sat in a second-row seat with a case stocked with 100 premade, pithy and thoroughly amusing written comments, each one 19 inches wide and 22 inches long. The Flyers certainly did not want him to cease his schtick. It was as much a part of a Philadelphia Flyers home game as a spirited donnybrook.

Not taking any chances, Philadelphia opted to play Kate Smith's famous version of "God Bless America" prior to the opening faceoff instead of "The Star-Spangled Banner" as the Smith song was a well-established, good-luck talisman for the club. That too was technically a violation of international sports protocols to play any song other than a country's national anthem, but nobody—especially anyone pulling for the Flyers—was going to object. And by the time the song was over, what could be done about it?

The Flyers faced two disadvantages on January 11. First, all-star goaltender Bernie Parent was unable to play due to an unusual injury—a pinched nerve in his neck. Parent had not played a single game for Philadelphia so far in 1975–76. He was scheduled to make his seasonal debut against the Kansas City Scouts on New Year's Day in Missouri, but Parent woke up that day still in great pain. His awaited return to the Philly net was indefinitely postponed. "The doctors keep telling me I'll be all right, but they don't say when," the frustrated goalie told the Associated Press. "It feels like a knife in my shoulder whenever I move."[25]

14. Game #8

For the Super Series game, Parent was replaced by Wayne Stephenson, the team's capable second-string netminder who was now the number-one man given Parent's lengthy absence. (In the January 17 issue of *The Sporting News*, hockey journalist Stan Fischler generously rated Stephenson as Bernie Parent's equal as an NHL goalie, if not better.) The 30-year-old Stephenson was perhaps more suited to the task than Parent would have been. For three frustrating years Stephenson was a member of the Canadian Nationals amateur team that only rarely beat the Soviets in international play during the 1960s. As it turned out, the Philadelphia goaltender would be almost a non-factor in the game. One scribe joked that Stephenson spent most of the game watching, from a distance, Vladislav Tretiak perform acrobatics.

The second problem the home team faced was that its roster had very little experience facing any Soviet opposition. There was Stephenson, of course, but only Flyer captain Bobby Clarke had been on either one of the Team Canada squads. (Clarke had famously rendered Valeri Kharlamov useless in 1972 with a timely slash. Word had trickled down to the Flyers that the Soviets were allegedly out for revenge.) Shero allowed Clarke to speak to the rest of the team at length and give them pointers from his experience in September 1972. Shero would say later, "Clarke told our guys that they would need patience. The Russians would hold the puck, even for a [whole] minute. He told them to stay where they were supposed to be and to not run around."[26]

Midway through the first period, the Flyers held a huge 12–1 advantage in shots and had successfully killed off a pair of minor penalties. Typically, the superb play of Central Red Army goaltender Vladislav Tretiak was solely keeping the visitors in the game.

Writing for the *New York Times*, Roger Kahn recalled how the game began. He penned,

> The Soviets began with a razzle-dazzle Icecapadeski in their own zone, which the Flyers ignored. Then, as they tried to move, the Flyers, notably Terry Crisp, forechecked beautifully. Up ice, the Flyer defensemen took their customary inhospitable view of rival forwards. The Soviets could control neither the puck nor the flow of the game. They had got off two shots to the Flyers' 12, when Ed Van Impe dumped Valeri Kharlamov.[27]

Then came a remarkable sequence of events that would be talked about forever among hockey fans who saw it live or on television—and new generations who have viewed it on YouTube. The Soviets, over the course of about 45 seconds, were subjected to what the 17 other NHL teams had faced when facing the reigning Stanley Cup champions during the past two seasons.

First, while the Soviets were on a power play with Ed Van Impe in the penalty box, André (Moose) Dupont halted Alexander Gusev at the Philadelphia blue line with a solid bodycheck that was unquestionably legal in any era of hockey. Ten seconds later Bill Barber rammed into Valeri Vasiliev in the corner to the right of Tretiak. (Today Barber might be called for hitting an opponent from behind into the boards, but there was no such rule on the books in the NHL in 1976—and the Soviets had agreed to abide by NHL rules on this tour.) About eight seconds after that, Barber struck again, driving Valeri Kharlamov into the boards with a bit of a crosscheck. Kharlamov hit the deck and looked to be a bit groggy. Again, in 1976 pro hockey, it was a trifling incident, not often whistled by an NHL referee. Fifteen seconds later, the *coupe de grace* was applied by Philadelphia. Boris Mikhailov carried the puck over the Flyers' blue line just as Ed Van Impe came out of the home team's penalty box. Mikhailov passed the puck to Kharlamov who was utterly oblivious to the check he was about to receive. Van Impe, who would later categorize it as "a sucker pass," steamrolled the Soviet star wearing #17. Down went Kharlamov with his face to the ice. He was in no hurry whatsoever to get back onto his feet.

"It was perfectly legal," Van Impe noted after the game. "There was no reason why he should have stayed down; it was an act."[28] Years later, Van Impe amended his opinion slightly by saying that Kharlamov may have accidentally run into his elbow.

On both the local Flyers broadcast and the *Hockey Night in Canada* telecast, nobody holding a microphone saw anything too egregious about Van Impe's check on Kharlamov or the other three hits dished out by the Broad Street Bullies that preceded it. Every announcer and analyst opined that the body contact initiated by Van Impe was perfectly legal based on 1976 NHL norms. (In 2023 it would likely have been whistled for perhaps a high stick, an elbow or a head check—but not in the heyday of the Broad Street Bullies.) When Philadelphia gained control of the puck, referee Lloyd Gilmour stopped play with 8:39 left in the first period because of the apparent serious injury suffered by Central Red Army's most potent scorer.

Years later Van Impe recalled his famous check on Kharlamov,

> My penalty expired. I came back [onto the ice]. I could see the play developing in the corner. It was a pass that had to go through a defenseman. Kharlamov has his head down and he picked [the puck] up. I timed it. As soon as he touched the puck, I was right there. He didn't see me. I was right on top of him. We collided. I really don't think it was that hard a bodycheck. I'd been hit harder in league play.[29]

Van Impe also correctly pointed out to the media after the game that he thought Valeri Vasiliev had hit Bobby Clarke earlier in the first period at least as hard, but Clarke admirably rose to his feet on his own power and continued his shift.

As Kharlamov writhed face down on the ice, his teammate, Boris Mikhailov, violently banged his stick on the ice, disputing the non-call by Gilmour. On the WPIX broadcast of the game, Marv Albert openly wondered how hurt Kharlamov truly was, citing the "swan movement" that Mikhailov had performed in Boston Garden versus the Bruins three days earlier. "Those guys are actors," Philadelphia's André Dupont insisted in a postgame interview. "I think [Kharlamov] was playing Hamlet or something the way he went down."[30]

"It was no place for the squeamish," wrote Robert Fachet of the *Washington Post*, "and the Soviets decided it was no place for them."[31]

Jim Coleman of the *Calgary Herald* fully believed that the fellow wearing #17 for Central Red Army was working on his thespian skills, too. The reporter sarcastically penned, "Kharlamov won another Academy Award as he swooned to the ice and lay there obviously in extreme distress. When the Soviet trainer had carefully re-inflated Valeri with a bicycle pump, the Soviet delegation withdrew...."[32]

Kharlamov was sprawled on the Spectrum ice for about a minute. Teammates helped him to the visitors' bench. Kharlamov healed swiftly and was ready for play when the game resumed—which would not be for a while.

Numerous insulting gestures came from the Red Army bench. They were all directed toward referee Lloyd Gilmour who was utterly unmoved by the Soviets' complaints. When it was apparent that no penalty was forthcoming to the Flyers for their boisterous checks, coach Konstantin Loktev signaled for the Soviets on the ice—including Tretiak—to come to the bench to ponder their options. NHL linesman Matt Pavelich fortunately spoke fluent Russian, so he acted as Gilmour's translator. (Yuri Karandin, a Soviet, was the other linesman that afternoon. His English was weak.) The visitors were instructed to get back on the ice and resume the game promptly. They did not. Gilmour refused to cave in. He handed the Soviets a two-minute bench penalty for delay of game—a gutsy thing to do under the tense circumstances. When the penalty was announced, the Central Red Army team headed to their dressing room in a huff, and took all their equipment with them. A little bit more than 11 minutes of Flyer hockey had been enough to irreparably spoil their pleasant Sunday afternoon in Pennsylvania. Jim Coleman of the *Calgary Herald* said the visitors' walkout was "shades of Andrei Gromyko at the United Nations." Coleman noted that "Spectrum spectators showered [the departing Soviets] with quaint vocal maledictions."[33]

"They're going home! They're going home! Yeah ... they're going home!"[34] Bob Cole told several million *Hockey Night in Canada* viewers in what may have been his most famous call in a long and distinguished broadcasting career.

"Can you imagine?" asked Dick Irvin rhetorically. "Denis, it's been a short afternoon," Irvin said to Denis Potvin who was sitting beside him.[35] The Islanders star defenseman added that he too believed Van Impe's check was within the rules of the game, "I thought they'd have more pride than that,"[36] Potvin disapprovingly said of the visitors' apparent decision to call it quits halfway through the first period.

Amidst the chaos, Cole appropriately reminisced, "In '72, in Moscow we stayed and we took it all ... and in '74 there was always something with the officials. We always let the Soviets get their way."[37]

"They [the Soviets] just got frustrated, that's why they walked off the ice,"[38] Fred Shero recalled years later, claiming Central Red Army could not figure out a way to beat his version of a neutral zone defensive trap that was 20 years ahead of its time in the NHL.

Jim Coleman absolutely agreed with Shero's assessment of the Red Army's sudden walkout. "Personally," the western Canadian scribe wrote, "I believe [it] was the direct result of frustration. I never thought I'd see the day when an individual NHL team could check Red Army so thoroughly that the Russians would be forced out of their game plan. But the Philadelphia Flyers thoroughly spooked the Russians yesterday afternoon...."[39]

Central Red Army had some allies in the North American media. One was Stan Fischler, who thought the Flyers' style of play was reprehensible. Fischler wrote in the February 7 issue of *The Sporting News*, "[Philadelphia] demonstrated to the Russians that intimidation of the most blatant variety was required and was their prime order of business in a game refereed by Lloyd Gilmour as if his whistle had a bad case of frostbite."[40]

Central Red Army coach Loktev said after the game that he withdrew his team from the ice because "we just don't want to play this way. I didn't question the judgement of the referee on any particular call. We didn't like to play such hockey. We didn't want to damage our players. The [1976 Winter] Olympics are coming up."[41]

At the time of the walkout, referee Gilmour had issued five minor penalties in 11½ minutes. Three of them went to the home team.

Years later, Loktev later explained his decision. "I decided to stop this game," he said, "to show the North Americans this is not hockey. I understand my decision to do this was a very serious one.... But I didn't want to have the first line injured."[42]

Longtime Flyers announcer Gene Hart told his audience that he did not want to get political, but he had to say the Soviets leaving the ice reflected badly on their country. Marv Albert was stunned by what he was

14. Game #8

seeing—a team quitting in the middle of a major hockey game. "This is incredible ... unprecedented,"[43] he claimed. Actually, it was not. Flyers owner Ed Snider remembered,

> We found out later, after doing some research, that the Russians had walked off the ice at all levels of international competition, from time to time, and had gotten their way. They felt Ed Van Impe ought to be penalized for what was a marginal, possible penalty. They wanted to establish a certain intimidation of the official so that he would call absolutely everything in a hard-hitting game. They weren't used to that and they wanted no part of it.[44]

In fact, the most notable walkout in Soviet hockey history did not occur in an international game, but in a famous match in the Soviet Elite League in 1969 between Central Red Army and Moscow Spartak. The game would decide which club would capture that season's league championship.

Prior to 1977, IIHF rules dictated that the third period of games must be split into two 10-minute halves so that each team's goaltender spent 30 minutes guarding each goal. (It was an antiquated rule, harkening back to when many games in Europe were played outdoors and ice conditions often varied from one end of the rink to another.) It caused chaos on this day. Before an estimated television viewing audience of 100 million people in the Soviet Union, famed coach Anatoli Tarasov, in a fit of unbridled anger, pulled his Central Red Army Club off the ice when an apparent game-tying goal by Central Red Army's Vladimir Petrov was waved off by the referee. The official ruled that time had expired even though the arena's clock showed one second remaining before the break in the third period. The timekeeper agreed that the game clock in the arena was unofficial and his watch—which showed 10 minutes had expired—was accurate. Tarasov was not buying it. Such staunch defiance of authority in the Soviet Union was almost unprecedented. It certainly made for compelling television— but individual acts of moxie were not what the Soviet government wanted shown to the populace. The fuming Tarasov kept his Red Army club in the dressing room for about 30 minutes until he received a personal note from Soviet leader Leonid Brezhnev, who was in attendance at the game, politely advising him to get his players back onto the ice. The "or else" was tacitly understood. Tarasov acquiesced. Spartak scored an insurance goal and won the game, 3–1. Tarasov was excoriated by the state-run press for his stunt. He had to wonder if his days in charge of Soviet hockey were suddenly numbered. Indeed, a few days later, Tarasov was stripped of his title as a "merited coach" in the Soviet Union. However, it was quietly restored in time for Tarasov to again lead the Soviets to a 9–1 record and a gold-medal finish at the 1970 IIHF world championship tournament in Stockholm, Sweden.

Thus, Central Red Army's walkout in Philadelphia clearly was not unprecedented as Marv Albert claimed, but it certainly was unusual, at least in North America. The Flyers did not know quite what to do with themselves now that the Central Red Army team was suddenly absent. The home team's trainer helpfully dumped a bucketful of pucks on the ice so the home team could have a midgame warmup and stay loose during the delay. Referee Gilmour and his linesman skated lap after lap for the same reason. All the while, Shero stood emotionless behind the home team's bench. Shero later told Jack Dulmage of the *Windsor Star* that he was afraid that the Soviets would not continue the game ... then what? Philadelphia's omnipresent Sign Man kept busy during the interim. One of his creations simply said CHICKEN. Another amusingly stated TELL IT TO THE CZAR. A third one suggested the Flyers needed new worlds to conquer. It proclaimed BRING ON THE MARTIANS.

There was an impasse, but Alan Eagleson, Ed Snider and Clarence Campbell all headed to the Soviet dressing room and arrived there almost simultaneously. Reporters were not allowed near the peace talks. Businessman Snider got to the crux of the matter. He asked Campbell, the NHL's president, if the Soviet Ice Hockey Federation had been paid their $200,000 for the eight-game tour. Campbell said no, not yet. The solution was now obvious. Through an interpreter, Eagleson calmly informed the Soviets that they did not have to play the rest of the game; they could immediately go back home if they wished to do so—but if that was their choice, they would forfeit their $200,000 payment for not living up to the agreement they had signed. That quick lesson in American contract law did the trick. Money talked. Clarence Campbell always denied that the threat of withholding the Soviet's payment ever came up, but several reporters mentioned it in their stories the next day. Ed Snider said years later that he at least had mentioned the threat of making the Soviets accountable for the refunds his club would have had to give to the sellout crowd. That sum would have been considerably more than the $25,000 the visitors were being paid for this one game.

Be that as it may, after an absence of about 14, 16, 17 or 18 minutes (depending upon which newspaper one read the next day), the Central Red Army hockey club and its coaching staff grudgingly returned to the visitors' bench to a loud chorus of boos. The frenzied Flyer fans mockingly waved white handkerchiefs at the Soviet players, boisterously sang another impromptu version of "God Bless America," then followed it with an enthusiastic, old-time American football chant: "Hit 'em again! Hit 'em again! Harder! Harder!"

Hockey writer Frank Dolson humorously observed, "...And to think there are people who insist that sport is the surest road to international understanding and goodwill."[45]

14. Game #8

Jack Dulmage of the *Windsor Star* wrote, "The often-maligned bully boy Flyers did not destroy USA–Russian détente, but they had a full-blown international incident, anyway. If it doesn't knock Angola off the front pages of Moscow newspapers today, nothing will."[46]

Officially, the Soviets returned to continue the game because of "common sense,"[47] according to a statement issued by Bryan O'Neill, the NHL's executive director. The matter of potentially withholding the Soviets' money for not completing the tour was not officially mentioned. Flyers assistant coach Mike Nykoluk said he heard the Soviets complain that they "had not come to Philadelphia for a boxing match."[48] This comment was later confirmed by O'Neill and repeated by Dick Irvin on the *HNIC* telecast. "[It is] a very, very dicey moment on the international hockey scene,"[49] Irvin accurately stated.

Later, Clarence Campbell was asked by a curious reporter if the game would have been forfeited to the Flyers had Loktev's team not returned to the ice. Campbell, for some reason, thought the question was patently silly. He tersely replied, "I have no comment on such a hypothetical question."[50] Campbell later claimed he had said to the visitors, through an interpreter, that this was no way to terminate the series, "It's never justified for any team to leave the ice."[51]

The game resumed with the Soviets shorthanded because the delay-of-game penalty they had been assessed by referee Gilmour would be enforced. A mere 17 seconds into the Flyer power play, Philadelphia's Reggie Leach subtly deflected a long shot by Bill Barber past Tretiak to put the home team up, 1–0. The Spectrum exploded with cheers. Before the period was over, Rick MacLeish scored on a breakaway, doubling the Flyers' lead to 2–0. That was the way the first 20 minutes ended. Philadelphia had outshot Central Red Army by a wide margin in the opening period: 17–2.

Between periods, Bobby Clarke was interviewed outside the dressing room by Brian McFarland of *Hockey Night in Canada*. Clarke said that the Flyers had been mentally prepared by their coach to anticipate some sort of oddball incident—such as a walkout—as part of the Soviets' psychological games. He confirmed that he had indeed called the Soviets SOBs and he was not going to retract the insult, although he modified it somewhat to say the remark was directed at the Soviet Union's hockey officials rather than the players themselves. As an example, Clarke mentioned that the Central Red Army club had declined to accept gifts of new hockey sticks from the Flyers—which was news to many reporters covering Super Series '76. When McFarlane commented that it must be quite a bit different preparing for a game with touring Soviet teams than for games with the Boston Bruins or Montréal Canadiens, Clarke stated, "Those other teams have a bit of class; the Russians don't."[52] Fans of the Bruins and Canadiens surely did double-takes upon hearing those complimentary words spoken by the captain of the Philadelphia Flyers.

The Flyers continued to shut down the Soviets in the second period. Defenseman Joe Watson got a third goal for Philadelphia at 2:44 when he backhanded a Don Saleski rebound past Tretiak. Watson was an unlikely offensive hero, having gone goal-less in his previous 35 games. It was a tally Watson notched while the Flyers had André Dupont in the penalty box—making it the first shorthanded goal Watson had ever scored. (He would play 919 games in the NHL and never score another.) Afterward Shero joked that Watson's unexpected goal had set back Soviet hockey 25 years.

Philadelphia did a masterful job killing penalties. Four times Lloyd Gilmour called them for minor penalties between the 7:00 mark of the first period and 3:08 of the second. In those eight minutes playing shorthanded, Central Red Army did not manage to get a single shot on Wayne Stephenson, despite Valeri Kharlamov, Boris Mikhailov and Alexander Maltsev being on the ice for most of that power-play time.

Central Red Army managed to get one goal back, however. It came at 10:38 of the middle period, when Viktor Kutyergin scored against the otherwise unbeatable Flyer goaltender. It was slightly fluky in nature. Joe Watson later confirmed to reporters that the puck had deflected off his skate past the Philly netminder. After 40 minutes, Philadelphia was ahead, 3–1 and was clearly the better of the two teams.

There was no letup by Philadelphia in the final period. Another Flyer defenseman, rookie Larry Goodenough, notched the Flyers' fourth goal at 4:01. Over the final 16 minutes of play, the Flyers continued to play smart hockey. In a 2015 article, Philadelphia sports journalist John Kreiser recalled, "For the remaining 15:59, the Flyers put on a textbook show of smart, physical hockey. The slick Soviet-style focused on the quality of shots, not the quantity, but it's tough for any team to win when it's outshot 49–13."[53]

When the final minute of the game approached, Bob Cole told the *HNIC* audience, "I think it's fair to say that almost all of Canada was behind the Flyers from coast to coast."[54] Some fans at the Spectrum started to gleefully chant, "We're number one!"

The walkout and other peripheral distractions were what many people were discussing. However, the Associated Press report on the game got to its core. It said, "Before anyone forgets, the Philadelphia Flyers, champions of the National Hockey League, buried the Soviet Central Red Army team, champions of the Soviet Union, 4–1, in a game which the Russians cried 'uncle.' It wasn't Uncle Sam."[55]

Philadelphia's Rick MacLeish, who scored the game-winning goal for the Flyers, called the Red Army walkout "poor sportsmanship." André Dupont said of the defeated Soviets, "They looked like amateurs. They're not so great. They looked like fools today."[56]

"The brawlers were just too much for the slickers,"[57] opined an unnamed correspondent from the Associated Press. More than a decade later, Vladislav Tretiak confirmed that the Flyers' physical brand of hockey had utterly intimated Central Red Army to the point that they were merely skating rather than playing competitive hockey over the last 2½ periods at the Spectrum.

Mike Avenenti, covering Super Series '76 for United Press International, saw it that way too. He wrote, "The Soviets found the Philadelphia Flyers' home ice colder than their hometown of Moscow on Sunday. For the better part of two periods, the Soviets circled in a figure-eight at their blue line waiting to spring a man and begin their rush. But Bobby Clarke, Rick MacLeish and Bill Barber constantly broke up the eight with their forechecking."[58]

Avenenti's knowledge of international hockey was poor, however. In his report, he wrongly referred to Vladislav Tretiak as "a brilliant young rookie."[59] While the two adjectives were accurate, Tretiak was hardly a novice goaltender. Tretiak, who was 23 years old when he faced the Flyers, had been affiliated with the Central Red Army club since the age of 15 and had won multiple world championships with the Soviet national team in that period plus an Olympic gold medal at Sapporo in 1972. Some rookie!

Interestingly, despite the Soviets' contention that the Flyers were deliberately trying to injure their players by "hunting" them, the worst injury of the game was suffered by a Philadelphia Flyer—Bobby Clarke. He incurred a nasty gash above his left eye late in the third period following an accidental collision with Red Army's Viktor Kutyergin. Clarke brusquely pushed Kutyergin away when the Soviet player attempted to apologize to him. A photo of the heavily bleeding Flyer captain skating off the Spectrum ice appeared in many newspapers the following day. One such paper was the *Boston Globe*. Its coverage of the Flyers–Central Red Army game was considerably larger and more in-depth than what was given the hometown Bruins and their home-ice win over the Washington Capitals that same day!

Kreisner also pointed out in his retrospective piece on the game that the Soviets steadfastly—and somewhat stubbornly—refused to abandon their style of hockey which was clearly ineffective against Fred Shero's cleverly designed trap. "Even down three goals," he wrote, "Loktev wouldn't change his team's style of play; he continued to have his players circling, looking for the perfect scoring opportunity rather than playing dump and chase, and the Flyers succeeded in bottling up the neutral zone, preventing the Soviets from gaining any speed."[60]

The 4–1 final score actually flattered Central Red Army; it seemed that the Flyers were more than three goals ahead when the game ended. After the first Philadelphia goal was scored, the Soviet champions were never a threat to win the game. They lost their zest for the contest. Despite being the losing goalie for the first time in Super Series '76, Vladislav Tretiak was his usual superb self for the visitors. His excellent play in the Red Amy net kept the game from being an absolute rout for Philadelphia. "If it wasn't for Tretiak," Flyers forward Gary Dornhoefer said afterward, "I think we'd have hit double figures."[61] Teammate Joe Watson was a little more conservative with his estimate—but not much more. He suggested the game's final score "could have been 8–1 or 9–1"[62] with a different, less able man guarding the pipes for Central Red Army.

Jim Coleman concurred. He wrote, "If Tretiak was brilliant against the Montréal Canadiens and Boston Bruins, he attained even greater heights on Sunday afternoon. Without Tretiak in the Central Red Army net, this might have been the most crushing defeat in the history of Soviet hockey."[63]

There were dissenters. Journalist Dave Anderson was unimpressed by the behavior of the home team. He unflatteringly wrote in the *New York Times*, "The Flyers upheld the Spectrum's reputation as the cradle of licensed muggings. It was a triumph of terror over style. Naturally, it warmed the hearts of the Flyers' followers, who would cheer for Frankenstein's monster if he could skate."[64] (Anderson's assessment of the game was reprinted verbatim in Soviet newspapers—certainly a true rarity for a mainstream American journalist's work in the mid-1970s.)

Coach Fred Shero absolutely figured his club had won the game fair and square. He stated to various media personnel, "We beat a hell of a machine. Ninety-nine percent of the NHL didn't think we could do it." The winning man behind the bench felt compelled to add, "Yes, we are the world champions. If they had won, they would have been the world champions."[65] Konstantin Loktev begged to differ. "One game doesn't decide anything,"[66] the Soviet coach sternly maintained.

Immediately after the game concluded, NHL president Clarence Campbell optimistically announced that he was hopeful of arranging a tournament in the autumn featuring the Stanley Cup winners and the championship club of the Soviet Union. Remarkably, Campbell was apparently unfazed by all the peripheral hullaballoo at the game he had just witnessed. He called the Soviet walkout merely "an error in judgement."[67]

Young Flyer defenseman Jim Watson could barely contain his emotions after the game. He said, "I'm not being overdramatic when I say that this surpasses everything." It was his way of saying the Flyers' win over Central Red Army was, in his eye, more important than their pair of

14. Game #8   185

Stanley Cup wins in 1974 and 1975. "I think we did a lot for our team, the league and for Canada's national pride."[68] The day before the game, the Flyers' brother combo of Joe and Jim Watson had received a telegram from their small hometown of Smithers in northwest British Columbia. There were more than 200 names on it with accompanying good-luck wishes.

Also excited beyond the norm was Philadelphia team owner Ed Snider. He unexpectedly burst into a press conference that Fred Shero was having to offer his personal congratulations to his coach. Snider told him, "Forget the interviews. Freddy ... that was the greatest coaching job in the history of hockey. I love you, Freddy. You're fabulous."[69] Snider then turned around and left the room just as quickly as he had entered it—leaving Shero utterly speechless at the microphone for more than just a moment.

Almost overlooked in the hullaballoo was the conspicuously quiet Dave Schultz. He was unusually pacifistic all game for the victors. He drew no penalties, so he was barely noticed. "In such an important game, I did not dare get a penalty,"[70] Schultz openly confessed to the media with a broad smile on his face.

Ed Van Impe agreed that pride was a prime motivator for the Flyers that afternoon. The man who had flattened Valeri Kharlamov in the first period told Frank Dolson of Knight News Service, "Each player's personal pride was at stake, and the pride of his team, his city his country. We had to beat them to save face. It was important for us to beat them. It really was."[71]

Philadelphia defenseman Tom Bladon told Dolson, "We were wound up in the first period because the pressure was on us. Before the game, when they were playing 'God Bless America,' I could have almost cried out there. My legs were giving...."[72] At this point, Bladon became so emotional in mid-sentence that he was unable to continue with Dolson's interview. Bladon was not an American; he had been born in Edmonton in 1952.

Photographs from the goings-on in Philadelphia were plastered across the front pages of most Canadian newspapers the following day, along with full-length stories lauding the Flyers—something that would have been unthinkable nine months earlier. *The Montréal Gazette* was one such daily with Tim Burke's coverage of the game that everyone was discussing as the newspaper's lead story. (News of the death of famed and beloved British mystery novelist Agatha Christie was pushed to lesser pages in most Canadian dailies.)

"The Philadelphia Flyers salvaged Canada's pride in her national sport with a near-perfect hockey masterpiece here yesterday to beat Russia's best, the Central Red Army team of Moscow, 4–1," he began. Then Burke got into the gory details of the first period walkout by the visitors.

The Flyers fashioned their masterpiece yesterday amidst a swirl of controversy which came to a boil when Red Army coach Konstantin Loktev withdrew his team for 18 minutes after Flyers defenseman Ed Van Impe had decked his star Valeri Kharlamov with a "shoulder check."

The Russians complained bitterly about the Flyers' "headhunting" in the initial minutes of the first period and after the game said the Flyers played like "animals."[73]

Veteran sports journalist Milt Dunnell of the *Toronto Star* had no sympathy whatsoever for the complaining Soviets at the end of the game. The 70-year-old who had been covering Canada–Soviet hockey since the days of the East York Lyndies, wrote these blunt words in the next day's edition of his newspaper:

The Moscow Musketeers ... hauled their team off the ice. [Coach] Loktev knew the conditions before he came. Nobody loves playing in Philadelphia. Once he accepted a game with the Flyers, under NHL rules, with an NHL referee, he was in the same boat as the Toronto Maple Leafs or Vancouver Canucks when they come to town. Loktev wanted his team to know what it's like to play the Flyers in Philly under NHL conditions. Well ... that's what it's like.[74]

Philadelphia captain Bobby Clarke tried to put things into perspective—at least as he saw them. "This doesn't prove Canadian hockey is better than theirs," he said in the raucous, jubilant Flyers dressing room following the decisive victory. "It just means the Flyers are better than their best."[75] Clarke added, "Obviously the Russians have a great team. However, they don't go for body checks or checks into the boards."[76]

In the losers' dressing room, even Konstantin Loktev had some surprisingly positive comments about how the Flyers' tactics were effective in stifling his team's offense. "The Philadelphia Flyers are a good team who can play any type of hockey," the Central Red Army coach stated. "The way they play is the fault of the media. Freddy Shero is a very progressive coach. If we played the Flyers seven games, anyone could win."[77] Presumably, Loktev knew about Shero's travels to the Soviet Union to attend coaching clinics. Later Shero would travel again to Moscow for a coaching clinic and gleefully describe how his club thoroughly intimidated Loktev's team. His self-congratulatory speech was coolly received in the Kremlin.

Journalist Tim Burke praised the meticulous manner in which Shero had primed his Philadelphia squad for the most important game of Super Series '76. "It was one of the most remarkable displays of preparedness, discipline and unflappability in the annals of sports," gushed the Montréal scribe. "It elevated coach Fred Shero's systematic approach to the game beyond question."[78]

Interestingly, with the notable exception of the *New York Times*, the North American sports media generally agreed that it had been one of the

14. Game #8

Flyers' tamer games of the ongoing 1975–76 season. When told that the Red Army coach Loktev had accused the Flyers of playing "animal hockey," Bobby Clarke scoffed at the insult. "We've been called worse things than that," he snickered. "This wasn't even a rough game."[79] NHL referee-in-chief Scotty Morrison said Lloyd Gilmour had done an excellent job as referee, noting, "Gilmour will never have to work under more pressure."[80] Morrison also added that he thought the Soviets leaving the ice in the first period was merely a ploy to get Gilmour to call a one-sided game.

Despite the open hostility between Bobby Clarke and anything connected with Soviet hockey, the Flyer captain was surprised to see a messenger in the home team's dressing bearing a gift for him. Vladislav Tretiak had sent him an album of Russian music. "Just what I've always wanted," Clarke sarcastically said to Red Fisher. "I'd better give him something in return." Tretiak fared very well in the gift exchange, according to the *Montréal Star* scribe. Whereas the record "goes for a couple of rubles on Gorky Street"[81] according to Fisher, Clarke sent the Red Army goalie his new digital watch. It was quite an expensive trinket in 1976, probably valued in excess of $200.

Clarke then held court in the winning team's dressing room. "I don't really know how to describe what we did today. I don't think this team has ever played a more disciplined game at a time we needed it more—for everybody. I was disappointed with the rest of the league—except for [the] Canadiens and Buffalo. I thought [the other NHL teams] would do better."[82]

In an article published on the NHL's website on the 38th anniversary of the game, Flyers beat writer Brad Kurtzberg called the Philadelphia victory over Central Red Army, without qualification, "one of the proudest moments"[83] in the team's history. Jack Dulmage of the *Windsor Star* concurred. He similarly claimed without reservation that the Flyers had "delivered one of the greatest hockey performances of modern times."[84]

Flyer goalie Wayne Stephenson was absolutely beaming with delight after the game. He had a right to be happier than perhaps any of his victorious teammates because of his history of frustration with the Soviets as an amateur player. "I think we beat them twice in all the years the National Team played against them," Stephenson recalled, "in the 1967 Centennial Tournament in Winnipeg and once at the *Izvestia* tournament in Russia. But this is really something else. It is nice to play against them behind this particular team." Stephenson made a point of emphasizing his belief. "If this Soviet Army team regularly played in the NHL," he said, "they wouldn't last two weeks."[85]

Bob Kelly and Don Saleski both pointed out to the media that the Soviets were subtle artists with their sticks—but not necessarily for the purposes of passing the puck and scoring goals. The latter displayed the evidence to Tim Burke of the *Montréal Gazette*: a fresh, nasty welt on his chest. Saleski commented, "That came from that little sawed-off runt, number 11 [Boris Alexandrov]. Just after Joe Watson's goal, he gave me the worst spear I ever got in my life. It was so hard that his stick broke."[86]

Not too surprisingly, behind the Iron Curtain the opinions about the game varied tremendously from what was generally being written and said by Canadian and American hockey journalists. A Soviet youth newspaper, *Komsomolskaya Pravda*, published a satirical cartoon portraying the Flyers as bestial creatures brandishing caveman-style clubs rather than hockey sticks. "The professionals wanted revenge at any price," its caption said. In an accompanying article penned by correspondent A. Pumpyanski, the newspaper claimed that the Flyers' play went "beyond the limit of fouling" which was wrongly sanctioned by Canadian referee Lloyd Gilmour. It further stated that the Flyers–Central Red Army game was built up by "tendentious propaganda ... as a game that would stand for the whole tournament." The newspaper emphasized that the two Soviet teams had won the eight-game series with five wins, two losses and a tie. No mention whatsoever was made in the article of the first-period walkout by the Soviet Union's top club team, a curious omission to be sure.

Three days before the Flyers–Central Red Army game, on January 8, the six-team Canada Cup tournament, to be held in various Canadian and American locales in September, had been confirmed. All five countries invited by the Canadian federal government had agreed to participate. (They were the United States, Sweden, Finland, Czechoslovakia, and the Soviet Union.) There were some worries that the Soviets' participation might now be in jeopardy because of the goings-on at the Philadelphia Spectrum on January 11. Those concerns did not pan out.

Despite the hostility surrounding the finale of Super Series '76, Soviet hockey officials made a positive gesture to budget-conscious hockey fans in the Washington, D.C., area. The Soviets announced that before heading for home on Tuesday, their two touring clubs would play each other in a special exhibition game at the Capital Center in Landover, Maryland, on Monday. (They certainly did not consider playing the lowly Washington Capitals as part of their tour, as the Caps were undeniably one of the NHL's bottom-feeders in 1975–76.) It would be general admission only, with tickets selling for a measly $3 apiece. It was certainly a bargain price. During the eight Super Series games, some tickets had a face value considerably beyond that of a regular NHL game. For example, the highest-priced tickets for the Central Red Army game at Boston Garden cost $13.50 each, $4.50 above the top $9 price one would have to pay to see the 1975–76 Boston Bruins at home on any other occasion that season.

That was a 50 percent increase. It was a hike in price that shocked longtime Boston hockey writer Francis Rosa. The scribe was even more surprised by how quickly the prized ducats for the January 8 game at Boston Garden sold out.

Frank Dolson concluded his report on the Flyers' impressive and important 4–1 victory over Central Red Army by noting, "The NHL's best had run roughshod over Russia's best. They wouldn't have to change the name of the Stanley Cup to the Stalin Cup, after all. At least not for a while."[87]

Larry McMullen, a journalist employed by the *Philadelphia Daily News* took a thoroughly cosmopolitan view of what happened at the Spectrum on the afternoon of January 11, 1976. He wrote, "If the Russians are upset by anything that happened in Philadelphia, it has to do with the Canadian way of life."[88]

Joe Watson declared, "For guys like me, this was the greatest game of our careers. Other guys on the club are great, and they'll get a chance, probably, to play those guys again. But I'm just an ordinary player, and for me it was my only chance. That's why it's the height of my career."[89]

Decades after the Flyers–Central Red Army game was played, it still generates heated discussion among hockey followers. Was it a disgraceful display of Philadelphia's goon tactics or was it a brilliant display of tough Flyers hockey masterminded by coach Fred Shero? Perhaps it was something in between? Opinions vary, of course. In 2016 Michael Farber of *Sports Illustrated* recalled the general sentiment of typical NHL fans about Philadelphia going into their January 11, 1976, tilt versus Central Red Army. "The Broad Street Bullies might have been the barbarians at the gate," he said, "but they were *our* barbarians."[90]

Scoring Summary

Red Army 0+1+0 = 1
Philadelphia 2+1+1 = 4

First period

1. Philadelphia: Leach (Barber) 11:38 (pp)
2. Philadelphia: MacLeish (Lonsberry) 17:37

Second period

1. Philadelphia: Joe Watson (Saleski, Kindrachuk) 2:44 (sh)
2. Red Army: Kutyergin (Popov) 10:38

Third period

3. Philadelphia: Goodenough (Clarke, Dornhoefer) 4:01

15

Aftermath 1976 to 1991
What It All Meant

When examining a historical event, one often encounters a wide variety of opinions. It is even more common for that to happen with sports history. Super Series '76 provided a great many discussion points and interpretations.

For the three NHL clubs that did not lose their games to the Soviets (Buffalo, Philadelphia and Montréal), their clashes with the Wings of the Soviet or Central Red Army remain, after all this time, cherished moments in their respective franchises' histories. Anniversaries of the games are routinely celebrated with lovingly written retrospective pieces on their websites. (Such stories provided plenty of excellent material for this book!) On the other hand, the five NHL teams that did lose their games to the Soviets seldom look back at them at all. Much like the Canadians who played in the 1974 Summit Series, the members of the losing NHL sides in Super Series '76 are rarely queried about those defeats. If glory is fleeting, as the saying goes, the relevance of the NHL's losses in exhibition games to foreigners from behind the Iron Curtain in the winter of 1975–76 seems to vanish even more quickly.

For some of the five NHL coaches who were behind their teams' respective benches and lost, it was a bad omen. Three had been fired by the end of 1976: Ron Stewart and Marc Boileau were both discharged within two weeks of dropping their games to the Soviets. Neither man ever coached again in the NHL. Billy Reay, the longtime coach of the Chicago Black Hawks got the ax from his club's upper management 34 games into the 1975–76 campaign. On Christmas Eve, the 58-year-old learned of his termination by finding a note that had been slid under the door of his Chicago Stadium office. Just to be sure Reay saw it, another copy of the pink slip was quietly put under the door of his apartment. It was one of professional sports' most callous and impersonal dismissals. Reay certainly deserved better. He had been the coach of the Black Hawks since 1963,

15. Aftermath 1976 to 1991

leading them to the Stanley Cup finals in 1965, 1971 and 1973, losing in hard-fought tussles to the Montréal Canadiens each time. At the time of his firing, Reay's 542 regular-season wins was the second-highest win total in NHL history. Like Ron Stewart and Marc Boileau, Reay also never coached another NHL club.

The two other coaches whose teams lost games to the Soviets in Super Series '76 more than survived—they thrived. Don Cherry's Boston Bruins finished atop the tough Adams Division in 1975–76 and advanced to the Stanley Cup semifinals where they lost to Philadelphia. It was the first of four divisional titles in a row for the colorful Cherry that included two consecutive trips to the Stanley Cup finals. (He is the most recent Bruins coach to achieve that feat.) Al Arbour of the New York Islanders fared spectacularly. His club advanced to five straight Stanley Cup finals from 1980 to 1984, winning the first four.

A few days after Super Series '76 concluded, Mark Mulvoy of *Sports Illustrated* wrote, "[It] had been a humbling experience for the once-lordly NHL. As they surveyed the defeats, some league officials and players attempted to pass off the Soviet triumphs as meaningless exhibitions and even went so far to suggest that the NHL ought to avoid such competition in the future."[1]

Aging NHL president Clarence Campbell preferred to be more selective in his analysis of the eight exhibition games. "As far as I'm concerned," he said, "the critical result of the series is that they did not defeat any one of our top three teams—Philadelphia, Montréal or Buffalo."[2] (Mulvoy interjected, "They're going to love Clarence in Boston."[3])

Red Fisher of the *Montréal Star* parroted Campbell when he wrote a summary of Super Series '76 on January 12 for his newspaper,

> The [Soviet clubs] were grand and talented visitors, but the Soviets do not represent a hockey season in this area—and should not. The Soviets won the series 5-2-1, but all the dialogue in the wake of Philadelphia's awesome wipeout of the Red Army team focused on the Soviets' failure to beat the National Hockey League's best three teams. Their best was unable to beat our best, which makes the overall results considerably less than important.[4]

But Campbell did acknowledge that the heady days of the NHL claiming unquestioned superiority in hockey were now long gone. "We cannot claim we're the best by brushing aside our principal rivals," he explained. "We cannot solve any credibility question by running from the Soviets. Why deceive people? Our own credibility has been waning, anyway. Some of our fat cats, plainly and simply, are not putting out. The age of affluence in hockey has watered down the zest of far too many players."[5]

In Mulvoy's feature article, one unnamed NHL executive concurred with Campbell, at least in part. He rhetorically asked the *SI* scribe, "How can we keep charging $12 for games against Washington, St. Louis and California when it's pretty obvious that we're not the best league in the world anymore?"[6]

Tom Fitzgerald of the *Boston Globe* had precisely the same concerns. He wrote on January 11, "As a businessman you'd have to wonder what the NHL and WHA proprietors think about the probable effect of current Russian successes on the already weak box office situation in many of their cities."[7]

Leigh Montville, also of the *Boston Globe*, with a sense of awe, wondered what new sports the Soviets would attempt to master next, having recently proven their obvious prowess in hockey, basketball, athletics and gymnastics. Much like the psychologically rattled Frank Mahovlich did in 1972, Montville seriously pondered whether American football might be the next enticing target for the unstoppable Big Red Machine of Soviet sports.

Ken Dryden told the *Boston Globe* that neither Canadian nor Soviet hockey had reached anything near perfection in his opinion. The Montréal goaltender said, "I think that both of us are a considerable distance from being the ultimate hockey team. We can both move a long way in that direction."[8]

If the Soviets' announced goal of using Super Series '76 to prepare their hockey team for the tournament at the 1976 Winter Olympics was indeed true, the plan worked out very well for them. At Innsbruck, the USSR thumped host Austria, 16–3, in a required qualifying game and then won all five of their games in the final stage—a six-team round robin—to capture their fourth consecutive Olympic goal medal and fifth overall. The Soviets were severely pressed in the final game, however. They needed a late rally to narrowly edge Czechoslovakia, 4–3, for the championship. The heroes of that last game were Valeri Kharlamov and Alexander Yakushev who notched two late goals a minute apart for the familiar victors.

During Super Series '76, Jack Dulmage of the *Windsor Star* wrongly forecasted an annual series between the championship clubs from the Soviet Union and the NHL. He wrote, "The present series is the final exhibition and is serving as a tune-up for what is to come—the best team of Russia versus the Stanley Cup champion across eight games ... four games in Moscow, four at the site of the Stanley Cup winner. It might not be just like that, but it will be something like that. The exact format has not been hammered down...."[9]

What did emerge from Super Series '76 was the first Canada Cup tournament that September. Hockey Canada struck a deal with the IIHF to return to its annual world championship tournament—with a

15. Aftermath 1976 to 1991

roster comprised of professional players—in return for it sanctioning a six-nation tournament to be held mostly in Canada, with two games contested in Philadelphia. IIHF officials would be on the ice. Alan Eagleson would act as tournament chairman. Each of the six participating nations (Canada, Czechoslovakia, the Soviet Union, Sweden, Finland and the United States) would play a round-robin with the top two advancing to a best-of-three final. For the first time in its long hockey history, Canada assembled its finest players without being handicapped with the restrictions of amateurism or self-inflicted NHL/WHA squabbles. Replete with future Hall-of Famers, Team Canada 1976 is often considered the most formidable team the country ever iced. Bobby Orr, Guy Lafleur, Gilbert Perrault, Denis Potvin and Bobby Hull were merely the tip of the Canadian iceberg. The squad was so daunting that 34-year-old Phil Esposito publicly grumbled about the lack of ice time he was getting from head coach Scotty Bowman.

While Canada was deadly serious about winning the tournament, the Soviets were less so. Perceiving the Canada Cup to be not quite on the same level of importance as their chief international rivals did, they chose

Sam Pollock (left), longtime general-manager of the Montréal Canadiens, poses with the Canada Cup and tournament chairman Alan Eagleson (Toronto Star Photograph Archive, Courtesy of Toronto Public Library).

not to send their best players. Instead, the Soviet Union sent an "experimental team" to the event. A few veterans remained in Moscow in order to give promising younger players extra exposure to international play. Among those left at home was superstar Valeri Kharlamov, who was recuperating from injuries he sustained in an automobile accident. The result was that the Soviets lost round-robin games to both Canada and Czechoslovakia and played to a 3–3 tie with Sweden. They failed to qualify for the tournament's best-of-three finals.

In its games, the Canadians had little trouble beating Finland, Sweden and the United States, but they surprisingly lost 1–0 to the Czechs, whose veteran goalie, Vladimir Dzurilla, was nothing short of sensational in that memorable contest. (In retrospect, the result should not have been a huge shock. Czechoslovakia had won the 1976 IIHF world championship in Poland that spring. However, in the Canada Cup tourney, the wildly unpredictable Czechs had tied the United States and lost to Sweden in the round robin!) Suddenly, the Canadians were in danger of not qualifying for the finals of their own tourney if they could not defeat the Soviet Union in their last outing of the round-robin. In a game which truly amounted to a sudden-death semifinal, Canada came through with a 3–1 win over the Soviets in Toronto. The Soviets, as they had after their loss to the Czechs and their tie with the Swedes, complained about biased officiating. Bobby Orr was named the game's top Canadian. (The 1976 Canada Cup proved to be a wonderful finale to the 28-year-old Orr's truncated career. Now a member of the Chicago Black Hawks, Orr was named the tournament MVP, but he did not play much afterward. Damaged knees sadly forced him into retirement at age 30.)

Canada beat Czechoslovakia in two straight games to win the tournament. The first one was a sound 6–0 thumping. The Czechs did much better in the second game, however. They held the lead until the final three minutes of the third period when Philadelphia's Bill Barber tied the game, 4–4, with just 2:13 left on the clock. Overtime was needed to settle things. Toronto's Darryl Sittler scored the winner in the extra period by exploiting Dzurilla's habit of coming far out of his net to challenge shooters. Sittler faked a shot and deftly moved around the Czech goalie to fire the puck into the gaping, open net. (Before the overtime period began, Team Canada's assistant coach, Don Cherry, had advised the players to try that maneuver if the opportunity arose.) With the victory, Canada could once again claim to be at the top of the hockey world. The vanquished Czechs nevertheless made good on a promise uttered by coach Karel Gut—to prove that there was more to international hockey than just the Soviets and the Canadians. That they certainly did.

The reciprocal act for the Canada Cup—having a Canadian team return, in 1977, to the IIHF world championships for the first time since 1969—did not work out nearly as well for Canada. Although they were free to send an all-professional roster for the first time ever, the realities of the NHL schedule made putting together a contending team almost impossible. The tournament (held in Austria) lasted from April 21 to May 8; it was the same time the Stanley Cup playoffs were in full swing. Thus, only players whose NHL teams had not qualified for those playoffs could play for Canada. Phil Esposito was the most notable recruit. Canada ended up finishing in fourth place. They played the Soviet Union twice, losing badly both times, 11–1 and 8–1. (The Soviets had their usual array of top talent in their lineup, of course.) In Canada, the lopsided losses prompted the old refrain of "Why participate when we can't send our best players?" It was a lament that harkened back to Stockholm in 1954 and the underachieving East York Lyndies. After the 11–1 shellacking, a journalist reporting from Vienna declared, "There was general consensus that Canada had sent better amateur teams in previous world championships than the one that was humiliated last night."[10] Although it sent teams overseas every spring, Canada would not win the IIHF tournament until 1994—some two and a half years after the dissolution of the Soviet Union.

Sequels of Super Series '76 took place every so often in NHL arenas over the next 15 years, each one being less meaningful than the one before. The novelty of the event began to wear off quickly, however. NHL teams often resented the extra game foisted upon them in an already busy and grueling league schedule. There was ample evidence of the decline in public interest in these games and their prestige.

During the 1978–79 season, the Montréal Canadiens were supposed to play the Soviet Wings, but they handed the unwanted task to their top farm team instead—the Nova Scotia Voyageurs. This would have been unfathomable in 1975. That same year, when the Boston Bruins hosted the Wings on January 9, they were granted special permission to use three goaltenders in the game—one for each period. Clearly, giving seldom-used, third-string goalie Jim Pettie some extra work was far more important to Boston than winning the game. When the game was played, the Bruins were enraged over the subtle stick fouls employed by the visitors: spears, butt-ends, and slashes to the back of their legs. Peter McNab openly called the Wings of the Soviet "a dirty crew"[11] in a postgame interview and said neither he nor his teammates wanted to risk serious injuries by playing them again.

The big international hockey event in 1979 was the Challenge Cup. It pitted the Soviet Union's national team in a best-of-three series versus what was billed as Team NHL. (Three Swedes were in the lineup; all the other players on Team NHL were Canadians.) The league had scrapped its annual All-Star Game in 1978–79 to fit the special series into its schedule. The three games were contested in the space of four days to minimize the disruption of NHL play. All three contests took place in New York City. The Soviets took this event very seriously, holding several practices in the Netherlands on an ice surface that matched the dimensions of Madison Square Garden's.

Team NHL won the opener on Thursday, February 8 by a 4–2 score. However, the Soviets rebounded to narrowly win 5–4 on Saturday (after trailing the game 4–2 in the second period) and then triumphed in a 6–0 laugher in the clincher on Sunday, February 11. The Soviets had outscored the NHL's top stars 9–0 over the last 90 minutes of play. Interestingly, Soviet coach Viktor Tikhonov opted to use backup goalie Vladimir Myshkin instead of veteran Vladislav Tretiak in the deciding game. Myshkin recorded the shutout—the first one ever suffered by North American pros at the hands of the Soviets. Boston goaltender Gerry Cheevers did not look especially sharp for the NHLers. Boris Mikhailov made a point of flaunting the trophy at Alan Eagleson and boasting, "Soviets number one.... Canadskis number two!"[12] E.M. Swift of *Sports Illustrated* declared the final five periods of action "were so one-sided in favor of the USSR that the Soviets seemed to become bored by it all."[13] Swift ended his article—which was titled "Run Over by the Big Red Machine"—by suggesting that the USSR's national team be handed the Stanley Cup.

Sadly, the career of John McCauley, widely rated as the NHL's best referee in 1979, was imperiled shortly after the third game concluded. He was sucker-punched by an irate fan while dining at a restaurant not far from Madison Square Garden, suffering permanent damage to his right eye. The assailant became irked when McCauley merely opined that the defeated NHL players could learn plenty about hockey from their victorious Soviet opponents. McCauley refereed sporadically for two years before retiring. Even after five surgeries, McCauley's depth perception was irreparably damaged and he never truly regained the form that made him one of the NHL's most respected whistle-blowers. He died young and suddenly on June 3, 1989, following emergency gall bladder surgery. McCauley was just 44 years old. He was the NHL's supervisor of officials at the time of his shocking passing.

Results proved that Canadian hockey on the international scene was clearly in a funk as the 1980s began. In 1980, Canada returned to Olympic hockey for the first time since 1968, the era when Father David Bauer was optimistically trying to produce winning teams with youthful Nats and a system that simply could not compete with the "masked professionals" from the communist bloc. Canada sent a team to Lake Placid comprised of amateurs—as per Olympic rules—comprised of a few young prospects

15. Aftermath 1976 to 1991

and older players mostly from the nation's dying Senior A circuits. At the tournament where American college boys performed their famous "miracle on ice" to win the gold medal, the Canadian squad struggled mightily. They finished sixth in the 12-team event and failed to qualify for the medal round. Canada could only defeat no-hopers Japan, Poland and the Netherlands, while losing to the Soviets, Finns and Czechs.

Further embarrassment came the following year, in 1981, when the second installment of the Canada Cup was played. In the tournament final, which was just a one-game affair this time, the Soviets drubbed the hosts, 8–1, at the Montréal Forum. The game was scoreless after 20 minutes, but Canadian goalie Mike Liut played poorly and allowed five third-period goals to the comrades. Canada's stockpile of famous NHL superstars mustered a pitiful four shots on goal in the final 20 minutes. Canada had beaten the USSR in the preliminary round, 7–3. Some observers figured the Soviets had "played possum" in that game to lull the Canadians into a false sense of superiority. If that was the case, the ruse worked wonderfully. Just like old times, Vladislav Tretiak was superb guarding the Soviet net. He was named the tournament MVP.

The event featured several embarrassing episodes for the host nation. Two games scheduled for Quebec City were abruptly shifted to Ottawa after advance ticket sales were unexpectedly dismal. (One was a tournament semifinal!) At the USA–Finland game in Montréal, the Italian national anthem was accidentally played instead of the Finnish one. The worst and most petty peripheral story, however, came at the end of the tournament: At Montréal's Mirabelle Airport, the Soviets were prevented from taking the championship trophy home by a group of Canadian hockey officials, including Alan Eagleson, who were bolstered by local police! Hockey Canada's poohbahs claimed the trophy was legally Canadian property and had to remain in its nation of origin. The Soviets loudly squawked, claiming such an action was a violation of international sporting protocols and traditions—which it certainly was. In response, a miffed Winnipeg trucking company owner named George Smith embarked on a one-man fund-raising campaign to have a replica of the snazzy, shiny trophy created for the deserving tournament champions. Hundreds of people responded positively and rallied to Smith's idea when it was publicized by a story that ran in the *Winnipeg Free Press* and other local media.

For a while, Hockey Canada's president Lou Lefaive escalated the situation. He considered suing Smith for copyright violations! Lefaive telephoned Smith personally to advise him to halt his maverick plan to give away an alternate Canada Cup. "If someone wants to send $11,000 worth of nickel to Moscow, that's not my business," Lefaive told the media. "But if it's a replica of the Canada Cup, we could take legal action against the manufacturer."[14]

Lefaive eventually relented in the face of growing adverse publicity as the whole scenario made his organization appear to be small-minded and vindictive. Calling his version, "the People's Canada Cup," Smith eventually amassed the required funds for a new trophy to be created. He personally presented it to the Soviet embassy in Ottawa where delighted diplomats praised the outstanding sportsmanship and fair-mindedness of the Canadian hockey fans who contributed to Smith's cause. The odd kerfuffle was, of course, an unexpected propaganda boon for the Soviet Union.

Despite the Canada Cup setback in 1981, Canadian hockey did have a resurgence in the next decade, however. The host country won Canada Cups in 1984, 1987, and 1991. (Some observers maintain the high quality of hockey on display in the Canada–Soviet games at the 1987 event has never been duplicated to this day.) Canada also became the preeminent power in international junior hockey, winning a bevy of world titles beginning in 1982. That was the first year Hockey Canada put together a true national junior team rather than sending a mere club team. The team was formed well enough in advance so the players could get accustomed to each other at a training camp.

In February 1987, there was a second confrontation between the Soviet Union's national squad and a team Comprised of NHL all-stars. This time the event was called Rendez-Vous '87. As in 1979, the mid-season event replaced the traditional NHL All-Star Game which was starting to lose its former luster. Rendez-Vous was a two-game affair with both matches played in Quebec City. The result was inconclusive. The NHL team won the February 11 opener, 4–3. Two nights later, the Soviets won, 5–3. Soviet coach Viktor Tikhonov could have claimed victory on goal difference, but he graciously chose not to do so. Instead, Tikhonov told the media, "The NHL didn't win and neither did we, the person that won was hockey itself. Both games were like holidays, like festivals, two of the greatest hockey games you'll ever see."[15] Tikhonov also cleverly combined a compliment and an insult to North American professional hockey by saying, "If I had Team NHL, I would never lose a game."[16]

However, by 1990–91, there was practically no demand for the Soviet-NHL exhibition games at the club level anymore. That year's Super Series games drew embarrassingly small crowds to NHL buildings. Fan apathy was made perfectly clear when hardly anyone bought tickets to see the Boston Bruins face the Soviet club Khimik on December 16. Esteemed *Boston Globe* hockey writer Francis Rosa penned the following day,

> No more love-hate. No more good guys-bad guys.
>
> The NHL should tell the Soviets to take your vodka and go home. No one cares anymore.
>
> Actually, they've been told the Super Series, which stopped over in Boston

15. Aftermath 1976 to 1991

last night, will not be renewed in the immediate future. Good thing, too, for it is a series whose time has passed. There were just 2,820 [fans] at the Garden to watch the Bruins lose to Khimik, 5–2—and there wasn't even a snowstorm.[17]

In a telling sidebar story that illustrated how little the NHL teams now cared about the Super Series concept, Rosa pointed out that two prominent Bruins were given permission to skip the exhibition game: John Carter and Craig Janney. Carter and his fiancée scheduled their wedding for that day while Janney was present as his teammate's best man. Six minor leaguers were hastily elevated to the parent club to round out Boston's lineup versus Khimik.

Overall, in their 98 total games played in the various Super Series encounters, the touring Soviet teams compiled a very impressive record of 55 wins, 33 losses, and 10 ties versus the North American pro clubs. Shutouts also favored the Soviets by a 6–3 margin, including a 0–0 draw between Dynamo Moscow and the Hartford Whalers in Super Series '91. (Two games were resolved in overtime with the NHL winning one and the Soviets the other.) The Buffalo Sabres' famous 12–6 victory over the Wings of the Soviet in January 1976 was the only one where a team reached double digits in goals. No team recorded more than eight goals in a game in any of the other 97 contests.

The Soviet Union, of course, collapsed as a single polity in 1991, splitting itself into many nations largely based on ethnic lines. The shackles of communism ceased to exist when 1992 began. The old Soviet players were now free to ply their trade as professional athletes. They did with alacrity, of course. Hockey players flooded into North America and western Europe. In the third decade of the 21st century, with players from all countries now freely honing their craft in the NHL and in various hockey countries all over the world, there is a debate as to whether "Soviet hockey" still exists as it once did. Former USSR goaltender Vladislav Tretiak, now a Russian hockey official, disagrees that his country's style of hockey training and preparations has waned since the disintegration of the old Soviet Union. "I don't agree that it's fading away," he firmly told an interviewer in 2020. "I think those players who played in the old Soviet Union and coach now, they teach what they were taught. I think it's a mix of styles now, a blend between Soviet and Canadian hockey. Look at what's going on in Canada—they don't play pure Canadian brand of hockey anymore. It's not like it's 1972."[18]

Although Tretiak never played a single game for an NHL team, he certainly benefited from greater personal freedom that existed in the Gorbachev era of the Soviet Union to earn a living in another country. Tretiak was hired as a goaltending coach in 1990 by the Chicago Blackhawks, which allowed him the opportunity to instruct such prominent NHL netminders as Ed Belfour, Dominik Hasek and Jocelyn Thibault. (Belfour went on to wear Tretiak's famous #20 as a tribute to his instructor. Other goalies including Evgeni Nabokov, also wore that number in Tretiak's honor.) He also ran a school in Toronto called the Vladislav Tretiak Elite School of Goaltending. In keeping with the Soviet idea of fitness being essential to all hockey players, the school was considered one of the most physically punishing goaltending academies in the world. Students could be refused admittance if they were not deemed to be in top condition. Tretiak also operated a goalie school in Montréal during the 1990s where he trained José Théodore and Martin Brodeur. A busy man, Tretiak also ran a goalie hockey camp in Detroit Lakes, Minnesota, in the early 2000s. He was probably the most popular Soviet player among fans in Canada during the height of the Canada–Soviet hockey rivalry.

In 1989, the 37-year-old Tretiak was inducted into the Hockey Hall of Fame in Toronto—the first Soviet player to receive that lofty honor. Others from his country would follow. Valeri Kharlamov (who died at age 33 in an August 1981 automobile accident) was enshrined posthumously in 2005. Alexander Yakushev joined them in 2018. All three inductees, of course, were prominent Soviet players during Super Series '76.

With the fall of the Iron Curtain, the "Us Against Them" mentality in international hockey has largely faded into sports history. Certainly, a great rivalry still exists between Russia and Canada at all levels of hockey—and probably always will. However, the holiday season of 1975–76 was perhaps the apex of the geopolitical element overriding the sport's encounters. The atmosphere surrounding Super Series '76 cannot be repeated. The world has changed considerably in the decades since that memorable December night when people across Canada delayed the start of their New Year's Eve parties because they considered it something akin to a patriotic duty to watch Central Red Army play the Montréal Canadiens on television. In the 21st century, Russian hockey players are now embraced as beloved NHLers wherever they are employed. Fans seldom think about anyone's nationality. Players from Eastern Europe are no longer perceived as suspicious enemy agents on ice skates championing the superiority of a dangerous and threatening ideology. The Broad Street Bullies no longer have to be deployed in a seek-and-destroy mission to preserve the stature of the National Hockey League.

In the overall scheme of things, that is probably a positive step in human relations. Yet, for those hockey fans who experienced the heyday of North America's hockey pros vying with the Soviet Union's vaunted "amateurs," something is now absent from the sport. Perhaps a leading Cold War figure, Lyndon Johnson, said it best when he opined, "Yesterday is not ours to recover, but tomorrow is ours to win or lose."[19]

Chapter Notes

Introduction

1. Dick Irvin, *Hockey Night in Canada* rerun of December 31, 1975, Central Red Army–Montréal Canadiens game, December 31, 1994.

Chapter 1

1. "The IHLC Results: Canada 12–1 Sweden: April 26, 1920," theihlc.com.
2. *Ibid.*
3. *Ibid.*
4. "IIHF World Hockey Championships 1953: Zurich, Basil Summary," legendsofhockey.net.
5. Peter Brown, "The Unseen Hand of Lloyd Percival," CBC.ca, February 7, 2022.
6. Vladislav Tretiak, *Tretiak: The Legend* (New York: Penguin, 1987), 13–14, 16.

Chapter 2

1. Tommy Shields, "Round and About," *Ottawa Citizen*, March 6, 1954, 21.
2. "Canada's Chances in Puck Meet May Be Clear After First Game," *Montréal Gazette*, February 27, 1954, 10.
3. Lawrence Martin, "Hockey's Red Dawn," *The Beaver*, December 2009–January 2010, 17.
4. "Russia Drubs East York 7–2 to Win World Hockey Tourney," *Montréal Gazette*, March 8, 1954, 25.
5. Larry Millson, "Lyndhursts' Heartache Hasn't Diminished," theglobeandmail.com, March 1, 2004.
6. "Russia Drubs East York 7–2 to Win World Hockey Tourney," *Montréal Gazette*, March 8, 1954, 25.
7. *Ibid.*
8. *Ibid.*
9. Michael McKinley, *It's Our Game: Celebrating 100 Years of Hockey Canada* (Toronto: Viking, 2014), 151–152.
10. Larry Millson, "Lyndhursts' Heartache Hasn't Diminished," theglobeandmail.com, March 1, 2004.
11. Lawrence Martin, "Hockey's Red Dawn," *The Beaver*, December 2009–January 2010, 17.
12. "Penticton Vees Celebrate 60-Year Anniversary of World Hockey Championship Win," CBC News website, March 7, 2015.
13. Ivan McLelland, *Gold Mine to Gold Medal and Beyond*, self-published in Canada, 2012, 313.
14. *Ibid.*, 311.
15. *Ibid.*, 346.
16. *Ibid.*
17. Denis Fodor, "The Russians Become Ex-Champs," *Sports Illustrated* (online archives), March 14, 1955.
18. Jack Stepler, "'Gashouse Gang' Wrecked Soviets' Hockey Supremacy," *Ottawa Citizen*, March 7, 1955, 1.
19. Emanuel Sequeira, "1955 World Championship Vees Were the 'Cinderella Kids,'" *Pentiction Western News* (online archives), March 5, 2015.
20. *Ibid.*
21. *Ibid.*
22. Jack Stepler, "'Gashouse Gang' Wrecked Soviets' Hockey Supremacy," *Ottawa Citizen*, March 7, 1955, 1.
23. "Canadian Sextet's Prexy Says Russians 'Quit Cold,'" *Boston Globe*, March 7, 1955, 17.
24. *Ibid.*
25. Steve Douglas, *The World of Sport,*

recorded by CBC Television, March 6, 1955.
26. Arch MacKenzie, "Hockey's Cold War Won by B.C. Team," Toronto *Globe & Mail*, March 7, 1955, 2.
27. Arch MacKenzie, "Strong Feeling Among Fans, Vs, Canada Should Quit Ice Tourney, *Montréal Gazette*, March 8, 1955, 18.
28. Jack Stepler, "'Gashouse Gang' Wrecked Soviets' Hockey Supremacy," *Ottawa Citizen*, March 7, 1955, 1.
29. "The Team and the Town," *The British Columbian*, March 8, 1955, 4.
30. "Massey, PM Join in Praise," *Ottawa Citizen*, March 7, 1955, 1.
31. "Swedes ... And Their Goalie ... Stymie Terries," *Windsor Star*, March 14, 1962, 23.
32. "Russians Beat Smokies 4–2 to Win World Hockey Title," Toronto *Globe & Mail*, March 18, 1963, 17.
33. Rod Currie, "CAHA Head Agrees New Deal is Needed After Smokies Wind up in Fourth Spot," *Ottawa Citizen*, March 18, 1963, 15.
34. *Ibid.*
35. Lloyd Percival, interview on *The Day It Is*, CBC Television, 1968.
36. Douglas Fisher, "He Was a Man Ahead of His Time," *Ottawa Citizen*, July 30, 1974, 29.
37. Peter Brown, "The Unseen Hand of Lloyd Percival," CBC.ca, February 7, 2022.
38. Gary Mossman, *Lloyd Percival: Coach and Visionary* (Woodstock, ON: Seraphim Editions, 2013), 9.

Chapter 3

1. Tim Burke, "Hull No, I Won't Go, Bobby Tells Hockey Canada," *Montréal Gazette*, April 22, 1972, 15.
2. *Ibid.*
3. *Ibid.*
4. *Ibid.*
5. *Ibid.*
6. *Ibid.*
7. *Ibid.*
8. Phil Esposito, *September 1972*, Markham, ON, Polygram Video, 1997.
9. Lawrence Martin, *The Red Machine: The Soviet Quest to Dominate Canada's Game* (New York: Doubleday, 1990), 98.
10. Todd Denault, *The Greatest Game* (Toronto: McClelland & Stewart, 2010), 72.
11. Vladislav Tretiak, *Tretiak: The Legend* (New York: Penguin, 1987), 52.
12. Todd Denault, *The Greatest Game* (Toronto: McClelland & Stewart, 2010), 94.
13. John Robertson, "Hockey Changed Forever After Summit Series," *Kitchener-Waterloo Record*, September 26, 1996, C3.
14. Roy MacSkimming, *Cold War: The Amazing Canada-Soviet Hockey Series of 1972* (Vancouver: Greystone Books, 1996), 42.
15. John Robertson, "Hockey Changed Forever After Summit Series," *Kitchener-Waterloo Record*, September 26, 1996, C3.
16. *Ibid.*
17. Ted Blackman, "A Dark Day: Sept. 2, 1972, When Pride Turned to Trauma," *Montréal Gazette*, September 3, 1972, 1.
18. *Ibid.*
19. *Ibid.*
20. *Ibid.*
21. John Robertson, "Hockey Changed Forever After Summit Series," *Kitchener-Waterloo Record*, September 26, 1996, C3.
22. Ted Blackman, "A Dark Day: Sept. 2, 1972, When Pride Turned to Trauma," *Montréal Gazette*, September 3, 1972, 1.
23. *Ibid.*
24. Harold Kaese, "Russians Prove Discipline Pays," *Boston Globe*, September 4, 1972, 73.
25. Francis Rosa, "Canada Wins, 4–1; Espos Star," *Boston Globe*, September 5, 1972.
26. Dick Beddoes, *Pal Hal* (Toronto: Macmillan of Canada, 1989), 175.
27. Roy MacSkimming, *Cold War: The Amazing Canada-Soviet Hockey Series of 1972* (Vancouver: Greystone Books, 1996), 85.
28. Phil Esposito, *September 1972*, Markham, ON, Polygram Video, 1997.
29. *Ibid.*
30. Milt Dunnell, "Summit Series Game 4: Canadians Hit Rock Bottom vs. Soviets as Boos Rain Down in Vancouver," *Toronto Star* digital archives, September 9, 1972.
31. *Ibid.*
32. Dick Beddoes, *Pal Hal* (Toronto: Macmillan of Canada, 1989), 193.
33. *Ibid.*, 195.
34. Ed Snider, "Flyers and Soviets, 1976: When Al Capone's Mob Ambushed the Bolshoi Ballet Dancers," puckstruck.com, January 12, 2016.

35. Brian Conacher, *As the Puck Turns: A Personal Journey Through the World of Hockey* (Mississauga: John Wiley & Sons Canada, 2007).
36. Francis Rosa, "Soviets Provoke, Espo Hits Back—Scores, Too," *Boston Globe*, September 27, 1972, 31.
37. "For Canada, An Extra Holiday," *Boston Globe*, September 29, 1972, 52.
38. Maurice Tougas, "Henderson has scored for Canada!" *In This Corner* (blog), September 28, 2012.
39. Francis Rosa, "Team Canada: No. 1 After All," *Boston Globe*, September 29, 1972, 52.
40. John Robertson, "Canada's Supreme Moment Came in Moscow," *Kitchener-Waterloo Record*, September 25, 1997, C2.
41. Vladislav Tretiak, *Ice-Breaker: The 1972 Summit Series* (2022 documentary).
42. Francis Rosa, "Team Canada: No. 1 After All," *Boston Globe*, September 29, 1972, 52.
43. "For Canada, An Extra Holiday," *Boston Globe*, September 29, 1972, 52.
44. Phil Esposito, *September 1972* (video set).
45. Craig Custance, "Alexander the Great: Yakushev Finally Takes His Rightful Place in the Hall of Fame," theathetic.com, November 9, 2018.
46. Roy MacSkimming, *Cold War: The Amazing Canada-Soviet Hockey Series of 1972* (Vancouver: Greystone Books, 1996), 3.
47. "Turned-on Canada Greets Her Heroes," *Windsor Star*, October 2, 1972, 2.
48. *Ibid.*
49. John Robertson, "Hockey Changed Forever After Summit Series," *Kitchener-Waterloo Record*, September 26, 1996, C3.
50. Jack Dulmage, "A Short Bus Ride," *Windsor Star*, December 30, 1975, 20.
51. Harry Sinden, *Hockey Showdown: The Canada-Russia Hockey Series* (Toronto: Doubleday Canada, 1972), 117.
52. Ken Dryden and Mark Mulvoy, *Face-Off at the Summit* (Toronto: Little, Brown, 1973), 185.
53. Todd Denault, *The Greatest Game* (Toronto: McClelland & Stewart, 2010), 116.

Chapter 4

1. Rick Westhead, "In Russia, Fond Memories for a Hockey Series Forgotten by Canadians," www.tsn.ca, December 11, 2014.
2. *Ibid.*
3. *Ibid.*
4. Jim Coleman, "Tretiak Can't Be That Great Forever," *Ottawa Citizen*, September 18, 1974, 25.
5. Francis Rosa, "Team Canada, Soviets Tie 3-3," *Boston Globe*, September 18, 1974, 56.
6. Vladislav Tretiak, "Press Room 1974: Game #1," www.chidlovski.com.
7. Francis Rosa, "Team Canada, Soviets Tie 3-3," *Boston Globe*, September 18, 1974, 56.
8. Lance Hornby, "Looking back at 40th Anniversary of Canada-Soviet Hockey Series," Torontosun.com, September 11, 2014.
9. Rick Westhead, "In Russia, Fond Memories for a Hockey Series Forgotten by Canadians," www.tsn.ca, December 11, 2014.
10. *Ibid.*
11. Don Chevrier, 1974 Canada-Soviet Series Game #4 Telecast, CTV Television, September 23, 1974.
12. Lance Hornby, "Looking back at 40th Anniversary of Canada-Soviet Hockey Series," Torontosun.com, September 11, 2014.
13. Rick Westhead, "In Russia, Fond Memories for a Hockey Series Forgotten by Canadians," www.tsn.ca, December 11, 2014.
14. Brodie Snyder, "Press Room 1974: Game #6," www.chidlovski.com.
15. Lance Hornby, "Looking back at 40th Anniversary of Canada-Soviet Hockey Series," Torontosun.com, September 11, 2014
16. Jim Coleman, "Russians' Victory Far from Sweet," *Calgary Herald*, October 7, 1974, 57.
17. Wayne Overland, "Russia Beats Another Invader," *Calgary Herald*, October 7, 1974, 1.
18. Jim Coleman, "Russians' Victory Far from Sweet," *Calgary Herald*, October 7, 1974, 57.
19. *Ibid.*
20. *Ibid.*
21. Lance Hornby, "Looking back at 40th Anniversary of Canada-Soviet Hockey Series," Torontosun.com, September 11, 2014.

22. *Ibid.*
23. Rick Westhead, "In Russia, Fond Memories for a Hockey Series Forgotten by Canadians," www.tsn.ca, December 11, 2014.
24. *Ibid.*

Chapter 5

1. "International Hockey Opens to Pros," *Montréal Gazette*, April 21, 1975, 42.
2. *Ibid.*
3. "Soviets-NHL to Meet Again," *Calgary Herald*, May 30, 1975, 23.
4. *Ibid.*
5. Frank Brown, "Russians Meet N.Y. Rangers in Opener of 8-Game Tour," *Boston Globe*, December 28, 1975, 67.
6. Brad Kurtzberg, "How We Remember the Philadelphia Flyers–Red Army Game 38 Years Later," bleacherreport.com, January 2, 2014.
7. "Soviets-NHL to Meet Again," *Calgary Herald*, May 30, 1975, 23.
8. Al Strachan, "Put Up or Shut Up, Russians are Coming!" *Montréal Gazette*, November 11, 1975, 18.

Chapter 7

1. Robin Herman, "N.H.L. Teams Not Taking Soviet Series Lightly," *New York Times*, December 28, 1975, 137.
2. Frank Brown, "Russians Meet N.Y. Rangers in Opener of 8-Game Tour," *Boston Globe*, December 28, 1975, 67.
3. *Ibid.*
4. *Ibid.*
5. Stan Fischler, "Jury Still Deliberating Over Espo-Park Deal," *The Sporting News*, January 10, 1976, 14.
6. Carl Martin, Central Red Army–New York Rangers telecast, *Hockey Night in Canada*, CBC Television, December 28, 1975.
7. Al Strachan, "Red Army Humbles Rangers 7–3," *Montréal Gazette*, December 29, 1975, 19.
8. Harry Sinden, Central Red Army–New York Rangers telecast, *Hockey Night in Canada*, CBC Television, December 28, 1975.
9. Al Strachan, "Red Army Humbles Rangers 7–3," *Montréal Gazette*, December 29, 1975, 19.
10. Dick Irvin, Central Red Army–New York Rangers telecast, *Hockey Night in Canada*, CBC Television, December 28, 1975.
11. Al Strachan, "Red Army Humbles Rangers 7–3," *Montréal Gazette*, December 29, 1975, 19.
12. "Red Army Socks Rangers by 7–3," *Bangor Daily News*, December 29, 1975, 24.
13. *Ibid.*
14. "Rangers Get First Goal, But Soviets Get Most, 7–3," *Boston Globe*, December 29, 1975, 26.
15. Parton Keese, "Rangers Trounced, 7–3, Here As Soviet Army Opens Tour," *New York Times*, December 29, 1975, 21.
16. "Rangers Get First Goal, But Soviets Get Most, 7–3," *Boston Globe*, December 29, 1975, 26.
17. Wes Gaffer, "Russians Bewilder Rangers in Uneven Exhibition, 7–3," *New York Dily News*, December 29, 1975, 53.
18. "Rangers Get First Goal, But Soviets Get Most, 7–3," *Boston Globe*, December 29, 1975, 26.
19. Hal Walker, "Hal Walker," *Calgary Herald*, December 29, 1975,
20. *Ibid.*
21. Al Strachan, "Red Army Humbles Rangers 7–3," *Montréal Gazette*, December 29, 1975, 19.
22. *Ibid.*
23. *Ibid.*
24. *Ibid.*
25. Parton Keese, "Rangers Trounced, 7–3, Here As Soviet Army Opens Tour," *New York Times*, December 29, 1975, 21.
26. *Ibid.*
27. Al Strachan, "Red Army Humbles Rangers 7–3," *Montréal Gazette*, December 29, 1975, 19.
28. *Ibid.*
29. Jack Dulmage, "Rangers Ready with Excuses," *Windsor Star*, December 29, 1975, 22.
30. Stan Fischler, "Rangers Had Better Wake Up," *The Sporting News*, January 31, 1976, 25.
31. Al Strachan, "Refereeing? Well, It's Better...," *Montréal Gazette*, December 29, 1975, 19.
32. *Ibid.*
33. *Ibid.*
34. *Ibid.*
35. Mark Mulvoy, "This Was Détente, Philly Style," *Sports Illustrated*, January 19, 1976, 21.

36. John S. Rodosta, "Soviet Skaters Give Lesson in Hockey," *New York Times*, December 29, 1975, 23.
37. Parton Keese, "Rangers Trounced, 7–3, Here As Soviet Army Opens Tour," *New York Times*, December 29, 1975, 21.
38. John S. Rodosta, "Soviet Skaters Give Lesson in Hockey," *New York Times*, December 29, 1975, 23.
39. Al Strachan, "Red Army Humbles Rangers 7–3," *Montréal Gazette*, December 29, 1975, 19.
40. *Ibid.*
41. Jack Dulmage, "Rangers Ready with Excuses," *Windsor Star*, December 29, 1975, 22.
42. *Ibid.*
43. Jack Dulmage, "A Short Bus Ride," *Windsor Star*, December 30, 1975, 20.
44. Andy O'Brien, "Let's Face the Facts," *Montréal Star*, January 9, 1976, C3.

Chapter 8

1. Al Strachan, "Penguin Mentor Unimpressed," *Montréal Gazette*, December 29, 1975, 19.
2. *Ibid.*
3. *Ibid.*
4. *Ibid.*
5. *Ibid.*
6. Bob Whitley, "Pens Face Soviets—No Détente," *Pittsburgh Post-Gazette*, December 29, 1975, 17.
7. *Ibid.*
8. *Ibid.*
9. Robin Herman, "Russian Wings Beat Penguins, 7–4," *New York Times*, December 30, 1975, 17.
10. Ian MacLaine, "Kulagin: They Learn Quickly," *Windsor Star*, December 30, 1975, 21.
11. Robin Herman, "Russian Wings Beat Penguins, 7–4," *New York Times*, December 30, 1975, 17.
12. Bill Heufelder, "Penguins Start Poorly, Lose to Soviet Wings," *Pittsburgh Press*, December 30, 1975, 18.
13. Ian MacLaine, "Kulagin: They Learn Quickly," *Windsor Star*, December 30, 1975, 21.
14. Bill Heufelder, "Penguins Start Poorly, Lose to Soviet Wings," *Pittsburgh Press*, December 30, 1975, 18.
15. *Ibid.*

16. *Ibid.*
17. *Ibid.*
18. Ian MacLaine, "Kulagin: They Learn Quickly," *Windsor Star*, December 30, 1975, 21.
19. *Ibid.*
20. *Ibid.*
21. Peter White, "Penguins Learn Too Late to Avert 7–4 Defeat," *Globe & Mail*, December 30, 1975, 27.
22. "Another Russian Team Beats NHL Penguins, 7–4," *Boston Globe*, December 30, 1975, 25.
23. Ian MacLaine, "Kulagin: They Learn Quickly," *Windsor Star*, December 30, 1975, 21.
24. *Ibid.*
25. *Ibid.*
26. *Ibid.*
27. *Ibid.*
28. *Ibid.*
29. Peter White, "Penguins Learn Too Late to Avert 7–4 Defeat," *Globe & Mail*, December 30, 1975, 27.
30. Robin Herman, "Russian Wings Beat Penguins, 7–4," *New York Times*, December 30, 1975, 17.
31. Ian MacLaine, "Kulagin: They Learn Quickly," *Windsor Star*, December 30, 1975, 21.
32. *Ibid.*
33. *Ibid.*
34. *Ibid.*
35. Jack Dulmage, "A Short Bus Ride," *Windsor Star*, December 30, 1975, 20.
36. Bob Verdi, "Russians are Coming! Wings vs. Hawks Tonight," *Chicago Tribune*, January 7, 1976, Section 4, 1.

Chapter 9

1. Jim Coleman, "The night Time Stood Still in the Forum," *Ottawa Citizen*, January 2, 1976, 19.
2. John Robertson, "Canadians–Red Army Match Was as Good as Hockey Gets," *Kitchener-Waterloo Record*, October 27, 1994, C1.
3. Gare Joyce, "Greatest Game: Red Army–Canadiens '75," sportsnet.ca, March 9, 2015.
4. John Robertson, "Les Canadiens vs. the Soviets: Here's One Root for the Home Team," *Montréal Gazette*, December 5, 1975, 82.

5. Todd Denault, *The Greatest Game* (Toronto: McClelland & Stewart, 2010), 207.
6. Al Strachan, "Pressure? Don Awrey Tells How It Really Is," *Montréal Gazette*, December 26, 1975, 15.
7. "Tretiak Receives Praise," *Windsor Star*, December 27, 1975, 20.
8. Al Strachan, "Dryden Can't Hide Feelings About Beating Russians," *Montréal Gazette*, December 31, 1975, 18.
9. Bob Morrisey, "Savard Sees Dangerous Signs Behind Our Brand of Hockey," *Montréal Gazette*, December 31, 1975, 18
10. Dick Irvin, Central Red Army–Montréal Canadiens telecast, *Hockey Night in Canada*, December 31, 1975
11. Jack Dulmage, "Never This Good," *Windsor Star*, January 2, 1976, 28.
12. John Robertson, "Canadians–Red Army Match Was as Good as Hockey Gets," *Kitchener-Waterloo Record*, October 27, 1994, C1.
13. Todd Denault, *The Greatest Game* (Toronto: McClelland & Stewart, 2010), 229.
14. Howie Meeker, Central Red Army–Montréal Canadiens telecast, *Hockey Night in Canada*, December 31, 1975.
15. Dave Reynolds, *Ibid*.
16. Vladislav Tretiak, *Tretiak: The Legend* (New York: Penguin, 1987), 84–85.
17. Bertrand Raymond, "Les Larmes de Steve Shutt: Pas du Chic," *Journal de Montréal*, January 3, 1976, 54.
18. Danny Gallivan, Central Red Army–Montréal Canadiens telecast, *Hockey Night in Canada*, December 31, 1975
19. Todd Denault, *The Greatest Game* (Toronto: McClelland & Stewart, 2010), 235.
20. Dick Irvin, Central Red Army–Montréal Canadiens telecast, *Hockey Night in Canada*, December 31, 1975.
21. John Ferguson, *Ibid*.
22. Todd Denault, *The Greatest Game* (Toronto: McClelland & Stewart, 2010), 239.
23. Dick Irvin, Central Red Army–Montréal Canadiens telecast, *Hockey Night in Canada*, December 31, 1975.
24. John Robertson, "Canadians–Red Army match was as good as hockey gets," *Kitchener-Waterloo Record*, October 27, 1994, C1.
25. Todd Denault, *The Greatest Game* (Toronto: McClelland & Stewart, 2010), 242.
26. Danny Gallivan, Central Red Army–Montréal Canadiens telecast, *Hockey Night in Canada*, December 31, 1975.
27. Dick Irvin, *Ibid*.
28. *Ibid*.
29. *Ibid*.
30. Red Fisher, "Canadiens Explode Soviet Supermen Myth," *Montréal Star*, January 2, 1976, C-4.
31. Dick Irvin, Central Red Army–Montréal Canadiens telecast, *Hockey Night in Canada*, December 31, 1975.
32. Gare Joyce, "Greatest Game: Red Army–Canadiens '75," sportsnet.ca, March 9, 2015.
33. *Ibid*.
34. Todd Denault, *The Greatest Game* (Toronto: McClelland & Stewart, 2010), 257.
35. Jim Coleman, "The Night Time Stood Still in the Forum," *Ottawa Citizen*, January 2, 1976, 19.
36. Todd Denault, *The Greatest Game* (Toronto: McClelland & Stewart, 2010), 256.
37. Howie Meeker, Central Red Army–Montréal Canadiens telecast, *Hockey Night in Canada*, December 31, 1975.
38. Peter Mahovlich, *Ibid*.
39. Todd Denault, *The Greatest Game* (Toronto: McClelland & Stewart, 2010), 260.
40. *Ibid*., 259.
41. *Ibid*., 261.
42. *Ibid*., 258.
43. Scott Abbott, "Super Effort, But Disappointing," *Winnipeg Free Press*, January 2, 1976, 43.
44. Robin Herman, "Russians Tie Canadiens, 3–3," *New York Times*, January 1, 1976, 43.
45. *Ibid*.
46. Todd Denault, *The Greatest Game* (Toronto: McClelland & Stewart, 2010), 258
47. Pat Hickey, "Remembering the 1975 New Year's Eve Classic," *Montréal Gazette* (online archives), December 31, 2020.
48. *Ibid*.
49. *Ibid*.
50. *Ibid*.
51. Jim Coleman, "The Night Time

Stood Still in The Forum," *Ottawa Citizen*, January 2, 1976, 19.
  52. Robin Herman, "Russians Tie Canadiens, 3–3," *New York Times*, January 1, 1976, 43.
  53. Mark Mulvoy, "This Was Détente, Philly Style," *Sports Illustrated*, January 19, 1976, 21.
  54. *Ibid*.
  55. Jack Dulmage, "Never This Good," *Windsor Star*, January 2, 1976, 28.
  56. Gare Joyce, "Greatest Game: Red Army-Canadiens '75," sportsnet.ca, March 9, 2015.
  57. "Soviets Roar Back, Tie Canadiens, 3–3," *Boston Globe*, January 1, 1976, 63.
  58. *Ibid*.
  59. Glenn Cole, "Tretiak an Iron Curtain," *Winnipeg Free Press*, January 2, 1976, 43.
  60. Scott Abbott, "Super Effort, But Disappointing," *Winnipeg Free Press*, January 2, 1976, 43.
  61. Robin Herman, "Russians Tie Canadiens, 3–3," *New York Times*, January 1, 1976, 43.
  62. Todd Denault, *The Greatest Game* (Toronto: McClelland & Stewart, 2010), prologue.
  63. *Ibid*., 199.
  64. "The Real Party Was at the Forum," *Montréal Star*, January 2, 1976, 1.
  65. Jack Dulmage, "Never This good," *Windsor Star*, January 2, 1976, 28.
  66. John Robertson, "Canadians-Red Army Match Was as Good as hockey gets," *Kitchener-Waterloo Record*, October 27, 1994, C1.

Chapter 10

  1. "Sabres Crow Over Soviet Wings," *Boston Globe*, January 5, 1976, 22.
  2. Bill Hewitt, Soviet Wings–Buffalo Sabres telecast, *Hockey Night in Canada*, January 4, 1976.
  3. Brian McFarlane, *Ibid*.
  4. *Ibid*.
  5. *Ibid*.
  6. Howie Meeker, *Ibid*.
  7. Peter McNab, *Ibid*.
  8. Robin Herman, "Sabres Trounce Soviet Wings, 12–6," *New York Times*, January 5, 1976, 42.
  9. Peter White, "Sabres Prove Russians Human, Shoot Down Wings 12–6," *Globe & Mail* (online archives), January 5, 1976.
  10. Jim Coleman, "Jim Coleman," *Calgary Herald*, January 5, 1976, 22.
  11. "Sabres Crow Over Soviet Wings," *Boston Globe*, January 5, 1976, 22.
  12. *Ibid*.
  13. *Ibid*.
  14. Hal Walker, "Hal Walker," *Calgary Herald*, January 5, 1976, 22.
  15. "Sabres Use Wings to Get NHL Flying," *Calgary Herald*, January 5, 1976, 22.
  16. *Ibid*.
  17. Robin Herman, "Sabres Trounce Soviet Wings, 12–6," *New York Times*, January 5, 1976, 41.
  18. Mike Harrington, "Hall Inductee Alexander Yakushev Has Vivid Memories of 12–6 Loss to Sabres in 1976 Exhibition Game," *Buffalo News* (online archive), November 9, 2018.
  19. Robin Herman, "Sabres Trounce Soviet Wings, 12–6," *New York Times*, January 5, 1976, 41.
  20. Mark Mulvoy, "This Was Détente, Philly Style," *Sports Illustrated*, January 19, 1976, 21.
  21. Brian McFarlane, Soviet Wings–Buffalo Sabres telecast, *Hockey Night in Canada*, January 4, 1976.
  22. Robin Herman, "Sabres Trounce Soviet Wings, 12–6," *New York Times*, January 5, 1976, 41.
  23. "Sabres Use Wings to Get NHL Flying," *Calgary Herald*, January 5, 1976, 22.
  24. Chuck Svoboda, "Korab's Stiff Checks Helped Soften up Wings," *Winnipeg Free Press*, January 5, 1976, 24.
  25. Robin Herman, "Soviet Players Go Shopping U.S. Style," *New York Times*, January 10, 1976, 13–14.
  26. Chuck Svoboda, "Korab's Stiff Checks Helped Soften up Wings," *Winnipeg Free Press*, January 5, 1976, 24.
  27. *Ibid*.
  28. Chris Ryndak, "Sabres Classics: Buffalo Downs Soviet Wings in 1976 Exhibition Game," nhl.com, May 21, 2020.
  29. Dick Irvin, rerun of Montréal-Red Army game, *Hockey Night in Canada*, December 31, 1994.
  30. Jim Coleman, "Jim Coleman," *Calgary Herald*, January 5, 1976, 22.
  31. Robin Herman, "Sabres Trounce Soviet Wings, 12–6," *New York Times*, January 5, 1976, 41.

Chapter 11

1. Dennis Passa, "Penalties Ground Chi-Hawks," *Calgary Herald*, January 8, 1976, 58.
2. *Ibid.*
3. Rob Verdi, "Soviet Wings Beat Hawks; Did Ref?" *Chicago Tribune*, January 9, 1976, 1.
4. *Ibid.*
5. *Ibid.*
6. *Ibid.*
7. *Ibid.*
8. Bob Verdi, "Russians are Coming! Wings vs. Hawks Tonight," *Chicago Tribune*, January 7, 1976, Section 4, 1.
9. *Ibid.*
10. *Ibid.*
11. *Ibid.*
12. *Ibid.*
13. Rob Verdi, "Soviet Wings Beat Hawks; Did Ref?" *Chicago Tribune*, January 8, 1976, 1.
14. Dennis Passa, "Penalties Ground Chi-Hawks," *Calgary Herald*, January 8, 1976, 58.
15. *Ibid.*
16. "Soviet Wings Upend Black Hawks, 4–2," *Boston Globe*, January 8, 1976, 26.
17. "Russians Grab Third Victory in NHL Series," *Pittsburgh Press*, January 8, 1976, 22.
18. "Soviet Wings Upend Black Hawks, 4–2," *Boston Globe*, January 8, 1976, 26.
19. "Chicago Moans About Soviet Referee," *Boston Globe*, January 8, 1976, 29.
20. Brodie Snyder, "Soviet Wings Clip Hawks 4–2," *Montréal Gazette*, January 8, 1976, 13.
21. Rob Verdi, "Soviet Wings Beat Hawks; Did Ref?" *Chicago Tribune*, January 8, 1976, 1.
22. Jack Dulmage, "Icy Détente Brings End to Super Series," *Windsor Star*, January 12, 1976.
23. Robin Herman, "International Touch to Russians' Outfits," *New York Times* (online archives), January 8, 1976.
24. *Ibid.*
25. *Ibid.*
26. *Ibid.*
27. *Ibid.*
28. *Ibid.*
29. "Soviets' Voice Says Hawks Couldn't 'Restrain' Wings," *Chicago Tribune*, January 8, 1976, C1.
30. Rob Verdi, "Soviet Wings Beat Hawks; Did Ref?" *Chicago Tribune*, January 8, 1976, 1.

Chapter 12

1. Tom Fitzgerald, "It's Just a Game of Hockey But..." *Boston Globe*, January 7, 1976, 50.
2. *Ibid.*
3. Christie Blatchford, "Christie Blatchford," *Globe & Mail*, January 9, 1976, 30.
4. Tom Fitzgerald, "It's Just a Game of Hockey But..." *Boston Globe*, January 7, 1976.
5. Christie Blatchford, "Christie Blatchford," *Globe & Mail*, January 9, 1976, 30.
6. Stan Fischler, *The Sporting News*, January 10, 1976.
7. John Powers, "It is Good to Play the Best, Eh Tovarich?" *Boston Globe*, January 9, 1976, 26.
8. Brain MacFarlane, Central Red Army–Boston Bruins telecast, *Hockey Night in Canada*, January 8, 1976.
9. Phil Esposito, *Ibid.*
10. *Ibid.*
11. *Ibid.*
12. *Ibid.*
13. *Ibid.*
14. John Powers, "It is Good to Play the Best, Eh Tovarich?" *Boston Globe*, January 9, 1976, 25–26.
15. *Ibid.*
16. Tim Burke, "Bruins Frustrated by 'Iron Curtain,'" *Montréal Gazette*, January 9, 1976, 25.
17. Mark Mulvoy, "This Was Détente, Philly Style," *Sports Illustrated*, January 19, 1976, 21.
18. Brian McFarlane, Central Red Army–Boston Bruins telecast, *Hockey Night in Canada*, January 8, 1976.
19. Tim Burke, "Bruins Frustrated by 'Iron Curtain,'" *Montréal Gazette*, January 9, 1976, 25.
20. Mark Mulvoy, "This Was Détente, Philly Style," *Sports Illustrated*, January 19, 1976, 21.
21. Tim Burke, "Bruins Frustrated by 'Iron Curtain,'" *Montréal Gazette*, January 9, 1976, 25.
22. Mark Mulvoy, "This Was Détente, Philly Style," *Sports Illustrated*, January 19, 1976. 21.

23. Phil Esposito, Central Red Army–Boston Bruins telecast, *Hockey Night in Canada*, January 8, 1976.
24. Danny Gallivan, *Ibid*.
25. Brian McFarlane, *Ibid*.
26. Phil Esposito, *Ibid*.
27. Al Colletti, "Reds Clinch Super Series," *Windsor Star*, January 9, 1976.
28. John Powers, "It is Good to Play the Best, Eh Tovarich?" *Boston Globe*, January 9, 1976, 25.
29. Al Colletti, "Reds Clinch Super Series," *Windsor Star*, January 9, 1976, 24.
30. *Ibid*.
31. Gil Peters, "Soviets Top Bruins, 5-2," *Bryan Times*, January 9, 1976, 6.
32. Tim Burke, "Bruins Frustrated by 'Iron Curtain,'" *Montréal Gazette*, January 9, 1976, 25.
33. Ernie Roberts, "Pure Hockey, Russian Style," *Boston Globe*, January 9, 1976, 26.
34. John Powers, "It is Good to Play the Best, Eh Tovarich?," *Boston Globe*, January 9, 1976, 25.
35. *Ibid*.
36. *Ibid*.
37. Mark Mulvoy, "This Was Détente, Philly Style," *Sports Illustrated*, January 19, 1976, 20–21.
38. Ernie Roberts, "Pure Hockey, Russian Style," *Boston Globe*, January 9, 1976, 26.
39. *Ibid*.
40. *Ibid*.
41. *Ibid*.
42. Howie Meeker, Central Red Army–Boston Bruins telecast, *Hockey Night in Canada*, January 8, 1976.
43. Dave Hodge, *Ibid*.
44. Tim Burke, "If Bruins Keep the Heat On, Soviets to Face a Real 'Grind,'" *Montréal Gazette*, January 8, 1976, 13.
45. Ernie Roberts, "Pure Hockey, Russian Style," *Boston Globe*, January 9, 1976, 26.
46. Ernie Roberts, "Stanley Cup Open to All?" *Boston Globe*, January 10, 1976, 21.
47. Leigh Montville, "What Will the Soviets 'Play' next?" *Boston Globe*, January 11, 1976, 78.
48. Mark Mulvoy, "This Was Détente, Philly Style," *Sports Illustrated*, January 19, 1976, 20–21.
49. *Ibid*., 21.

Chapter 13

1. Neil Campbell, "Leafs Upset Islanders, 5–3," *Windsor Star*, January 9, 1976, 24.
2. "Secret Workout for NY," *Windsor Star*, January 10, 1976, 18.
3. Jim McKay, "Flyers Get Back on the Track," *Windsor Star*, May 13, 1975, 39.
4. Robin Herman, "Soviet Players Go Shopping U.S. Style," *New York Times*, January 10, 1976, 13–14.
5. Robin Herman, "Islanders are Beaten by Soviet Wings, 2–1," *New York Times*, January 11, 1976, S3.
6. Al Colletti, "Broken Goalie Stick Costs Islanders," *Windsor Star*, January 12, 1976, 30.
7. Robin Herman, "Islanders are Beaten by Soviet Wings, 2–1," *New York Times*, January 11, 1976, S3.
8. *Ibid*.
9. Al Colletti, "Broken Goalie Stick Costs Islanders," *Windsor Star*, January 12, 1976, 30.
10. Robin Herman, "Islanders are Beaten by Soviet Wings, 2–1," *New York Times*, January 11, 1976, S3.
11. *Ibid*.
12. Al Colletti, "Broken Goalie Stick Costs Islanders," *Windsor Star*, January 12, 1976, 30.
13. Robin Herman, "Islanders are Beaten by Soviet Wings, 2–1," *New York Times*, January 11, 1976, S3.
14. Stan Fischler, "Speaking Out on Hockey," *The Sporting News*, February 7, 1976, 30.
15. Al Colletti, "Broken Goalie Stick Costs Islanders," *Windsor Star*, January 12, 1976, 30.
16. "Objects Thrown at Soviet Wings," *Boston Globe*, January 11, 1976, 68.
17. *Ibid*.
18. *Ibid*.
19. Robin Herman, "Islanders are Beaten by Soviet Wings, 2–1," *New York Times*, January 11, 1976, S3.
20. Al Colletti, "Broken Goalie Stick Costs Islanders," *Windsor Star*, January 12, 1976, 30.
21. *Ibid*.

Chapter 14

1. "Longtime NHL referee Lloyd Gilmour dead at 82," nhl.com, August 18, 2010.

2. Al Strachan, "Army-Flyers May Get a Bell-yful from Hood," *Montréal Gazette*, January 9, 1976, 25.
3. *The Broad Street Bullies* (HBO documentary film), 2010.
4. *Ibid.*
5. *Ibid.*
6. *Ibid.*
7. *Ibid.*
8. *Ibid.*
9. Ray Kennedy, "Wanted: An End to Mayhem," *Sports Illustrated* (online archive), November 17, 1975.
10. *Ibid.*
11. Fred Shero, Central Red Army–Philadelphia Flyers telecast, *Hockey Night in Canada*, January 11, 1976.
12. Tom Fitzgerald, "Will Red Army See a Bit of Itself on Meeting Flyers?" *Boston Globe*, January 11, 1976, 69.
13. Jack Dulmage, "Icy Détente Brings End to Super Series," *Windsor Star*, January 12, 1976, 1.
14. Mark Mulvoy, "This Was Détente, Philly Style," *Sports Illustrated*, January 19, 1976, 21.
15. John Kreiser, "When the Flyers Beat the Red Army," *Philadelphia Inquirer* (online archives), January 23, 2015.
16. John Powers, "It is Good to Play the Best, Eh Tovarich?" *Boston Globe*, January 9, 1976, 26.
17. Rod Smith, *Sportsdesk* (TSN sports news telecast), January 11, 2016.
18. Brad Kurtzberg, "How We Remember the Philadelphia Flyers–Red Army Game 38 Years Later," bleacherreport.com, January 11, 2014.
19. Mark Mulvoy, "This Was Détente, Philly Style," *Sports Illustrated*, January 19, 1976, 20–21.
20. *The Broad Street Bullies* (HBO documentary film), 2010.
21. John Kreiser, "When the Flyers Beat the Red Army," *Philadelphia Inquirer* (online archives), January 23, 2015.
22. *The Broad Street Bullies* (HBO documentary film), 2010.
23. *Ibid.*
24. Mark Mulvoy, "This Was Détente, Philly Style," *Sports Illustrated*, January 19, 1976, 20–21.
25. Tom Fitzgerald, "Will Red Army See a Bit of Itself on Meeting Flyers?" *Boston Globe*, January 11, 1976, 69.
26. "Flyers Stop Sulky Soviets, 4–1," *Bangor Daily News*, January 12, 1976, 18.
27. Ed Snider, "Flyers and Soviets, 1976: When Al Capone's Mob Ambushed the Bolshoi Ballet Dancers," puckstruck.com, January 12, 2016.
28. "Flyers Stop Sulky Soviets, 4–1," *Bangor Daily News*, January 12, 1976, 18.
29. Ed Van Impe, *The Broad Street Bullies* (HBO documentary film), 2010.
30. Jim Coleman, "Flyers Hit Heights and Red Army," *Calgary Herald*, January 12, 1976, 12.
31. Robert Fachet, "Flyers Intimidate Soviet Army, 4–1," *Washington Post*, January 12, 1976, C-1.
32. Jim Coleman, "Flyers Hit Heights and Red Army," *Calgary Herald*, January 12, 1976, 12.
33. *Ibid.*
34. Bob Cole, Central Red Army–Philadelphia Flyers telecast, *Hockey Night in Canada*, January 11, 1976.
35. Dick Ivin, *Ibid.*
36. Denis Potvin, *Ibid.*
37. Bob Cole, *Ibid.*
38. *The Broad Street Bullies* (HBO documentary film), 2010.
39. Jim Coleman, "Flyers hit heights and Red Army," *Calgary Herald*, January 12, 1976, 12.
40. Stan Fischler, "Speaking Out on Hockey," *The Sporting News*, February 7, 1976, 30.
41. "Flyers Stop Sulky Soviets, 4–1," *Bangor Daily News*, January 12, 1976, 18.
42. John Kreiser, "When the Flyers Beat the Red Army," *Philadelphia Inquirer* (online archives), January 23, 2015.
43. Marv Albert, broadcast of Flyers–Red Army game, WPIX-TV, January 11, 1976.
44. *The Broad Street Bullies* (HBO documentary film), 2010.
45. Frank Dolson, "Flyers Pull out All the Stops," *Boston Globe*, January 12, 1976, 18.
46. Jack Dulmage, "Icy Detent Brings End to Super Series," *Windsor Star*, January 12, 1976, 4.
47. "Flyers Stop Sulky Soviets, 4–1," *Bangor Daily News*, January 12, 1976, 18.
48. Dick Irvin, Central Red Army–Philadelphia Flyers telecast, *Hockey Night in Canada*, January 11, 1976
49. *Ibid.*
50. Jim Coleman, "Flyers Hit Heights

and Red Army," *Calgary Herald*, January 12, 1976, 12.
51. *Ibid.*
52. Bobby Clarke, Central Red Army–Philadelphia Flyers telecast, *Hockey Night in Canada*, January 11, 1976.
53. John Kreiser, "When the Flyers Beat the Red Army," *Philadelphia Inquirer* (online archives), January 23, 2015
54. Bob Cole, Central Red Army–Philadelphia Flyers telecast, *Hockey Night in Canada*, January 11, 1976.
55. "Losing Russians in Walkoff Huff," *Pittsburgh Post-Gazette*, January 12, 1976, 12.
56. *Ibid.*
57. *Ibid.*
58. Mike Avenenti, "Aggressive Flyers Triumph, 4-1, over Russian Army Puck Team," *Berkshire Eagle*, January 12, 1976, 16.
59. *Ibid.*
60. John Kreiser, "When the Flyers Beat the Red Army," *Philadelphia Inquirer* (online archives), January 23, 2015.
61. *Ibid.*
62. Jim Coleman, "Flyers Hit Heights and Red Army," *Calgary Herald*, January 12, 1976, 12.
63. *Ibid.*
64. Dave Anderson, "A Hockey Lesson for Dr. Kissinger," *New York Times*, January 12, 1976, 33.
65. Jim Coleman, "Flyers Hit Heights and Red Army," *Calgary Herald*, January 12, 1976, 12.
66. *Ibid.*
67. *Ibid.*
68. Tim Burke, "Flyers Salvage Canada's Pride," *Montréal Gazette*, January 12, 1976, 1.
69. *Ibid.*
70. "Flyers Seen as Animals … Hungry for Victory," *Calgary Herald*, January 12, 1976, 12.
71. Frank Dolson, "Flyers Pull Out All the Stops," *Boston Globe*, January 12, 1976, 18.
72. *Ibid.*
73. Tim Burke, "Flyers Salvage Canada's Pride," *Montréal Gazette*, January 12, 1976, 1.
74. Donald Wood, "Red Fever: The 35th Anniversary of the Flyer–Red Army Game," bleacherreport.com, January 11, 2011.

75. Brad Kurtzberg, "How We Remember the Philadelphia Flyers–Red Army Game 38 Years Later," bleacherreport.com, January 11, 2014.
76. Jim Coleman, "Flyers Hit Heights and Red Army," *Calgary Herald*, January 12, 1976, 12.
77. *Ibid.*
78. Tim Burke, "Flyers Salvage Canada's Pride," *Montréal Gazette*, January 12, 1976, 1.
79. "Flyers Seen as Animals … Hungry for Victory," *Calgary Herald*, January, 12, 1976, 12.
80. *Ibid.*
81. Red Fisher, "Flyers Prove They're Still the Best," *Montréal Star*, January 12, 1976, C-1.
82. *Ibid.*
83. Brad Kurtzberg, "How We Remember the Philadelphia Flyers–Red Army Game 38 Years Later," bleacherreport.com, January 11, 2014.
84. Jack Dulmage, "Icy Detent Brings End to Super Series," *Windsor Star*, January 12, 1976, 4.
85. Jim Coleman, "Flyers Hit Heights and Red Army," *Calgary Herald*, January 12, 1976, 12.
86. Ed Snider, "Flyers and Soviets, 1976: When Al Capone's Mob Ambushed the Bolshoi Ballet Dancers," puckstruck.com, January 12, 2016.
87. Frank Dolson, "Flyers Pull Out All the Stops," *Boston Globe*, January 12, 1976, 18.
88. Ed Snider, "Flyers and Soviets, 1976: When Al Capone's Mob Ambushed the Bolshoi Ballet Dancers," puckstruck.com, January 12, 2016.
89. *Ibid.*
90. Michael Farber, *Sportsdesk* (TSN sports news telecast), January 11, 2016.

Chapter 15

1. Mark Mulvoy, "This Was Détente, Philly Style," *Sports Illustrated*, January 19, 1976, 20.
2. *Ibid.*
3. Jack Dulmage, "Icy Detent Brings End to Super Series," *Windsor Star*, January 12, 1976, 4.
4. Red Fisher, "Canadiens Explode Soviet Supermen Myth," *Montréal Star*, January 2, 1976, C-4.

5. *Ibid.*
6. Mark Mulvoy, "This Was Détente, Philly Style," *Sports Illustrated*, January 19, 1976, 20.
7. Tom Fitzgerald, "Will Red Army See a Bit of Itself on Meeting Flyers?" *Boston Globe*, January 12, 1976, 69.
8. Ernie Roberts, "Pure Hockey, Russian Style," *Boston Globe*, January 9, 1976, 26.
9. Jack Dulmage, "A Short Bus Ride," *Windsor Star*, December 30, 1975, 20.
10. "Ouch! Team Canada Iced 11-1 and It Stings," *Montréal Gazette*, April 25, 1977, 1
11. Francis Rosa, "…And the Game: Russians Spoil the Party, 4-1," *Boston Globe*, January 10, 1979, 35.
12. E.M. Swift, "Run Over by the Big Red Machine," *Sports Illustrated*, February 19, 1979, 19.
13. *Ibid.*
14. "The President of Hockey Canada Warned Sports Fan," UPI online archives, September 16, 1981.
15. E.M. Swift, "Détente on Ice," *Sports Illustrated*, February 23, 1987, 13.
16. *Ibid.*
17. Francis Rosa, "Bruins—Ho Hum—Fall to Khimik," *Boston Globe*, December 17, 1990, 47.
18. Gillian Kemmerer, "Six Shots on Vladislav Tretiak," thecaviardiploamt.com, January 19, 2020.
19. Lyndon Johnson, BrainyQuote.com.

Bibliography

Books

Beddoes, Dick. *Pal Hal: A Biography of Harold Ballard.* Toronto: Macmillan of Canada, 1989.
Conacher, Brian. *As the Puck Turns: A Personal Journey Through the World of Hockey.* Mississauga: John Wiley & Sons Canada, 2007.
Denault, Todd. *The Greatest Game.* Toronto: McClelland & Stewart, 2010.
Dryden, Ken, and Mark Mulvoy. *Face-Off at the Summit.* Toronto: Little, Brown, 1973.
MacSkimming, Roy. *Cold War: The Amazing Canada–Soviet Hockey Series of 1972.* Vancouver: Greystone Books, 1996.
Martin, Lawrence. *The Red Machine: The Soviet Quest to Dominate Canada's Game.* New York: Doubleday, 1990.
McKinley, Michael. *It's Our Game: Celebrating 100 Years of Hockey Canada.* Toronto: Viking, 2014.
McLelland, Ivan. *Gold Mine to Gold Medal and Beyond.* Self-published in Canada, 2012.
Morrison, Scott. *The Days Canada Stood Still.* Toronto: McGraw-Hill Ryerson Limited, 1989.
Mossman, Gary. *Lloyd Percival: Coach and Visionary.* Woodstock, ON: Seraphim Editions, 2013.
Sinden, Harry. *Hockey Showdown: The Canada-Russia Hockey Series.* Toronto, Doubleday Canada, 1972.
Tretiak, Vladislav. *Tretiak: The Legend.* New York: Penguin, 1987.

Documentaries

The Broad Street Bullies, HBO documentary, 2010.
Go Vs Go! Toronto, Davart Productions, 1955.
Ice-Breaker: The 1972 Summit Series, Canada, 2022.
September 1972, Markham, ON, Polygram Video, 1997.

Newspaper Archives

Bangor Daily News
Berkshire Eagle
Boston Globe
The British Columbian
Bryan Times
Buffalo News
Calgary Herald
Cambridge Reporter
Chicago Tribune
Ellensburg Daily Record
Kitchener-Waterloo Record
Le Journal de Montréal

London Free Press
Montréal Gazette
Montréal Herald
Montréal Star
New York Daily News
New York Times
Ottawa Citizen
Ottawa Journal
Penticton Western News
Philadelphia Daily News
Philadelphia Inquirer
Pittsburgh Post-Gazette
Pittsburgh Press
St. John's Daily News
Schenectady Gazette
Toledo Blade
(Toronto) Globe & Mail
Toronto Star
Toronto Sun
Vancouver Sun
Washington Post
Windsor Star
Winnipeg Free Press

Periodicals

The Hockey News
The Sporting News
Sports Illustrated

Websites

BBC.com
Bleacherreport.com
ESPN.com
Globeandmail.com
Legendsofhockey.net
NHL.com
SI.com
Thecaviardiplomat.com

Index

Ahearne, Bunny 34, 41, 76
Albert, Marv 177, 178–179, 180
Ali, Muhammad 13
Anderson, Dave 184
Anisin, Vyacheslav 102, 163, 164
Arbour, Al 161–165, 191
Arpin, Louis 54–55
Avenenti, Mike 183
Awrey, Don 41, 110, 117

Baader, Franz 47, 49
Babich, Yevgeny 28
Babinov, Sergei 163
Backstrom, Ralph 66, 69, 72, 73
Barber, Bill 170–183, 194
Bauer, Father David 31, 196
Beasley, Mercer 11
Béchard, Claude 113
Beddoes, Dick 21, 38, 44–45, 48, 94
Bedrick, Jill 165
Belfour, Ed 200
Berenson, Red 35
Bergman, Gary 42, 48, 49
Bird, Clem 25
Blackman, Ted 41, 42–43
Bladon, Tom 185
Blair, Wren 98, 99
Bobrov, Vsevolod 10, 24–25, 41, 42, 43, 52
Boileau, Marc 97–105, 190, 191
Bowman, Scotty 94–95, 115–120, 193
Bregg, Formo 25
Bregg, June 25
Bregg, Merv 25
Brezhnev, Leonid 2, 50, 179
Brodeur, Denis 29
Brodeur, Martin 29, 200
Bronson, Charles 2
Brown, Frank 84–85
Brown, Tom 61, 69
Bucyk, Johnny 149

Burke, Tim 35, 153, 156, 158, 185–186, 188
Byron, Wally 9

Carter, John 199
Cherry, Don 149–157, 191
Chevalier, Jack 170
Chevrier, Don 63
Christie, Agatha 185
Christie, Frankie 128
Chuvalo, George 13
Clancy, King 111, 135–136
Clement, Bill 169
Clements, Earl 15
Cole, Bob 173, 177–178, 182
Colletti, Al 164
Conacher, Brian 40, 41, 48
Conacher, Lionel 19–20
Crha, Jiri 72
Crisp, Terry 175
Crowder, Harry 15
Currie, Greg 18

Dahlberg, Uwe 49
D'Amico, John 86, 150
Davidson, Bob 37
Davidson, John 87–92
Denault, Todd 55
Desjardins, Gerry 128–131
Doak, Gary 149
Dr. Zhivago (movie) 127
Dolson, Frank 180, 185, 189
Dornhoefer, Gary 184
Doucet, Roger 113, 119
Douglas, Steve 25, 26
Drapeau, Jean 1–2
Drew, George 28
Drobny, Jaroslav 16
Dunnell, Milt 46, 186
Dupont, André 169, 176, 177, 182, 183
Dzurilla, Vladimir 194

215

Index

Eastwood, Clint 2
Edestrand, Darryl 153, 155
Eisen, Harry 19
Ellis, Ron 36, 40, 42, 48
Esaw, Johnny 42, 45
Eskenazi, Jerry 38

Fachet, Robert 177
Farber, Michael 189
Fedosov, Boris 33
Ferguson, Elmer 19
Ferguson, John 49, 112, 114, 150
Field, Russell 56
Finley, Charlie 144
Fisher, Douglas 32, 43
Fitzgerald, Tom 147, 149, 192
Fogolin, Lee 129
Forbes, Dave 151–152
Ford, Gerald 2
Forristal, Frosty 50
Francis, Emile 85
Fredrickson, Frank 9

Gaffer, Wes 91
Gairdner, Bill 13
Galand, Moe 17
Gare, Danny 129, 130, 131
Gault, John 58
George, W.B. 9–10, 18
Gilbert, Gilles 150–155, 162
Gilbert, Rod 40, 84, 90, 92
Gilbertson, Stan 104
Gilmour, Lloyd 167–188
Goldsworthy, Bill 35, 45, 46
Goodenough, Larry 182
Gratton, Gilles 65, 72
Greschner, Ron 88, 93
Gromyko, Andrei 177
Guevremont, Jocelyn 128, 130
Gut, Karel 194

Hackel, Stu 169–170
Haggroth, Lennart 29–30
Halderson, Haldor (Slim) 9
Harrington, Mike 133
Harris, Billy (player) 165
Harris, Wally 113–123
Hart, Gene 178
Hasek, Dominik 200
Hatskin, Ben 44
Heufelder, Bill 101
Hewitt, Bill 8, 127, 134
Hewitt, Foster 8, 25, 38, 41, 48
Hewitt, W.H. 8
Hickey, Pat 120–121
Hodge, Dave 130, 158

Hodge, Ken 149, 151, 154, 157
Holmqvist, Leif 65
Holocek, Jiri 72
Hood, Bruce 167
Houle, Réjean 162
Howatt, Garry 164
Howlett, Jack 19
Hull, Dennis 34, 138, 139, 140, 141, 142
Hull, Joanne 44
Hunter, Bill 58–72, 124
"Hymn of the Soviet Union" (song) 113

Imlach, Dorothy (Dodo) 135
Imlach, Punch 127–136
Ivan, Tommy 144

Jackson, Bo 10
Janney, Craig 199
Jarrett, Doug 87
Jarvis, Doug 113, 115
Jaws (movie) 2
Jennings, Bill 93–94
Johannesson, Brian 7
Johannesson, Konnie 7
John, Elton 157
Johnson, Lyndon 200
Johnston, Ed 45
Joyce, Gare 108, 118
Juckes, Gordon 56, 76, 77

Kaese, Harold 43
Kahn, Roger 175
Kapustin, Sergei 130–131
Keese, Parton 91, 92
Kelly, Bob 169, 187–188
Keon, Dave 35
Khrushchev, Nikita 113, 140
Kidd, Bruce 32
Koloskov, Viacheslav 113, 135
Kompalla, Josef 47, 49, 50
Kosygin, Alexei 2
Kotov, Sergei 130
Kreiser, John 173, 182
Kromm, Bobby 30
Krylov, Yuri 26
Kukushin, Seva 13
Kulikov, Alexander 129, 130, 131
Kurtzburg, Brad 80
Kuzin, Valentin 26
Kuzkin, Viktor 40
Kuznetsov, Victor 144

Lader, Martin 90–91
Lafleur, Guy 108, 116, 121, 193
Laforge, Claude 168–169

Lambert, Yvon 114
Lapointe, Guy 42, 110, 116
Larouche, Pierre 102, 103
Leach, Reg 170, 181
Lefaive, Lou 197–198
Lefley, Chuck 167
Lemaire, Jacques 114, 116, 117
Lennon, Frank 51
Leonardi, Dave 174
Ley, Rick 62, 68
Liut, Mike 197
Lockhart, Don 17, 20
Lorentz, Jim 129, 136
"Love Will Keep Us Together" (song) 1

MacDonald, Lowell 99
MacGregor, Bruce 67
MacKenzie, Arch 27
MacLaine, Ian 100–101, 103, 104–105
MacLeish, Rick 170, 181, 182–83
MacSkimming, Ray 39, 51, 53
Marcotte, Don 149
Marks, John 143
Martin, Carl 85
Martin, Lawrence 36
Martin, Pit 138–139, 145
Martin, Rick 127–144
Massey, Raymond 28
McAvoy, George 25
McCauley, John 196
McKay, Jim 162
McKenzie, John 60
McLellan, Johnny 37
McLelland, Ivan 21–26
McLeod, Don 62, 65, 72
McMullen, Larry 189
McNab, Peter 130, 131, 132, 157, 195
Mellanby, Ralph 119–120
Middleton, Rick 157
Mikita, Stan 36, 140–143, 145
Mkrtychan, Grigory 26
Monteville, Leigh 158–159, 192
Morrison, Scotty 187
Mulvey, Grant 140
Myshkin, Vladimir 196

Nabokov, Evgeni 200
Nattrass, Susan 35
Neilson, Jim 34
Nielsen, Robert 18–19
Nystrom, Bob 164

O'Neill, Bryan 181
Overland, Wayne 71
Ozerov, Nikolai 145

Paladiev, Evgeny 43
Parent, Bernie 170–171, 174, 175
Parisé, J.P. 50
Parker, Frankie 11
Passa, Dennis 140
Patterson, Tammy 148
Pavelich, Matt 86, 145, 177
Percival, Lloyd 11–13, 31–32, 45
Perreault, Gilbert 127, 128, 133
Peters, Gil 156
Petrov, Vladimir
Pettie, Jim 195
Picard, Noel 168
Plager, Barclay 168
Plager, Bob 168
Plante, Jacques 37–38
Plasse, Michel 100, 101, 162
Polis, Greg 90
Pollock, Sam 115, 122
Popov, Vladimir 88, 117
Porter, Art 30
Potvin, Denis 163–164, 173–174, 178, 193
Powers, John 153, 156, 172
Puchkov, Nikolai 26
Pupyanski, A. 188

Rasko, Vladimir 142
Reay, Billy 138, 139, 190–191
Redly, Elizabeth 165
Redmond, Dick 138, 140, 141, 142, 143
Repniev, Vladimir 128, 130
Resch, Glenn 163–166
Reynolds, Dave 112, 119, 128, 130 131
Rigazio, Don 23
Risebrough, Doug 118, 122
Roadknight, Mabel 53
Robert, René 129, 133
Roberts, Ernie 156, 158
Roberts, Jim 109
Robertson, John 109
Robinson, Larry 118
Rodosta, John S. 94
Rolfe, Dale 170
Rota, Darcy 142
Roubell, Lloyd 30

St. Laurent, André 164
St. Laurent, Louis 28
Saleski, Don 169, 182, 187–188
Sanderson, Derek 56
Savard, André 132, 157
Savard, Serge 110, 116, 120
Savin, Sergey 10–11
Schmautz, Bobby 151, 152, 154, 155
Schock, Ron 104
Schoenfeld, Jim 127

Schultz, Dave 93, 169–70, 185
Sciamonte, John 61
Scott, George C. 153
Seiling, Rod 41
Selwood, Brad 62
Shchepek, Voitech 66
Sheppard, Gregg 151, 158
Shero, Fred 94–95, 168–189
Shields, Tommy 17
Shuvalov, Viktor 25–26
Silver, Johnathan 165
Silver, Sharon 165
Sims, Al 152. 154, 155
Sittler, Darryl 194
Smith, Billy 166
Smith, Dallas 151
Smith, Floyd 133, 135
Smith, Gary 33
Smith, George 197–198
Smith, Kate 174
Smith, Pohla 101
Smith, Rod 3, 172
Smythe, Conn 20
Snider, Ed 169–185
Snyder, Brodie 143
Soetaert, Doug 89
"Somewhere, My Love" (song) 127
Spencer, Brian 130, 131
Spragge, Reg 19
Stanfield, Fred 131
Stapleton, Pat 58, 71
Starovoytov, Andrey 56, 71
Stephenson, Wayne 175, 182, 187
Stepler, Jack 27
Stewart, Ron 85, 88, 89, 90, 91, 93, 95, 150, 190, 191
Stickle, Leon 50
Storey, Red 38
Subrt, Miloslav 76
Svensson, Elnar 9

Tallon, Dale 140, 141
Tarala, Hal 24–25
Tarasov, Anatoli 11, 13–14, 14, 36, 52, 171, 179
Terrell, Ernie 13
Théodore, José 200
Thibault, Jocelyn 200
Thomson, Bobby 52
Tikhonov, Viktor 196, 198
Torpey, Frank 25, 148
Torrey, Bill 162
Tougas, Maurice 50
Tremblay, J.C. 56, 61
Trottier, Bryan 163, 164
Trudeau, Pierre 39, 52, 54, 60
Tsygankov, Gennady 154, 155

Unger, Eric 18
Uvarov, Alexander 24, 26

Vadnais, Carol 85, 90, 93, 147
Valtonen, Jorna 65
Van Impe, Ed 175–178, 186
Vickers, Steve 86, 87, 90
Vikulov, Vladimir 87–88, 90

Walker, Hal 91, 133
Warwick, Bill 25
Warwick, Grant 23–29
Watson, Jim 185
Wayne, John 43
Welch, Raquel 45
Westwick, Bill 19
White, Bill 141, 145
White, Peter 103, 104, 142
Whitley, Bob 99
Wilson, Dunc 89
Wilson, Murray 113

Yourkewicz, Al 23, 24, 26

Zimin, Evgeny 39, 41